LOUGHREA, 'THAT DEN OF INFAMY'

Loughrea,
'that den of infamy'
during the
Land War in Co. Galway,
1879–82

Pat Finnegan

FOUR COURTS PRESS

This book was set in 10.5 on 12.5 point Ehrhardt by
Mark Heslington, Scarborough, North Yorkshire for
FOUR COURTS PRESS
7 Malpas Street, Dublin 8, Ireland
www.fourcourtspress.ie
and in North America for
FOUR COURTS PRESS
c/o ISBS, 920 N.E. 58th Avenue, Suite 300, Portland, OR 97213.

© the author and Four Courts Press 2014

A catalogue record for this title
is available from the British Library.

ISBN 978-1-84682-511-8 | hbk
ISBN 978-1-84682-512-5 | pbk

All rights reserved. No part of this publication may be reproduced,
stored in or introduced into a retrieval system, or transmitted,
in any form or by any means (electronic, mechanical,
photocopying, recording or otherwise), without the
prior written permission of both the copyright
owner and publisher of this book.

Printed in Great Britain
by TJ International, Padstow, Cornwall

Contents

	LISTS OF FIGURES AND TABLES	6
	LIST OF ABBREVIATIONS	7
	PREFACE AND ACKNOWLEDGMENTS	9
	INTRODUCTION	11
1	The establishment of the Irish National Land League	14
2	The agricultural crisis of 1879–80	21
3	Local and national political developments, 1879–80	30
4	Stopping the hunt	42
5	Rent, evictions and outrages	50
6	Agrarian secret societies and the Fenian organization	62
7	The Land War and the response of the government	76
8	Serious incidents in south Galway, May 1881 to June 1882	88
9	Suppression of the Land League	103
10	Analysis of arrests of suspects in Co. Galway	114
11	Political and social consequences of agrarian unrest in 1882	125
12	The Prevention of Crime (Ireland) Act 1882	131
13	The foundation of the Irish National League	146
14	Conclusion	151
Appendix 1: Transcript of the diary of John Sweeny		159
Appendix 2: Persons from the Loughrea and Athenry police districts arrested under the Protection of Person and Property (Ireland) Act 1881		164
Appendix 3: Persons arrested after the Irish National League meetings in Clostoken and Ballymana in December 1882		167
	BIBLIOGRAPHY	168
	INDEX	175

Figures and tables

Figures

1	A number of those present at the Loughrea meeting, 15 August 1884	74
2	Map of the murder triangle	89
3	Exterior of a portable hut for police in Mayo	121
4	Interior of a police hut	121
5	Loughrea prisoners released from Kilmainham Jail on 17 August 1882	127
6	Diary of John Sweeny	160

Tables

1	Population changes in the Loughrea and Gort Poor Law Unions	12
2	Population change in some south Galway townlands, 1841–51	13
3	Average weather conditions	22
4	Produce of crops in Loughrea and Gort	22
5	Livestock in Loughrea and Gort	22
6	Numbers of families evicted and readmitted as caretakers or tenants	54
7	Evictions without readmission as caretakers or tenants	55
8	National outrage statistics, 1879–83	59
9	Galway East and West Riding outrages, 1879–83	60
10	Analysis of agrarian and political murders, 1880–2	60
11	National statistics of evictions and outrages, 1879–82	61
12	Number of persons arrested in the Loughrea and Athenry police districts in 1881 and 1882 under the PPP (Ireland) Act 1881	114
13	Occupations of persons arrested in Co. Galway under the PPP (Ireland) Act 1881	115
14	Comparison of the percentages of arrests within the agricultural sector	116
15	Comparison of the percentages of arrests between Clark's study and the Co. Galway figures in the present study and the values in the national and Co. Galway labour forces	116
16	Categories of offences under the PPP (Ireland) Act 1881	117
17	Arrests under the PPP (Ireland) Act 1881 during 1881 and 1882	118
18	Police districts with the most arrests under the PPP (Ireland) Act 1881	120

Abbreviations

AG	attorney general
BL	barrister-at-law
BTDA	Ballinasloe Tenants' Defence Association
CBS	crime branch special
CC	Catholic curate
CI	county inspector
CSO	chief secretary's office
DI	district inspector
DM	divisional magistrate
DMP	Dublin Metropolitan Police
FCR	Fortnightly Crime Report
GAA	Gaelic Athletic Association
HC	head constable (in text)
HC	House of Commons
ILL	Irish Land League
INL	Irish National League
IRB	Irish Republican Brotherhood
JP	justice of the peace
LGB	Local Government Board
MHRC	Mansion House Relief Committee
MP	Member of Parliament (UK)
n.d.	no date (given)
NAI	National Archives of Ireland
NUIG	National University of Ireland, Galway
PDA	Property Defence Association
PLG	Poor Law Guardian
PLU	Poor Law Union
PP	parish priest
PPP (Ireland) Act	Protection of Person and Property (Ireland) Act
QC	queen's counsel
Revd	Reverend
RIC	Royal Irish Constabulary
RM	resident magistrate
RP	registered papers
SI	sub inspector
SRM	special resident magistrate
UCD	University College Dublin
UCG	University College Galway (now NUIG)

Preface and acknowledgments

After my grandfather's release from prison in 1902, he married Alice Sweeny and thereafter lived and died in Dunkellin Street, Loughrea. John Sweeny, Alice's father, was an active Fenian from the early 1870s and later the secretary of the Loughrea branch of the Land League. His house was the venue for branch meetings and his wife Bridget (O'Neill) looked after the family and public bar and shop during his two periods in jail. Growing up in the house in Dunkellin Street, reading documents such as John Sweeny's notebook (see Appendix 1) and letters sent by leading figures such as John Dillon, Timothy Harrington, William O'Brien and others, inevitably aroused an interest in the Land League. In addition, my father, P.J. Finnegan, had an extensive knowledge of the period and my sister, Anne O'Máille, chose that period for her MA thesis and that work was a valuable introduction to the local history of the time.

In my own researches I found that seven members of the extended Sweeny and Finnegan families were jailed as suspects under the Protection of Person and Property (Ireland) Act in 1881–2. Loughrea was judged to be one of the most 'disturbed' towns in Ireland. The title of this book, *Loughrea, 'that den of infamy'*, refers to that time and derives from a letter that a notorious magistrate, Clifford Lloyd, wrote to Earl Spencer in July 1882. Clifford Lloyd had recently arranged for the arrest of twenty-three suspects from the town in connection with the killing of John Blake and Thady Ruane just outside the town. Clifford Lloyd was determined to make the people of the town pay under the provisions of a new coercion act. No evidence was presented connecting any of those arrested with the killings and none of the suspects was prosecuted in the courts.

I am deeply grateful to two local historians, Maura Lyons and Gerry Cloonan, for sharing their extensive knowledge with me and for their generous hospitality on my numerous visits to their homes. Fergus Campbell, Reader in History at the University of Newcastle upon Tyne, took an inspirational interest in the project and his support and advice was very important to me. Professor James Donnelly, University of Wisconsin–Madison, during his sabbatical visits to NUIG provided very valuable critical advice and encouragement. Dr John Cunningham, Dr Tony Varley and many other former colleagues and friends were also helpful and encouraging. Kieran Hoare made me aware of the diary of Peter Broderick that gives a unique insight into the experience of imprisonment of the suspects in Galway jail. Marie Boran and Geraldine Curtin and all the staff of the James Hardiman Library of NUIG were of immense help in guiding my efforts in a completely new area of enquiry. I was also greatly assisted by the staff of the National Library of Ireland, the Dublin City Library, the Dublin Diocesan Archive, the British Library, the Galway County Library in Nun's

Island and particularly by the staff of the National Archives of Ireland. I wish to gratefully acknowledge the grant by NUIG toward publication of the book.

I am deeply grateful to Michael Potterton and Martin Fanning of Four Courts Press.

I owe a great debt of gratitude to my family. My late wife Máire was an unfailing support and tolerated my preoccupation with the project. My children, Emer, Nuala and Niall and my sister Anne showed a continuous interest and provided critical readings of the manuscript. The support of my sister Alice, brother Paul and sister Mary was always welcome.

Marianne ten Cate was again a careful and painstaking proof reader and the book bears all the hallmarks of the considerable expertise of her editing skills.

Introduction

During the Land War of 1879–82, Galway was frequently referred to as a dangerously disturbed area. Of particular concern was the fact that eight individuals were killed in the police districts of Loughrea and Athenry between May 1881 and June 1882. The killings spanned the range of what were referred to as agrarian crimes and included a landlord (Walter Bourke of Rahasane House, near Craughwell) and his bodyguard, the land agent of Lord Clanricarde and his servant, a policeman and three men whose deaths were related to land disputes. In addition, agrarian outrages were frequent, with numerous attacks in which firearms were used on people and houses, public disorder and intimidation to prevent the payment of rent. The authorities responded to this social and political crisis by introducing the Protection of Person and Property (Ireland) Act in March 1881[1] and the Prevention of Crime (Ireland) Act in July 1882.[2] Known as the Coercion Act and the Crimes Act respectively, they resulted in the arrest and internment without trial of 111 men in the two police districts. Clifford Lloyd, who was one of the special resident magistrates appointed by Chief Secretary Forster, and also the most controversial, was put in charge of Co. Galway in July 1882. He said of Loughrea that it was a 'den of infamy and must be made to pay under the new act'.[3] Large numbers of police and soldiers were present in the area; numerous police huts were set up and frequent day and night patrols gave rise to a feeling that the community was under siege.

A number of factors led to the troubled state of the community. Like other parts of Ireland, the district was affected by the profound societal changes that had occurred from before the Great Famine. In evidence given to the Devon Commission in 1844, Revd John Macklin, PP of Carrabane, a townland halfway between Loughrea and Athenry, referred to the increase in grazing farms and the decline in more labour-intensive tillage farming. Most tenants in the area had holdings of between five and ten acres and there had been many evictions forcing people to move to the bogs and the town of Loughrea. James Hardiman Burke of the St Clerans estate also reported consolidation of farms.[4] Between 1841 and 1861, emigration and the increased death rate owing to starvation and disease caused a marked reduction of the population (table 1, p. 12).

Over the period of twenty years, the population decrease in the Loughrea Union was 59 per cent and in the Gort Union it decreased by 53 per cent, with the main reduction occurring between 1841 and 1851. Typical population

---

1 Protection of Person and Property (Ireland) Act, 44 & 45 Vict., c. 14, 1881.   2 Prevention of Crime (Ireland) Act, 45 & 46 Vict., c. 25, 1882.   3 BL Spencer papers, 77080, Lloyd to Jenkinson, 7 July 1882. Charles Dalton Clifford Lloyd (1844–91), RM 1874–81 and 1885, SRM 1881–3.   4 HC 1845, xxi, 1, Devon Commission.

Table 1 Population changes in the Loughrea and Gort Poor Law Unions, 1841–61 (sources: Kinealy, 'The response of the Poor Law to the Great Famine in Co. Galway', p. 390; Lane, 'The Encumbered Estates Court and Galway land ownership, 1849–58', p. 412).

	1841	1851	1861	Total change
Loughrea	71,774	38,735	29,138	-59%
Gort	43,543	26,759	20,501	-53%

changes in some of the townlands within the Loughrea and Gort Unions are shown in table 2 (p. 13).

The Encumbered Estates (Ireland) Act of 1849 was introduced in an attempt to solve the bankruptcy of Irish estates. Under the act, solvent members of the aristocracy such as lords Clanricarde, Clancarty, Ashtown, Dunsandle and Malahide, as well as many landed gentry made extensive acquisitions.[5] Other purchasers who were interested in commercial farming came from England and Scotland. Shopkeepers were also active in the purchase of encumbered and evicted properties and they became deeply involved in the expanding cattle trade.

Between March and December 1851, 1,223 occupiers were cleared in Galway East Riding and 3,570 in Galway West Riding.[6] The reduction in the amount of land devoted to labour-intensive tillage farming resulted in a decrease in employment for labourers and a major increase in emigration. The consolidation of holdings meant the creation of a distinct group known as graziers and the development of social and class conflicts with the small tillage farmers. The number of sheep and cattle on the land increased dramatically and, with increasing prices and low labour costs, the large farmers and graziers prospered. However, there is good evidence that the same level of prosperity did not extend to the small farmers.[7]

Galway experienced a period of relative prosperity between 1863 and 1876, with a succession of good harvests and a significant improvement in the prices for stock and agricultural produce. Social conditions also improved, with a marked increase in literacy rates, and the politicization of local communities was greatly facilitated by the proliferation of national and local newspapers. The political control exerted by landlords on parliamentary elections began to wane and nationalists increasingly challenged their dominance on the boards of Poor Law Unions. The period of prosperity ended with a succession of bad harvests in the late 1870s, and the agricultural crisis of 1879–80 generated fears of

5 Padraig G. Lane, 'The Encumbered Estates Court and Galway land ownership, 1849–58' in Moran and Gillespie (eds), *Galway: history and society* (1996), pp 395–419. 6 Padraig G. Lane, 'The general impact of the Encumbered Estates Act of 1849 on Counties Galway and Mayo', *Journal of Galway Archaeological and Historical Society*, 33 (1972–3), 44–74. 7 Paul Bew, *Land and the national question in Ireland, 1858–82* (Dublin, 1978), pp 25–33.

Table 2 Population change in some south Galway townlands, 1841–51 (source: de Lourdes Fahy, *Kiltartan: many leaves, one root*, p. 86).

	1841	1851	Change
Ardrahan	4,191	2,887	-31%
Kilchreest	1,579	954	-40%
Killeeneen	1,531	1,014	-34%
Killora	1,618	1,180	-27%
Kilogilleen	1,074	699	-35%

another major famine. This crisis coincided with the foundation of the Irish National Land League (referred to below as the Land League) and the new organization quickly generated widespread enthusiasm for land tenure and constitutional reform.

1 The establishment of the Irish National Land League

Throughout the nineteenth century, the ownership of land and the wealth and the political power derived from it were central political concerns in Ireland. The opposing Irish and British attitudes to property constituted the essence of the problem. The deeply held belief on the part of the Irish was that the land was theirs and had been appropriated by an alien power, whereas the British reverence for the rights of property was unshakeable.

Daniel O'Connell's political activities concentrated on Catholic emancipation and repeal of the Union. The Repeal Association did promote a programme of agrarian reform that included 'the sale of holdings on crown estates to the occupying tenants in small lots, and a scheme for creating peasant proprietors on reclaimed wasteland'. However, O'Connell's declaration in parliament in favour of fixity of tenure did not translate into any action on the land question.[1] The Young Irelanders were also concerned with the problem of land tenure and Thomas Davis 'asserted that because the issue of tenure was a life-or-death matter for the people, it should not be postponed until Ireland had won its national rights'. He also advocated that Irish tenants should become peasant proprietors.[2] In 1848, one member of the group, James Fintan Lalor, voiced his views on land reform with great fervour:

> A mightier question moves Ireland today ... the soil of Ireland for the people of Ireland, to have and to hold from God alone who gave it ... Ireland's most vital need was ... to found a new nation and raise up a free people ... based on a peasantry rooted like rocks in the soil.[3]

Lalor's statement entered popular use in 1870 when the slogan 'The land for the people' appeared on a threatening notice posted on the door of the chapel at Aughamore, Co. Mayo. The signature was the familiar one associated with agrarian secret societies: 'Rory of the Hill and his merry men all'.[4]

In the 1850s, the Irish tenant leagues sought the granting of the '3 Fs' – fair rent, fixity of tenure and free sale – as a basis for land tenure to be attained through legislation. In James S. Donnelly's opinion, 'the distinctive contribution' of the leaders of the movement was

---

1 James S. Donnelly Junior, 'The land question in nationalist politics' in Hachey and McCaffrey (eds), *Perspectives on Irish nationalism* (1989), pp 84–5. 2 Cited in ibid., p. 86. 3 Cited in T.W. Moody, *Davitt and Irish revolution, 1846–82* (Oxford, 1981), p. 36. 4 NAI CSO RP 1870/3528, RM Morris Reade to under secretary, 21 Feb. 1870.

their readiness to put themselves at the head of a popular agrarian campaign. It was this characteristic which marks the tenant-right movement of the early 1850s as the real beginning of an agrarian political tradition in which local, national and parliamentary activities were closely intertwined.[5]

However, the Irish tenant leagues mainly represented the interests of large grain farmers in the southern half of the country and not the impoverished tenant farmers of the west. Furthermore, the lack of political progress on the land tenure question inevitably led to the decline of support for these organizations. The Fenian movement was also inspired by the words of Lalor and, in his study of the Fenians, R.V. Comerford refers to 'a virtually universal assumption at the time that a successful political revolution would result in a redivision of Irish land'.[6]

Land tenure reform came to prominence with the debates on William Ewart Gladstone's Land Act of 1870. The act aimed to provide a greater degree of tenure, similar to the conditions in Ulster. It also allowed for improvements to the property and free sale of the tenant's interest in the property. In practice, the 1870 Land Act failed because landlords issued leases with restrictive clauses that excluded the potential benefits.

The farmers' clubs and tenants' associations, established in the 1870s, also put forward the '3 Fs' as their initial demand. In May 1876, Matthew Harris, James Kilmartin, Michael Malachy O'Sullivan and others founded the Ballinasloe Tenants' Defence Association and at its inaugural meeting James Kilmartin PLG advocated agitation on the land issue in order to emancipate 'the tenant farmers from the thraldom of landlord tyranny'.[7] The BTDA soon became involved in the organization of land meetings in east Galway and south Roscommon.[8] Later in 1876, James Daly, editor of the *Connaught Telegraph*, who had been advocating land tenure reform, called for the establishment of a similar association in Mayo.[9] Daly was impressed by the radical policies of the BTDA and regularly attended meetings, along with his business partner Alfred O'Hea.[10]

Matthew Harris was a Fenian who had been active since 1865 and he was the Connacht representative on the supreme council of the Irish Republican Brotherhood. By 1878, Harris' thinking had already gone beyond the '3 Fs' and, in evidence to the select committee on the Landlord and Tenant (Ireland) Act

---

5 Donnelly, 'The land question in nationalist politics', p. 88.   6 R.V. Comerford, *The Fenians in context* (Dublin, 1985), p. 115.   7 *Connaught Telegraph*, 13 May 1876.   8 Gerard Moran, 'Laying the seeds for agrarian agitation in the west of Ireland' in King and McNamara (eds), *The west of Ireland* (2011), p. 74.   9 *Connaught Telegraph*, 5 Aug. 1876.   10 Gerard Moran, 'James Daly and the rise and fall of the Land League in the west of Ireland, 1879–1882', *Journal of the Irish Historical Society*, 39:114 (1994), 191.

1870, commonly known as the Bessborough Commission, he advocated peasant proprietorship and government intervention to provide funding for the purchase of landlords' estates.[11] It is significant that Harris was one of the people that Michael Davitt met when he visited Galway and Mayo in January 1878, soon after his release from Dartmoor prison.[12]

In 1878, Davitt had resumed his relationship with the Fenian movement, being elected to the supreme council of the IRB to represent the north of England. Later that year, Davitt undertook an extended visit to America during which he familiarized himself with all strands of Irish-American opinion. He became well acquainted with John Devoy, who was responsible for the telegram transmitted to Ireland for Charles Kickham and published in the *New York Herald Tribune* on 25 October 1878. This document outlined the plan for a new departure, which would allow the Fenians and constitutional nationalists to cooperate in order to achieve mutually desirable ends. The main proposals were:

> First, abandonment of the federal demand, and substitution of a general declaration in favour of self-government. Second, vigorous agitation of the land question on the basis of a peasant proprietary, while accepting concessions tending to abolish arbitrary eviction. Third, exclusion of all sectarian issues from the platform. Fourth, Irish members to vote together on all imperial and home questions, adopt an aggressive policy, and energetically resist coercive legislation. Fifth, advocacy of all struggling nationalities in the British Empire and elsewhere.[13]

Controversy surrounded the telegram because of Kickham's rejection of the proposals and doubts about Charles Stewart Parnell's attitude to them, but in practice it opened the way for close cooperation between the Fenians and the promoters of the land agitation.

The latter part of 1878 saw further political developments in Ireland with the establishment of the Mayo Tenants' Defence Association in October. John O'Connor Power addressed the inaugural meeting. He was a native of Ballinasloe and had, in 1861, emigrated to Lancashire, where he met Davitt and joined the IRB. He became a member of parliament in 1874 and later a member of the IRB supreme council.[14] In his speech, he used the phrase 'the land of Ireland for the people of Ireland', which was to become one of the popular slogans of the Land League. On the same occasion, John James Louden, a barrister from Westport, said that there was a need for 'the passing of a law which will settle the land

---

11 HC 1878 (249), xv, 1, Report from the select committee on the Irish Land Act 1870. 12 Moody, *Davitt and Irish revolution, 1846–82*, p. 193. 13 D.B. Cashman, *The life of Michael Davitt, founder of the National Land League* (London, n.d.), p. 57. 14 Moody, *Davitt and Irish revolution, 1846–82*, p. 47.

question forever – which will make the land the property of those who occupy and cultivate it'.[15]

Throughout this period, O'Connor Power and James Daly promoted the alliance of tenant farmers with aggressive parliamentarians in support of the land agitation and national independence.[16] In November, Parnell addressed a meeting of the BTDA. During his speech, he acknowledged that tenants should become 'possessors of their own farms' and peasant proprietorship, rather than the '3 Fs', should be the basis for a future settlement of the land question.[17] However, later that month he voiced a more cautious approach to the question in Tralee.[18]

In January 1879, Davitt travelled to Paris for a meeting of the IRB supreme council but he failed to get support for the 'new departure'. On his return to Mayo, he learned of the bad harvest of 1878 and fears of a famine in 1879 if the harvest failed again. In the early months of 1879, James Daly commenced preparations for a land meeting in Irishtown, Co. Mayo. A number of Fenians were actively involved, including John Walshe and P.W. Nally from Balla, and John O'Keane and Patrick J. Quinn from Claremorris.[19] The meeting was held on 20 April and was attended by a crowd variously estimated at seven thousand to thirteen thousand.[20] Davitt did not attend but drafted two of the resolutions.[21] There were two representatives from Galway on the platform, Matthew Harris and M.M. O'Sullivan, a teacher in Ballinasloe and also a Fenian. In the course of an eloquent speech, O'Sullivan advised the negotiation of a fair rent and, if agreement could not be reached with a landlord, that no rent should be paid. He concluded by saying:

> It is true; I would wish to see every man his own landlord – to see a system of peasant proprietorship established in the country, such as that which has enriched France, Belgium, Switzerland and Germany. I would give the landlords the full purchase money but I would abolish the system.

He went on to say that he did not approve of the shooting of landlords.[22]

The second mass meeting followed in Westport on 8 June, with Davitt and Parnell in attendance. Three days prior to the meeting, Archbishop John McHale of Tuam wrote to the *Freeman's Journal* expressing concerns about the 'combinations in this diocese, organized by a few designing men, who, ... seek only to promote their personal interests'.[23] Harris and O'Sullivan were again on

---

15 *Connaught Telegraph*, 26 Oct. and 2 Nov. 1878. 16 Donald E. Jordan, *Land and popular politics in Ireland* (Cambridge, 1994), p. 211. 17 *Freeman's Journal*, 4 Nov. 1878. 18 *Freeman's Journal*, 18 Nov. 1878. 19 Michael Davitt, *The fall of feudalism in Ireland* (London and New York, 1904), p. 147. 20 *Connaught Telegraph*, *Tuam Herald* and *Western News*, 26 Apr. 1879. 21 Moody, *Davitt and Irish revolution, 1846–82*, p. 291. 22 *Connaught Telegraph*, 26 Apr. 1879. 23 *Freeman's Journal*, 5 June 1879.

the platform in Westport. In the first resolution, Davitt asserted the right of the country to self-determination. O'Sullivan went further, stating that 'moral force is truly a great power, but becomes a greater power when backed up by physical force'. Parnell demanded ownership of the land and coined another of the Land League's slogans: 'You must show the landlords that you intend to hold a firm grip of your homesteads'.[24]

Further mass meetings followed in Milltown, Co. Galway, and in Claremorris, Co. Mayo, on 13 July.[25] Archbishop McHale again wrote to the *Freeman's Journal* and cast aspersions on 'a few unknown, strolling men, who, with affected grief, deploring the condition of the tenantry, seek only to mount to place and preferment on the shoulders of the people'.[26] In reply, Davitt alluded to his family's connection with Mayo and referred to his own prison experiences, stating that the only preferment he could expect for his actions was a return to prison.[27] On this occasion, there was evidence of clerical support with Canon Ulick Bourke in the chair and eleven other priests on the platform. However, prior to the meeting suspicions were voiced by James Daly who claimed that Bourke's purpose was the undermining of the independence of the tenant movement. This view may have prompted the organizers to refuse to include any proposals that were sectarian.[28] According to Donald Jordan, the terms for clerical involvement in the developing land movement were outlined by Matthew Harris at a meeting in Balla when he referred to his resolution which supported 'a closer union between the priests and the people' but also stated that the 'proposed union must be one in which the people, not the priests, would determine the course of events'.[29] A succession of meetings during June and July culminated in the foundation of the National Land League of Mayo on 16 August 1879. The purpose of the organization was to 'supplant the Tenants' Defence Associations and create an aggressive movement which would try to rally the country in a fight against the whole land system'.[30]

The political agitation quickly spread throughout Co. Galway and during September and October meetings were held in Clifden, Tuam, Claregalway and Currandula.[31] The first land meeting in south Galway was held in Gort in October and from the start there was a significant clerical presence at the meetings. Bishop McEvilly of Galway and, from November 1881, archbishop of Tuam, was 'opposed to any form of agitation ... and allowed no distinction between the outrages carried out by secret societies and the more restrained form of agitation encouraged by the Land League'. Moreover, 'while personally hostile to the league ... he was anxious that priests be present at meetings' in

---

24 *Connaught Telegraph*, 14 June 1879. 25 *Freeman's Journal*, 14 June 1879. 26 *Freeman's Journal*, 10 July 1879. 27 *Freeman's Journal*, 11 July 1879. 28 Jordan, *Land and popular politics in Ireland*, pp 239–40. 29 Ibid., pp 241–2. 30 Davitt, *The fall of feudalism*, p. 164. 31 NAI, CSO, RP 1880/34686.

order to exercise 'control and restraint'.³² In contrast, the Land League enjoyed the unequivocal support of the bishop of Clonfert, Patrick Duggan. He had already expressed strong views on the land question and in evidence to the Richmond Commission spoke in favour of a peasant proprietary. Bishop Duggan became an admirer and close friend of Davitt.

A development of profound importance was Parnell's agreement to join the movement, and on 21 October 1879, the Irish National Land League was established with Parnell as president. Michael Davitt, Thomas Brennan and Andrew Kettle became the secretaries and M.M. O'Sullivan became assistant secretary. Patrick Egan, Joseph Biggar and W.H. O'Sullivan were appointed treasurers. There were two Catholic priests present at the meeting, but fourteen were nominated on the committee. Matthew Harris and Richard Kelly, proprietor of the *Tuam Herald*, represented Galway. The objects of the league were

a) to bring about a reduction of rack-rents;
b) to facilitate the obtaining of the ownership of the soil by the occupiers.

It was agreed that the objects of the league could be best attained by promoting organization among the tenant farmers; by defending those who might be threatened with eviction for refusing to pay unjust rents; by facilitating the working of the Bright clauses³³ of the Land Act during the winter; and by obtaining such a reform in the laws relating to land as would enable every tenant to become the owner of his holding by paying a fair rent for a limited number of years. It was also agreed that none of the funds should be used for the purchase of any landlord's interest in the land or for furthering the interests of any parliamentary candidate. Parnell was requested to proceed to America for the purpose of obtaining assistance from the Irish-American community.

Davitt's 'appeal to the Irish race for the sustainment of the movement was approved with an order that it be circulated'.³⁴ The appeal was addressed to Irish-Americans and referred to the land system as 'barbarous, unjust and reprehensible'. It demanded 'ownership of the soil by the occupiers in substitution of the landlords' but did not seek confiscation but 'a fair compensation ... to those who shall be called upon to agree to such transfer for the settlement of the agrarian strife of the country and the supreme good of its people'. In order to achieve this aim, the landless farmers must organize to assert their rights and financial support would be required from Irish exiles.³⁵ In his retrospective

---

32 Liam Bane, 'John McEvilly and the Catholic Church in Galway, 1857–1902' in Moran and Gillespie (eds), *Galway: history and society* (1996), p. 435.   33 John Bright MP (1811–89) introduced clauses in the 1870 land act for the payment of advances to tenants in order to purchase their holdings.   34 Davitt, *The fall of feudalism*, pp 171–2.   35 Cashman, *The life of Michael Davitt*, pp 103–7.

comments, Davitt acknowledged that the Fenian leaders in Ireland had opposed the new departure but he considered that the men of Clan na Gael in America 'were most favourable to it'.[36] Parnell and John Dillon soon departed for America to launch the appeal for financial support for the new organization.

36 Davitt, *The fall of feudalism*, p. 176.

2 The agricultural crisis of 1879–80

INTRODUCTION

The agricultural crisis of 1879–80 occurred after a period of relative prosperity that extended from 1863 to the mid-1870s. A marked increase in livestock production since the Great Famine had improved the income levels of graziers and larger farmers. In 1875 and 1876, the yields of hay and potatoes were exceptionally high and the reduction in emigration rates in 1876–8 may be one indication of the rising expectations of people identified by Donnelly.[1] However, the subsistence economies of the west of Ireland remained impoverished.

The weather in 1877 was very poor and resulted in a marked reduction in potato production in the Loughrea and Gort Poor Law Unions (PLUs),[2] but there was some improvement of conditions in 1878. The following year proved to be disastrous in terms of crop production, however, and this precipitated a severe agricultural crisis. The very inclement weather commenced in October 1878 with an exceptionally cold month and below average temperatures were recorded each month until October 1879. In addition, February 1879 was exceptionally wet and rainfall figures were well above average in June, July and August. The official report indicated that the mean temperature for the year was three degrees below average with 'unusually clouded skies and deficient sunshine and a rainfall considerably in excess of the average'.[3] Indeed, John Devoy, during his extended visit to Ireland in the spring of that year, claimed that he never saw a clear sky.[4] The weather during the final three months of 1879 was cold and dry, which helped to salvage some of the crops. However, the cold and wet conditions during the growing and harvesting seasons resulted in a very poor harvest. The weather statistics for the first nine months of the year are shown in table 3 (p. 22).

Table 4 (p. 22) shows the produce of crops per acre in the Loughrea and Gort PLUs in 1879 compared with the average output for the period 1876–8.

The production of oats was well below average; the potato crop was reduced by more than 50 per cent and the crop was also badly affected by disease. The hay crop was close to the average in quantity but the quality was poor and great amounts could not be harvested because of flooding.

Table 5 (p. 22) shows the changes in livestock numbers for 1880 compared with the average for 1876–8. The figures indicate the effects of the reduction in available fodder after the poor harvest of 1879 and, in the case of sheep, the

---

1 James S. Donnelly Junior, *The land and the people of nineteenth-century Cork* (London, 1975), p. 250. 2 HC 1878 [C.1938], lxxvii, 511. 3 HC 1880 [C.2534], lxxvi, 815. 4 NAI, Fenian A files, A 612, report of John Devoy (copy).

Table 3 Average weather conditions in the first nine months of 1879 compared with those of the first nine months of the years 1869–78 (source: HC 1880 [C.2534], lxxvi, 815. The weather data were recorded in Dublin; the records for Queen's College, Galway, which commenced in 1862, are lacking for the period 1872–80).

Period	Mean temperature	Cloud (per cent)	Rainfall (inches)	Rainy days
Jan.–Sept. 1869–78	50.7°F	59.6	2.2	144
Jan.–Sept. 1879	47.6°F	68.3	2.8	174

Table 4 Produce of crops in Loughrea and Gort PLUs, 1876–8 and 1879 (source: HC 1880 [C.2534], lxxvi, 815).

	Loughrea PLU			Gort PLU		
Crops	Average output 1876–8	Output 1879	Change	Average output 1876–8	Output 1879	Change
Oats (cwt per acre)	14.2	10.8	–24%	12.87	11.1	–14%
Potatoes (tons per acre)	2.9	1.3	–55%	3.66	1.6	–56%
Hay (tons per acre)	1.9	1.8	–5%	2.00	1.8	–10%

Table 5 Livestock in Loughrea and Gort PLUs, 1876–8 and 1880 (source: HC 1881 [C.2932], xciii, 685).

	Loughrea PLU			Gort PLU		
Livestock	Average 1876–8	Numbers in 1880	Change	Average 1876–8	Numbers in 1880	Change
Horses	3,724	3,994	+3%	2,588	2,596	+0.3%
Cattle	25,540	25,779	+0.9%	11,761	11,886	+1%
Sheep	108,751	92,492	–15%	65,270	56,320	–14%
Pigs	7,744	5,747	–26%	5,858	4,206	–28%

effects of the wet season that favoured diseases such as liver fluke. The number of sheep was reduced by 15 per cent in Loughrea PLU and 14 per cent in Gort PLU. Pig numbers fell by 26 per cent in Loughrea and 28 per cent in Gort. The failure of the potato crop resulted in a lack of fodder for pigs and there may have been an increased sale of pigs in order to pay the rent and increased killing of pigs for domestic consumption. A similar reduction in pig numbers was observed during the Great Famine, with small farmers forced to sell sheep and pigs without having the necessary finance to replace them.[5] The relatively small

5 James S. Donnelly Junior, *The great Irish potato famine* (Stroud, 2001), p. 76.

effects on cattle and sheep numbers may be explained by the poor sales of stock in the autumn of 1879. At the Ballinasloe fair of that year, 67 per cent of sheep and 65 per cent of cattle were sold; this was well below the average sales levels.[6]

The results outlined for the Loughrea and Gort PLUs closely parallel the figures for both crop production and livestock numbers throughout Co. Galway, the province of Connacht and nationally.

THE ESTABLISHMENT OF RELIEF FUNDS BY CHARITABLE BODIES AND THE LAND LEAGUE

With the evolving evidence of a poor harvest in 1879, the spectre of famine again appeared and there was an obvious need for relief measures. In early September, the Local Government Board (LGB) requested a report from their inspectors on the state of the harvest and whether there would be much distress and an unusual demand for relief during the coming winter. On receipt of the reports, the board informed Dublin Castle on 28 October 1879 that 'the potato crop was deficient in quantity, inferior in quality and affected with blight and that upon the whole there would not be more than half an average crop'. They also stated that the general harvest appeared to be inferior. 'The supply of turf appeared to be greatly deficient everywhere and much suffering and sickness was anticipated'. They concluded that 'there would be a considerable increase in pauperism during the winter season' and finally, they expressed the opinion 'that the Poor Law Unions would be equal to the demands'.[7]

'Many of the clerics who attended land meetings in the autumn of 1879 attributed their presence to the impending famine'[8] and from this early stage the Catholic clergy were at the forefront of the efforts to deal with the crisis. At a meeting of the Irish Catholic bishops on 24 October, there was unanimous agreement 'that the existing Poor Law was insufficient to cope with the coming crisis'. They warned that 'it is the urgent duty of the government to take effectual measures to save the people from a calamity'.[9] Throughout the winter, the LGB was in regular communication with Dublin Castle regarding the provision of loans to landholders for relief works and the need for emergency measures. The reports forecasting an impending famine aroused widespread interest and Palmer quotes numerous accounts from special correspondents for newspapers in England, America and the Continent that gave graphic accounts of the sufferings of the people, particularly in the west of Ireland.[10]

---

6 *Thom's Directory, 1882*, pp 693–4.　7 HC 1879 [C.2483] and [C.2506], Correspondence relative to measures for the relief of distress in Ireland.　8 Gerard Moran, 'Near famine: the Roman Catholic Church and the subsistence crisis of 1879–82', *Studia Hibernica*, 32 (2002–3), 161.　9 Norman Dunbar Palmer, *The Irish Land League crisis* (New Haven, CT, 1940), p. 78.　10 Ibid., pp 64–77.

In mid-December 1879, a charitable fund was established by the duchess of Marlborough, the wife of the lord lieutenant. She promoted the fund vigorously and contributions came from England, including £35,000 from the citizens of London, as well as from Canada, France and elsewhere.[11] The Mansion House Relief Fund, established by the lord mayor of Dublin, held its first meeting on 2 January 1880. Many prominent citizens joined the committee, including Archbishop McCabe of Dublin, who was also involved in the other committees.

The Mansion House Relief Committee (MHRC) met frequently to acknowledge the receipt of funds from all over the world and to decide regarding the distribution of money to local committees. A total of 840 local committees were founded and members included 1,404 Catholic clergymen and 835 Protestant ministers as well as other prominent citizens. The chairman of the Loughrea committee was Revd James Carroll and the other members were William Strattan (secretary), the Protestant rector, Revd Edward Rush, Revd P. Egan CC, Town Commissioner Dr John Burke, John Smyth JP, John O'Toole PLG, Columbus Kelly (printer) and M.E. Kelly (president of St Brendan's College). The treasurer was M.J. Nicholson of the National Bank. The first donation to the Loughrea committee of £100 was received in January, providing relief for 330 families comprising 1,320 persons and in every instance there was extreme distress if not absolute destitution.[12] Thereafter, the fund provided £25 to £75 at regular intervals. In addition, separate appeals were made by the nuns of the Convent of Mercy, Loughrea, for funds to aid children attending the school and those in the orphanage.[13]

Private donations were received by the bishops and religious organizations, an estimated £200,000 coming from Catholic sources. The *New York Herald Tribune* Fund was inaugurated in early January 1880 by a gift of $100,000 from James Gordon Bennett, the owner of the paper.[14] In addition, the Land League distributed £60,000 raised in America by Parnell and Dillon. The Land League distributed sums of money through their local branches and this also helped to recruit new members from the local communities and the establishment of new branches.

The Land League leaders gave a very guarded response to the work of the charitable organizations, with Davitt complaining to John Devoy that Parnell's persistent attacks on the Duchess of Marlborough Fund were 'arraying a phalanx of holy heroes against him'. At the same time, Davitt was wary of the charitable organizations, stating 'that vigilance is required to prevent the work of the past year being undone through the demoralising influences of meal and money'.[15]

11 Ibid., pp 85–6. 12 Mansion House Relief Committee Correspondence, CH 1/52/109, 30 Jan. 1880. 13 Mansion House Relief Committee Correspondence, CH 1/52/109, 11 Mar. 1880. 14 Palmer, *The Irish Land League crisis*, p. 84. 15 William O'Brien and Desmond Ryan (eds), *Devoy's post bag* (Dublin, 1948), Davitt to Devoy, 6 Feb. 1880, vol. 1, p. 483.

In January 1880, the parish priest of Athenry, Revd P.J. O'Brien, pleaded at a meeting of the Loughrea Board of Guardians for immediate relief works and outdoor relief for eighty families. While the meeting was taking place, two hundred labourers gathered in front of the workhouse, asking for relief work.[16] The local committee in Athenry was typical of many in the country, being chaired by Revd O'Brien and having Revd P.J. McPhilpin CC as treasurer. Communicating with the central committee on 2 February, the secretary indicated that 183 families of 474 persons required relief in the town and a further 222 families of 966 persons in the country portion of the parish.[17] Also in January, Revd Jerome Fahey, Peterswell, writing to Archbishop McCabe, reported that over one hundred families were in want and 'few of the land proprietors were inclined to provide employment'. In particular, he referred to the 'urgency of getting seed potatoes and the sum required is much greater than the bishop [McEvilly] can afford to send'.[18]

In a report sent from Loughrea to the Duchess of Marlborough Fund, the almost complete failure of the crops was recorded, with many families reported to be starving. An instance was given of one family of nine who 'were living on raw Indian meal because they did not even have the fuel to cook it'. The harvest of turf was greatly reduced due to the poor weather, which made bogs inaccessible. It was also reported that tenants had already eaten their seed potatoes, with none kept for sowing.[19] A more sanguine view was expressed by Colonel Deane, a temporary inspector for the LGB reporting to the same fund, having garnered his intelligence from gentlemen farmers he met at the February fair in Loughrea. He suggested that 'although there was no starvation, there was considerable want'.[20] Reporting from Gort a short while later, Colonel Deane said that

> the distress was much exaggerated. Nothing approaching starvation is anticipated and a judicious distribution of relief will enable the distressed classes to tide over the period which must elapse before regular work can be obtained.[21]

The bishop of Clonfert, Dr Patrick Duggan, was a leading figure in the efforts to support the people in his diocese and, writing to Archbishop McCabe on 2 March 1880, he referred to every parish requiring relief. 'In the towns, artisans of all descriptions are all but idle, as their employers are now unable to employ'. He also commented that 'only in some very few cases, landlords are aiding them'.[22] On 17 May 1880, Bishop Duggan wrote to the MHRC stating that for the previous week his house was 'surrounded from morning to night

16 *Irish Times*, 19 Jan. 1880. 17 Mansion House Relief Committee Correspondence, CH 1/52/78. 18 Dublin Diocesan Archive, McCabe Relief of Distress Papers, Correspondence. 19 *Irish Times*, 9 Jan. 1880. 20 *Irish Times*, 13 Feb. 1880. 21 *Irish Times*, 17 Feb. 1880. 22 Dublin Diocesan Archive, McCabe Relief of Distress Papers, 2 Mar. 1880.

with a clamorous and hungry crowd begging food or work'. He had already disbursed large sums that he had received from France, America and other places. 'There is no work to be had here, though the poor people are willing to earn their bread'.[23] He asked the Relief Committee to remember that 382 families comprising 1,172 persons were dependant on charitable donations.

There had been repeated demands on the government to implement relief measures and in March 1880 the Relief of Distress (Ireland) Act 1880 was enacted by parliament. Funding of £1.5 million was obtained from the Church Disestablishment Fund to provide public works by means of loans to landholders and the Board of Public Works. In addition, Major John Nolan, MP for Galway, introduced the Seed Supply Act, empowering PLUs to borrow money without interest for the purchase of seed potatoes and other seeds. This was of great importance because families had already consumed their store of potatoes leaving none for planting in the spring. At the end of April, the MHRC wrote to the LGB enquiring as to why the Relief of Distress Act had not been availed of in certain areas; for instance, in Swinford and Manorhamilton. The LGB replied that some unions had obtained orders authorizing outdoor relief for a limited time but did not consider it necessary that the orders be renewed. They further stated that 'the very liberal assistance afforded to the poor by means of funds obtained from charitable sources has in many places rendered it unnecessary for Boards of Guardians to administer outdoor relief to able-bodied persons.[24] In June, enquiries to the local relief committees in Galway, based on returns from seventy-five of the ninety committees, revealed that in more than half of the districts no public works had been projected and in twenty-seven districts they had not been started by 1 June.[25]

Great destitution prevailed among the labourers and small farmers on the Dunsandle estate. Lord Dunsandle responded with a reduction of 25 per cent in the May rents and he also supplied oats, potatoes and timber to his poorer tenants.[26] A meeting of tenant farmers near Clostoken appealed to their absentee landlord, Dr John Harrison of Chester, to exercise mercy in relation to the rent.[27] Also in May, destitute labourers marched through Loughrea to plead for help at the residence of Bishop Duggan. After giving them sums of money, he attended a meeting of the Board of Guardians to plead with the board to help the poor.[28] The response from the Board of Guardians was the passage of a resolution by a large majority stating that 'we are not justified in calling on the LGB for an order to enable us to give outdoor relief'.[29]

On 15 June, Dr Roughan, a LGB inspector, visited Loughrea and attended a meeting of the local relief committee, chaired by Bishop Duggan. The bishop

23 Mansion House Relief Committee, Minute Book, 20 May 1880. 24 Mansion House Relief Committee, Minute Book, 11 May 1880. 25 Mansion House Relief Committee, Minute Book, 12 June 1880. 26 *Irish Times*, 8 May 1880. 27 *Western News*, 15 May 1880. 28 *Western News*, 22 May 1880. 29 *Western News*, 5 June 1880.

said that he had heard of reports going to government denying the existence of distress in Loughrea and he was bound to state that great distress did exist there. Roughan refused to visit the impoverished areas; nevertheless, he heard of the problems from a number of poor people. That evening, an angry crowd of some two hundred people marched through the streets and later burned an effigy of the local relieving officer, James Rickham, because he had denied the existence of distress in Loughrea.[30]

In a debate in the House of Commons, the members for Co. Galway, Major Nolan and Mitchell Henry, criticized the disbursement of funds to landlords at interest rates of 1 per cent, compared with the loans from the Board of Works at rates of 6 per cent, which severely limited the number of applications for such loans when they were so desperately needed in the winter of 1880.[31] In the House of Commons on 28 June, when Parnell wished to move the Relief (Ireland) Bill, he received no support from Chief Secretary William Edward Forster, who declared that the PLUs could deal with the existing distress. However, Forster made a proposal to reduce the rate of interest charged to the unions for the purpose of outdoor relief.[32]

Bishop Duggan addressed the MHRC on 23 June and indicated that, in Loughrea, between 1,100 and 1,200 people were receiving relief from the local committee at a cost of £40 per week. He had received £7,000 from private sources and was distributing £600 per week for relief purposes to the priests of the diocese of Clonfert. He believed the Poor Law system was of no value in such a crisis because only seven persons out of a population of four thousand were receiving outdoor relief. In terms recalling the Great Famine, he said that 'he knew people who would elect to die rather than enter a poorhouse. To hold out the poorhouse as a mode of relieving distress at any time was simply inhuman'.[33] He said that his statements about distress in Loughrea applied also to the towns of Ballinasloe and Portumna and all the small towns and rural hamlets in his diocese. He referred to parliamentary questions tabled by Major Nolan in relation to carrying out baronial works. In reply, Nolan was informed by the chief secretary, W.E. Forster, that a sum of £5,000 had been borrowed for the purpose and that the officers of the Loughrea Board of Guardians had stated there was no distress requiring work.[34] One of the successful contributions by the government was the provision of gunboats that were deployed to deliver supplies to the islands off the west coast and remote areas on the coast. For a time, one of the boats was captained by the duke of Edinburgh.[35]

Although the prevalence of disease and death was much less than during the Great Famine, the national mortality figures showed that deaths in 1879 were 10

---

30 *Western News*, 19 June 1880.   31 *Western News*, 5 June 1880.   32 Ibid.   33 *Western News*, 3 July 1880.   34 Mansion House Relief Committee, Minute Book, 1 July 1880.   35 Palmer, *The Irish Land League crisis*, p. 95.

per cent above the yearly average for 1870–8 and in 1880 the figure was 8 per cent above average.[36] The MHRC sent a medical commission, composed of Drs George Sigerson and Joseph E. Kenny, to report on the causes of the fever epidemic in the west of Ireland. All around Loughrea, they found examples of typhus fever. In Oranmore, 132 cases were suspected and fourteen deaths had occurred, including that of the local medical practitioner, Dr Greally. In Athenry, there were thirty-four cases and four deaths and in Craughwell, Revd T.D. Geoghegan reported that two families were affected.

The death rates would almost certainly have been much higher but for the actions of the relief committees and the intervention of the PLUs. In February 1878, 51,720 people received relief in workhouses and this figure had increased to 60,341 by February 1880. There was an increase of 22 per cent in people receiving outdoor relief from 37,103 in 1878 to 47,418 in 1880 and by February 1881 there was a marked increase to 93,167. However, there was widespread anger that the PLUs had not done enough to relieve distress. The social effects of the crisis were also evident in the reduction in the number of marriages by 10 per cent in 1879 and 21 per cent in 1880. Furthermore, the birth rate fell by 5 per cent in 1879 and 10 per cent in 1880.

One of the features of the Great Famine was the dramatic increase in emigration. An increase also occurred during the agricultural crisis of 1879–80. In 1878, 41,626 people emigrated from Ireland but in 1879 the figure increased to 47,364 and a further massive increase occurred in 1880 when as many as 95,517 people emigrated.[37] Local newspaper accounts corroborated the bare national statistics when, in a single day, twenty young men and a large number of young women left for America from the Loughrea district.[38] In the same week, twenty young people from Killeenadeema emigrated and, on 25 May, another twenty boarded the train from Craughwell to Queenstown. A report in the *Western News* stated that the country between Loughrea and Craughwell contained some fertile land that was owned by a few graziers, with only a few scattered houses to be seen and the ruins of once comfortable homesteads visible along the road.[39]

The annual report of the LGB indicates that the limit of their ambitions in 1880 was to prevent starvation while tolerating 'much suffering from want'.[40] The attitude of the public bodies was in stark contrast to the life-saving disbursements by the charitable organizations. The final report of the Duchess of Marlborough Fund indicated that the total amount subscribed was £135,245, of which £36,983 was expended on the purchase of seed potatoes and other seeds.[41] The Mansion House Relief Fund raised £181,350 and the *New York Herald Tribune* Fund $341,000. The MHRC estimated that a total of £830,000

36 HC 1880 [C.2567], lxxvi, 1003 and HC 1881 [C.2894], xciv, 721. 37 HC 1878–9 [C.2221], lxxv, 703, HC 1880 [C.2501], lxxvi, 985 and HC 1881 [C.2828], xciv, 703. 38 *Western News*, 15 May 1880. 39 *Western News*, 29 May 1880. 40 HC 1880 [C.2603], Annual report of the local government board for Ireland, 13. 41 Moran, 'Near famine', 161.

was raised and distributed by all the charitable sources, including the funds received by the Irish bishops and money sent directly to individuals, and this undoubtedly helped to avert a major disaster.[42] In 1880, weather conditions improved and consequently the harvest showed some improvement on the previous year. There was an increased production of oats, potatoes and hay in the Loughrea PLU of 23, 38 and 5 per cent respectively.[43]

In a letter to Archbishop McCabe on 27 October 1880, however, Bishop Duggan remained very apprehensive regarding conditions in the country and reported 'that destitution was still evident in his diocese and the potato crop is materially damaged'. He wrote 'these are critical times, those threatened prosecutions [of Parnell and others] will only intensify this agitation on the land question and complicate our difficulty. God grant that great mischief does not follow'.[44]

---

[42] Moody, *Davitt and Irish revolution*, p. 356. [43] HC 1881 [C.2932], xciii, 685. [44] Dublin Diocesan Archives, McCabe Irish Bishops file, 1880.

3 Local and national political developments, 1879–80

THE LAND LEAGUE IN CO. GALWAY

Following the establishment of the Irish National Land League in October 1879, the land agitation movement gathered momentum in Co. Galway with the holding of public land meetings. A meeting in Athenry on 1 November 1879 was attended by six thousand people. The chairperson, Revd P.J. O'Brien PP, addressed the meeting in an extraordinary speech, replete with classical allusions that must have bemused many in the audience. The tone of the meeting was conservative and moderate resolutions were passed relating to home rule and relief for struggling tenants. Congratulatory references were made to Mitchell Henry and Major Nolan, the MPs for the county.[1] Three weeks later, they both addressed the Ballinasloe land meeting at which one resolution commended the abatement of rent offered by Galway landlords. Major Nolan offered 25 per cent, Mitchell Henry 20 per cent, Lord Dunsandle 15 per cent for tenants with holdings valued at less than £100 and 10 per cent on holdings of more than £100, Christopher Usher 20 per cent and Captain Smyth of Masonbrook remitted a whole year's rent. At the Ballinasloe meeting, the first resolution referred to the distress occasioned by a succession of bad harvests and the depreciation in the value of farming stock and agricultural produce.[2] There was no reference to Lord Clanricarde who had responded to a request from his Craughwell tenants for a reduction of rent with a threat to evict them all if they did not pay in full.[3] The resolutions at the meeting demanded action by the government to provide employment, protection from eviction and the right of free sale. It is of interest that Matthew Harris played little part in the proceedings and this may explain the moderate nature of the demands.

The land meeting on 6 January 1880 was the occasion of Davitt's first visit to Loughrea. Revd Carroll CC chaired the meeting and there were ten other clergymen on the platform as well as a number of townspeople and tenant farmers. In his speech to the large and enthusiastic crowd, Davitt called for national self-government and a radical solution to the land problem through the creation of peasant proprietors and the abolition of landlordism.[4] In a powerful speech, Matthew Harris advised that people should not be too grateful for generous gestures by landlords. Referring to the Land League as a social as well as a political agitation, he maintained that the 'time is coming when the lands of this country must be confiscated and will be ours'. The police note-taker

1 *Western News*, 8 Nov. 1879. 2 *Western News*, 29 Nov. 1879. 3 Ibid. 4 *Western News*, 10 Jan. 1880.

observed that a number of the clergymen and others on the platform dissociated themselves from some of the strong opinions expressed by Harris.[5] Interesting features of the south Galway meetings were the letters of apology from Bishop Duggan for his inability to attend. The letters, however, voiced strong support for the Land League and at the Loughrea meeting a letter stated that 'in order to prevent recurrent cycles of famine, the tenants must be rooted in the soil, at rents to be regulated by a competent and impartial tribunal. By degrees this will lead to a large increase in peasant proprietors'.[6]

During the early part of 1880, Land League members concentrated on the distribution of relief funds and Davitt later claimed that the involvement of local clergy in this process often led to the formation of branches of the Land League.[7] A branch of the Land League had been formed in Craughwell in late 1879, no doubt in response to Lord Clanricarde's threat of eviction, and new branches followed in Ballinasloe, Creggs, Mountbellew, Gurteen and Athenry.[8] The branch in Loughrea was not formally established until December 1880.

The tactical programme of the Land League developed throughout 1880. Protests were organized against evictions and support was provided for evicted tenants. Members were forbidden to take farms vacated by evicted tenants and anyone doing so should be regarded as a traitor. The potent weapon of social ostracism was given explicit support by Parnell in his speech in Ennis in September 1880,[9] when he advocated that 'a land grabber should be put into moral Coventry and isolated as if he was a leper of old'. Large crowds attempted to prevent process serving and evictions; strong passions were aroused during such events and often led to assaults on bailiffs, process servers, landlords and their agents. Land grabbers were intimidated by threatening letters and notices posted in the vicinity of their dwellings. Shots were fired into houses, animals were maimed and serious assaults occurred. Mass resistance to process serving and evictions achieved early success in Carraroe in January 1880, with a major confrontation between local people and large forces of police and military. At one location, the road between Spiddal and Carraroe was dug up, and at another a large boulder was placed on it to prevent access by the police and military. John Fenton, the local process server, and his police escort were attacked with stones and blackthorn sticks, forcing them to retreat to the barracks. Police reinforcements were recruited but a very large crowd from Carraroe and the surrounding districts confronted them and prevented the serving of the processes. At the end of May 1880, the controversy over process serving again arose and on that occasion a very large force of police and military, many of whom were transported to Carraroe by sea, was assembled to protect the process server. However,

---

5 NAI, Parnell Special Commission, box 4.   6 *Western News*, 10 Jan. 1880.   7 Davitt, *The fall of feudalism*, p. 211.   8 NAI CSO RP 1880/34686, Co. Galway ER. Summaries of reports received from RIC relative to the Land League.   9 *Freeman's Journal*, 20 Sept. 1880.

on this occasion the process server's son served the writs and there were no violent incidents. Shortly afterwards, during the debate in the House of Commons on the Compensation for Disturbance Bill, Forster stated:

> We feel bound to carry out the law, and enforce these evictions with any exercise of force however severely they may press upon this distressed people. So long as I remain where I am, and that law exists, it will be my hard duty to enforce it, because nothing can work so much harm in Ireland as to allow the law to be disobeyed or disregarded.[10]

The increase in agrarian crime later in 1880 influenced Forster to prepare the PPP (Ireland) Act 1881, designed to ensure the enforcement of the law and the suppression of the Land League.

NATIONAL DEVELOPMENTS

In April 1880, the general election resulted in the defeat of the Conservative government of Lord Beaconsfield (Benjamin Disraeli) and W.E. Gladstone's return to power. Parnell was elected for three constituencies, Cork city, Co. Mayo and Co. Meath, and a number of key supporters were elected for the first time. These included John Dillon, James J. O'Kelly, Thomas Sexton and T.P. O'Connor. Two hundred delegates from Land League branches attended a land conference on 29 April in the Rotunda, Dublin. The establishment of a peasant proprietary was adopted as the desired outcome of a permanent reform of land tenure and a department of land administration should be established to administer this reform. A proposal was approved for the introduction of a bill suspending for two years ejectments for non-payment of rent on all holdings valued at £10, this sum being changed to £20 by amendment.[11] It was also proposed that the right of recovery of a higher rent than Griffith's valuation[12] be suspended for the same period. At the conference, Matthew Harris, who had recently joined the central executive of the Land League, strongly opposed the interests of graziers while defending the interests of the small farmers.[13] At the end of May 1880, the Land League received a significant boost to its political fortunes when it received strong support in a speech by the influential Archbishop Croke of Cashel.[14]

---

10 Richard Hawkins, 'Liberals, land and coercion in the summer of 1880: the influence of the Carraroe ejectments', *Galway Archaeological and Historical Society*, 34 (1974–5), 40–57; Davitt, *The fall of feudalism in Ireland*, pp 213–19.   11 Davitt, *The fall of feudalism in Ireland*, pp 241–4.   12 Between 1852 and 1865, Sir Richard Griffith, commissioner of valuation, conducted a valuation of holdings in Ireland for the purposes of local taxation. This was generally known as Griffith's valuation and also as the poor law valuation.   13 *Freeman's Journal*, 30 Apr. 1880.   14 *Freeman's Journal*, 31 May 1880.

The Irish Parliamentary Party did not adopt the proposals from the land conference and the only outcome was a bill introduced by John O'Connor Power in the House of Commons that would give the tenant the right of compensation for eviction due to non-payment of rent. Thomas Brennan expressed concerns regarding the cost of legal proceedings for defending members of the Land League and the calls by John Dillon to 'Hold the harvest' rather than pay rent and face the possibility of mass evictions.[15]

During the summer of 1880, a major divergence of opinion occurred among the founders of the Land League in Co. Mayo. At a meeting described as anti-agitation, held in Irishtown on 27 June, James Daly proposed the following motion:

> That as Irish Nationalists we hereby express our disapproval of and dissent from the policy of parliamentary agitation, which has been deceptive, misleading, and inimical to the cause of Irish Nationality.[16]

According to Jordan, Daly was convinced that the Land League was providing inadequate aid for evicted tenants and that officers were profiting from Land League funds while promoting policies that could bring no relief to Mayo farmers.[17] The leading Fenians, P.W. Nally and John O'Keane, shared his views and they dissociated themselves from the land agitation.

AGRARIAN INCIDENTS IN SOUTH GALWAY

Land grabbing was reported in the Craughwell area during April 1880, when Michael Clasby, a local farmer and merchant, acknowledged that he had taken a grass farm; he claimed that there were many farms vacant in the area at the time.[18] In Loughrea, the first sign of agitation related to an attempt at land grabbing of the 'Walks' fields and the organization of a meeting to oppose it, at which speakers from the Land League would attend.[19] At the end of May, an event occurred in Craughwell that was to cast a long shadow over the coming years.[20] Thomas Cunniffe relinquished a holding of land in Carrigan that he had rented from Walter Bourke of Rahasane House. Peter Doherty (Senior) and his cousin, John Doherty, agreed to rent the land. Protests were reported immediately, the windows of the Dohertys' houses were broken, shots were fired and afterwards police patrols were provided for their protection.[21] The manner of

---

15 *Irish World*, 10 Apr. 1880.   16 *Freeman's Journal*, 28 June 1880.   17 Jordan, *Land and popular politics in Ireland*, p. 269.   18 *Western News*, 24 Apr. 1880 and 1 May 1880.   19 *Western News*, 29 May 1880.   20 See Pat Finnegan, *The case of the Craughwell prisoners during the Land War in Co. Galway, 1879–85* (Dublin, 2012).   21 *Western News*, 19 June 1880.

the agitation illustrates the vigour that characterized local protests. Placards were posted throughout the Craughwell area using highly polemical language:

> Despite the many appeals made to our brother farmers, those of them as are still deaf to the voice of reason and justice still wish to continue the evil work of land jobbing. The Irish National Land League warns farmers against such work – which is daily bringing unknown evils on the tenant farmer's cause. Still, regardless of those warnings, two wretches are to be found in our midst who have taken land contrary to the rules of the Land League. Let all honest and upright farmers in the locality shun such men's company. Let those soulless wretches be excluded from society as some unclean things! Let no tenants be found in the locality to assist or work for them. In a word, let the traitors who are in the camp be held up to the scorn and contempt of the civilised world. If this is done, Ireland will shortly be able to make a clean sweep of Irish landlords and Irishmen will ere long be able to live on the land that God and nature intended as theirs. Tenant farmers of Craughwell and surrounding districts be up and doing. Now or never is the time to show our heartless "rulers" that we want our rights or else. – Down with all land grabbers. The land for its lawful owners – the people. God save Ireland from her enemies.[22]

The police removed many of the placards denouncing land grabbers but, when the matter was raised at Loughrea Petty Sessions, the magistrate declared that the placards were not treasonable.[23]

The Athenry branch of the Land League was credited with a successful intervention in the case of Thomas Madden, who had recently taken possession of lands. In a letter to Walter P. Lambert of Castle Ellen, Madden stated that he was unable to retain possession 'on account of public opinion being against me and under no circumstances will I from this day forward be your tenant for the lands'.[24] Peter Blake of Hollypark House, Kilconierin, received a letter containing a threat to his life if he attempted to evict a widow whose request for a reduction of rent he had refused.[25]

RENEWED POLITICAL AGITATION, SUMMER AND AUTUMN 1880

Following the general election in April, Gladstone appointed W.E. Forster as chief secretary and Forster paid his first official visit to Ireland on 3 May 1880.

22 *Irish Times*, 10 July 1880. 23 *Western News*, 10 July 1880. 24 *Western News*, 3 July 1880.
25 Ibid.

He introduced to parliament the Compensation for Disturbance Bill, which proposed to amend the 1870 Land Act in order to give tenants the right to claim compensation if they were evicted for non-payment of rent due to adverse circumstances. The reason for its introduction was the 'undoubted severity of the distress from which the tenants of Ireland were suffering and the fact that many landlords were taking advantage of this distress in order to evict their poorer tenants'.[26] In fact, more than one thousand evictions had taken place in the first six months of 1880. The House of Commons passed the bill but in early August it was heavily defeated in the House of Lords by a majority of 231 with only fifty-one peers supporting it. Davitt's retrospective judgment was that 'a stubborn resistance to an equitable and humane proposal was to precipitate a conflict of savage antagonism in which landlordism would be bound to suffer for its short-sighted selfishness'.[27] Florence Arnold-Forster, niece of the chief secretary, observed in her journal that, as a result, 'it is to be feared the anti-rent agitation will have received a fresh impetus'.[28] Patrick Egan immediately advocated the radicalization of tactics at a meeting of the central executive of the Land League, when he proposed that landlords should be compelled to collect rents 'at the point of the bayonet'.[29]

During August 1880, when the agricultural crisis had abated, political activities revived with the resumption of large public meetings. The first land meeting was held on the property of Lord Dunsandle in Kiltulla on 22 August. The crowd was reported to be ten thousand with seven hundred men marching in military order from Loughrea. The Killeenadeema contingent carried a large green silk banner, bearing the inscription 'Killeenadeema to the front to crush the tyrants of our land'. The tone of the meeting was decidedly more militant than at earlier meetings and this became evident in a response from the crowd to a letter of apology from Mitchell Henry MP: 'We don't want counsel from a landlord'. The resolutions called on tenant farmers to keep a firm grip of their crops, demanded the abolition of the system of land tenure and denounced land grabbers. Peter Broderick of Athenry proposed the formation of a Land League branch in Kiltulla and several hundred people agreed to join.[30]

On the day after the Kiltulla meeting, close by at Riverville, a man called Martin Bermingham was evicted by Lord Dunsandle for non-payment of rent. Fifty policemen, under Sub Inspector Dominick Barry from Loughrea, accompanied the bailiff and sheriff for the eviction. A few hours later, a party of men restored the evicted man to his house.[31] In early September, Murty Hynes of Ballybane bought hay from the farm and police protection was immediately provided for him. A land meeting was announced for Riverville on 19 September

---

26 Thomas Wemyss Reid, *Life of the Rt Hon. W.E. Forster* (New York, 1970), ii, p. 244.
27 Davitt, *The fall of feudalism*, p. 261.   28 T.W. Moody & R.A.J. Hawkins (eds), *Florence Arnold-Forster's Irish journal* (Oxford, 1988), p. 10.   29 *Freeman's Journal*, 11 Aug. 1880.
30 *Freeman's Journal*, 23 Aug. 1880.   31 *Irish Times*, 25 Aug. 1880.

and a large crowd gathered, including contingents from Loughrea, Craughwell, Kiltulla, Athenry and Gurteen. At the start of the meeting, Harris proposed that Michael Fallon, recently evicted from his home in Moneen, Ardrahan, should act as chairman. Fallon was to become the focus of a long saga of eviction, repossession and imprisonment over the coming years (see below, p. 56). M.M. O'Sullivan, assistant secretary of the Land League, attended the meeting and proposed adherence to the principles of the Land League and the ostracism of Murty Hynes.[32] Joseph Huban, Loughrea, in proposing the first resolution, denounced the actions of Murty Hynes and called on the audience 'to confront that system of landlordism, and wage persistent war against it'. He advised to 'combine fearlessly ... openly and legally'.[33] Matthew Harris referred to the evils of landlordism and in particular to Lord Dunsandle, who 'had laid waste whole districts around this country'. There was evidence of surprise in the neighbourhood that the Land League was defending Bermingham because it was alleged in a letter from Murty Hynes' father that the Berminghams aided Lord Dunsandle in evictions.[34] Two days later, Murty Hynes yielded to public pressure and declared that he 'did not wish to have anything to do with the farm as it is against the rules of the Land League. I believe the Land League is the salvation of the Irish people'.[35] To celebrate the event, T.D. Sullivan[36] composed the ballad of 'Murty Hynes', which achieved considerable popularity at the time. It included the following two verses:

> For when upon the roadside poor Bermingham was sent,
> because with all his striving he could not pay the rent
> and keep ould Lord Dunsandle in horses, dogs and wines
> who comes and takes the houldin but foolish Murty Hynes.
>
> But when the noble Land League got word of this disgrace,
> they sent a man to Murty to raison out the case:
> I own my crime says Murty but I'll wash out the stain
> I'll keep that farm no longer; I'll give it up again.

The momentum of organization and enthusiasm was maintained at a meeting in Killeenadeema at the end of September, attended by T.P. O'Connor MP. M.M. O'Sullivan exhorted the people to show a new spirit in their dealings with the landlords: 'Don't doff your hats to the landlords and when you meet them hold up your heads'. Matthew Harris celebrated the victory over Murty Hynes,

---

32 *Irish Times*, 21 Sept. 1880. 33 *Irish Times*, 4 Jan. 1881; evidence given at state trials of Parnell, Harris and others. 34 *Irish Times*, 4 Jan. 1881. 35 *Western News*, 25 Sept. 1880. 36 Timothy Daniel Sullivan (1827–1914), nationalist politician and MP (1880–1900), poet and journalist, owner and editor of *The Nation* with his brother Alexander Martin. 'Murty Hynes' was published in *Green Leaves* (Dublin, 1886).

claiming that it would ensure that evicted farms would lie waste. Furthermore, the banners proclaimed the mood of militancy, 'England is our only foe' and 'The wise man arms to combat', indicating the strong Fenian influence in the area. J.J. Griffin from Gurteen castigated the actions of Lord Dunsandle in relation to the clearances on his estate in 1847 and praised the new attitude of outright defiance due to the influence of the Land League.[37] Speaking at a meeting in Attymon,[38] Martin O'Halloran, secretary of the Kiltulla Land League, advised that a fair rent should be paid and he regarded that to be the Griffith's valuation. This opinion was repeated at many local gatherings. Anticipating the tactic that was later adopted during the Plan of Campaign,[39] he suggested that, if the landlord would not accept a fair rent, the money be given to the local branches and sent as security to the Irish Land League. O'Halloran was one of the more dynamic Land League activists and, although he did not advocate violence directly, some of his remarks were ambiguous. However, Matthew Harris, in evidence to the Parnell Special Commission, denied that O'Halloran was a Fenian.[40] Denigration of Mitchell Henry MP, who had been re-elected to parliament in April, was a common theme at land meetings, even though, by then, he supported the '3 Fs' and peasant proprietary. At the Cappanoole meeting on 6 September, he was referred to as a wolf in sheep's clothing and there were calls for his defeat at the next election.[41] Parnell and others used strong language at a meeting in Galway on 24 October. During his speech, Parnell claimed that English-made law was responsible for the murder of landlords and he also declared:

> I would not have taken off my coat and gone to this work if I had not known that we were laying the foundations in this movement for the regeneration of our legislative independence.[42]

Matthew Harris made his controversial remark 'if the tenant farmers of Ireland shoot down landlords as partridges are shot in the month of September, that Matt Harris never would say one word against them'. When the chairman, Martin Tierney, expressed his disapproval of that comment, Harris explained 'that all he meant was that if landlords were shot, he would not do as he did in former times – come forward and denounce the men'. Harris also made reference to the tactic that became popular later that year, when he stated, as he had done at the Riverville meeting, that it was fully within the power of the people to prevent the landlords hunting throughout the county.

On 8 November, an estimated crowd of ten thousand assembled at Clostoken

37 *Western News*, 2 Oct. 1880.   38 *Western News*, 23 Oct. 1880.   39 The Plan of Campaign was a policy of withholding rents on selected estates between 1886 and 1891; in Co. Galway, the Dunsandle and Clanricarde estates were selected.   40 NLI, Parnell Special Commission, vol. 10, p. 198.   41 *Irish Times*, 7 Sept. 1880.   42 *Freeman's Journal*, 25 Oct. 1880.

in a continuous downpour of rain. M.M. O'Sullivan apologized for his inability to attend because there were ten other meetings taking place that day. He suggested that money spent on organizing meetings would be better spent on forming a branch of the Land League, and this duly happened.[43] O'Sullivan's advice also bore fruit on 1 December when a branch was formed in Loughrea, the twelfth branch within a radius of twelve miles of the town.[44]

An important land conference was held in Athenry on 19 November 1880. Revd Peter J. McPhilpin, vice president, said they wished to promote a more efficient organization by confining each branch within a parish boundary as a lot of extra duties had devolved on the Athenry branch. These related to its function as a land court with many cases referred to it for arbitration from outside the area, some from as far away as Oranmore and Clarinbridge.[45] RM W.J. Paul, Ballinasloe, reported the activities of the Athenry land court and also of the Gurteen land court to Dublin Castle.[46]

Delegates expressed approval for the decision of the Gurteen branch not to pay any rent above Griffith's valuation. Representation on the Boards of Poor Law Guardians was also discussed and Revd McPhilpin said it was one of the great reforms needed as at present it was a landlords' board and in the coming months the people could assert their power and elect their own representatives. Further evidence of the work of the highly organized Land League branch in Athenry was provided by another delegate conference on 4 February 1881, when the focus was on the selection of appropriate candidates for the elections to the board of Loughrea PLU, to be held the following month.[47] Land League candidates received strong support in the elections but did not achieve a majority on the board.

Local feelings were inflamed by the eviction of the widow Dempsey of Kylebeg on 17 November. A large number of volunteers, led by M.M. O'Sullivan, assembled during the night to roof the house and make it habitable again.[48] Three days later, Martin O'Halloran, the widow Dempsey and three others were arrested and brought before the magistrates in Loughrea. They were remanded in custody but a local hotel proprietor refused to supply cars to convey them to jail and it was reported that two thousand people paraded the streets to protest at the arrests.[49] At Killimor court, the accused were charged under the Whiteboy Act,[50] but the magistrate, Benjamin Hill, considered that insufficient evidence was presented and he discharged them.[51]

On 21 November, an estimated twelve thousand people attended a meeting in Ballymana. One hundred horsemen carrying swords, under the command of Michael Calligy and Captain Henry Pilkington PLG, formerly of the Donegal

43 *Irish Times*, 9 Nov. 1880. 44 *Western News*, 4 Dec. 1880. 45 *Western News*, 18 Dec. 1880. 46 NAI CSO RP 1881/1142. RM Paul to under secretary, 7 Jan. 1881. 47 *Western News*, 12 Feb. 1881. 48 *Western News*, 20 Nov. 1880. 49 *Irish Times*, 22 Nov. 1880. 50 15 & 16 George III, c. 21, section 2, Whiteboy Act 1831. 51 *Western News*, 27 Nov. 1880.

Rifles, headed a large contingent from Killeenadeema. Among the platform party were the chairman, Revd T.B. Considine, PP of Ardrahan, four other clergymen and Michael Clasby of Craughwell, even though he had been boycotted as a land grabber a few months earlier. Revd P.A. Callanan, a Carmelite priest and a native of Ballymana, addressed the meeting. In an extraordinary speech, full of nationalist rhetoric, biblical references and religious fervour, he was prepared to place the Land League firmly in the Garden of Eden when he said 'that the oldest and most venerable gospel of all is that of the land for the people. It is the holy gospel of nature according to Adam'.[52]

Another highly emotional meeting was held in Craughwell on 14 December 1880. The occasion was marked by a large demonstration, with contingents from Loughrea, Athenry, Gort, Clostoken and Ballymana and many other districts, bearing swords and sticks. The Athenry band was followed by an estimated one thousand horsemen and the Gort band by 1,200, headed by Revd T.B. Considine. The Land League executive was not represented. A group of people, described as nationalists (presumably Fenians), attempted to knock over the platform. Order was restored with the arrival of the clergy and the parish priest, Revd Geoghegan, chaired the meeting. The platform party included Peter Broderick (Athenry), Peter Sweeny (Loughrea), 'Colonel' John Newell (Carrigan),[53] J. Benn (Ballymore House, Craughwell)[54] and Martin O'Halloran. The resolutions condemned the action of the government in prosecuting the leaders of the Land League[55] and pledged allegiance to the principles of the Land League and unity against those trafficking in land. Revd Considine voiced agreement with a call for cheers for the Fenians, an expression he was later asked to explain at the Parnell Special Commission.[56] O'Halloran spoke about disarming the police and advised the crowd to boycott the police and herdsmen. As a result, he was prosecuted for 'using language calculated to stir up disorder and sedition' and he was bound over to be of good behaviour.[57] Sweeny composed a ballad extolling the exploits of O'Halloran and this became popular at the time.

> When the Land League was young in its might and its power
> And feudal oppression was strong,
> When men were as slaves, and like slaves had to cower
> 'Neath the heel of a hard grinding wrong,
> When hearts long pressed down swelled the gathering clan

---

52 Ibid. 53 John Newell was Fenian Head Centre for the barony of Dunkellin. 54 J. Benn was tenant of a large property, Ballymore House, owned by Lord Clanricarde; his wife became vice president of the Craughwell Ladies' Land League. 55 Parnell and thirteen others were charged with conspiracy to prevent the payment of rent. 56 NLI, Parnell Special Commission, vol. 7, p. 433. 57 NAI, Irish Land League (ILL) and Irish National League (INL) documents,

That sprung up vowed to do and to dare,
And toil in the march of their country's proud van
Wasn't Maurtheen O'Halloran there.[58]

In the latter half of 1880, other meetings were held throughout south and east Galway, and these were also attended by large and enthusiastic crowds. Venues included Mountbellew, Portumna, New Inn, Cappataggle, Killimor, Abbeygormican, Kilconnell, Leitrim, Ballymacward, Tynagh and Ahascragh. At all these meetings the land question dominated proceedings and, while there was condemnation of Britain and the expression of general nationalist sentiments, the only explicit call for national independence and a parliament in Ireland had been made by Davitt at the meeting in Loughrea in early 1880.

The local agitation had reached such a pitch that extra police were drafted in, with ten policemen stationed in Loughrea and three in all the adjoining stations. A meeting of traders and commissioners condemned the extra cost of these reinforcements.[59] At a public meeting in the town, Joseph Huban from Barrack Street, one of the leading Land League organizers, addressed the crowd as 'an Irish republican' who did not owe any allegiance to the British government.[60] He protested about the extra police but urged the people to stand together and 'they would soon bring England to her knees'. Constable James Linton, who was to be shot in Loughrea the following year, reported Huban's speech to Dublin Castle. Huban was prosecuted for seditious language and bound over to be of good behaviour for twelve months.[61]

The extra forces of police were not sufficient to prevent a serious disturbance in the town on 6 December, when an attempt was made to sell cattle belonging to Mrs Hannah Lewis of Ballinagar. She had refused to accept rent at Griffith's valuation and immediately afterwards ordered the tenants to be served with writs. A large crowd, led by two bell-ringers and Martin O'Halloran, assembled at the Fair Green and prevented the sale. The crowd escorted the drovers and cattle for a mile outside the town. In the evening, a tenant farmer who had paid his rent to a local landlord, was attacked and severely injured.[62]

Given the heightened passions because of evictions and the failure to pass the Compensation for Disturbance Bill, it is not surprising that agrarian crimes increased in frequency in the second half of 1880. John W. Lambert of Aggard House, the owner of an estate of 3,440 acres, was an early target when a large grave was dug in front of his house and a document was found close by, stating that if he 'did not cease persecuting his tenants' he would 'shortly be consigned to the grave'.[63] Lambert, in evidence to the Parnell Special Commission, said that he was boycotted for three years, tenants surrendered some six hundred

box 2. 58 *Western News*, 11 Dec. 1880. 59 *Irish Times*, 2 Dec. 1880. 60 NAI, ILL and INL documents, 1879–88, Cos A–L, carton 2. 61 *Western News*, 19 Feb. 1881. 62 *Freeman's Journal*, 7 Dec. 1880. 63 *Irish Times*, 13 Oct. 1880.

acres, walls were knocked, workmen left his employment and the houses of two herds were burned down. He was given police protection and 'Emergency Men' were sent from Liverpool to work for him. He complained that they knew nothing about the work and they were more of a nuisance.[64] His brother, Walter Lambert of Castle Ellen, Athenry, was also boycotted and his domestic staff and herdsmen were warned to leave his employment.[65] Other episodes included an armed attack on Captain Smyth of Masonbrook, Loughrea,[66] and an attack on a bailiff collecting rent.[67] For the second time in 1880, Peter Blake of Hollypark received a letter threatening him with instant death if he evicted a poor woman from his property. The letter was signed 'Rory of the Hills'. A young man employed by Blake was convicted of writing the letter on extremely flimsy evidence and sentenced to nine months' imprisonment with hard labour.[68]

The local availability of arms was enhanced with the larceny of fifteen rifles in transit from Limerick to Loughrea.[69] They were taken from a store at Craughwell railway station and it was believed by the police that Edward Barrett of Craughwell was the organizer of the raid.[70] The ready availability of arms and the appearance at many meetings of contingents marching in military order indicate the developing influence of the Fenian movement within the Land League organization.

---

64 NLI, Parnell Special Commission, vol. 1, pp 483–4. 65 *Irish Times*, 22 Nov. 1880.
66 *Irish Times*, 30 Aug. 1880. 67 *Irish Times*, 4 Oct. 1880. 68 *Irish Times*, 12 Dec. 1880.
69 *Irish Times*, 18 Nov. 1880. 70 NAI, CSO, RP 1883/153.

4 Stopping the hunt[1]

THE RESISTANCE TO HUNTING IN CO. GALWAY

The hunting of foxes and, to a much lesser extent, of stags was a widespread source of entertainment for gentry, magistrates, army officers and strong farmers who hunted with the approximately twenty packs in the country. It was also regarded as an assertion by the ascendancy of traditional dominance over their tenants. Lavish sums of money were expended on the purchase and feeding of horses and the payment of the servants needed to maintain them. In addition, it was of importance to the local economies due to the influx of visitors requiring accommodation and sustenance from local shopkeepers. On the other hand, the tenants resented the intrusion on their farms and the consequent damage to crops, fences and walls. Although the Land League executive never endorsed it officially, the tactic that became known as 'Stopping the hunt' was first advocated by Matthew Harris, a member of the central executive. He suggested this tactic in his speech at the Riverville meeting in September 1880. His speech included a forthright denunciation of the Persse family of Roxborough House, who had evicted Michael Fallon, the chairman of the meeting. Harris said in relation to the Persses: 'if they go on oppressing the people they will have to drop their hunting. [We] will not allow them to ride over the hearthstones of the people all over the country'.[2] A month later, Harris returned to the topic in his speech in Galway when he asserted that 'it is fully within the power of the people to forbid them hunting throughout this country'.[3]

In December 1880, the first interference with hunting took place at Ballydugan, Loughrea. The Galway Blazers arrived there under their master, Burton Persse of Moyode Castle, brother of Dudley Persse of Roxborough House. Before the first covert was drawn, a large number of farmers, many of them wearing Land League cards on their hats, gathered and proceeded to hold a meeting. After discussion, it was resolved to prevent the Blazers from hunting in the district. Although the farmers present at the meeting were all tenants, their sense of proprietary rights was evident from the resolution they passed:

> That, as we are willing to pay a fair rent for our land, we believe no man has a right to injure our lands, consequently we call on all tenant farmers

---

1 For valuable accounts of the agitation, see L.P. Curtis, 'Stopping the hunt' in Philpin (ed.), *Nationalism and popular protest in Ireland* (1987), pp 349–402; Heather Laird, *Subversive law in Ireland, 1879–1920* (Dublin, 2005), pp 60–102.   2 NAI, ILL and INL documents, carton 5.   3 *Freeman's Journal*, 25 Oct. 1880.

in this district to prevent a class calling themselves gentlemen and lords of the soil from hunting over their lands.⁴

At the Co. Galway Land Convention in October 1881, a spirited discussion developed about hunting, leading to the passing of the following resolution:

> That since the landlords and their agents were mainly instrumental in placing our fellow-countrymen in prison under the Coercion Act, this convention earnestly requests the farmers of Co. Galway to do all in their power to prevent all rack-renting landlords and their agents from fox-hunting on their lands.

The editor of the *Galway Vindicator* analysed the complexity of the issues involved, including the economic consequences to local people if hunting was stopped, unemployment of servants and grooms, reduced payments for hay and oats, loss of income for saddlers and shop keepers and, indirectly, harm to the whole community.⁵

On 16 December 1881, the County Galway Hunt, consisting of members of the Galway County Club, met in east Galway at Ballycrissane, where a crowd of four to five hundred people had gathered. Because of their determined attitude, Burton Persse, the master of the hunt, 'thought it prudent to ask would they allow the hunt to go on'. He received the emphatic answer: 'No, till the suspects are released'.⁶ The hunt moved to another area nearby but found the covert surrounded and it was reported that the crowd beat off the dogs.⁷ The traditional Christmas hunt of the Galway Blazers was arranged for St Stephen's Day at Kilcornan demesne, the home of the Redingtons of Clarinbridge. The hounds and the huntsmen came from Moyode Castle, the seat of Burton Persse. On arrival at the demesne gate, the hunt found it shut and blockaded with rocks, and a crowd of approximately five hundred was assembled in front of it. A poster on the gate stated:

> I hereby give notice to Mr Persse and all the club gentry not to dare venture Kilcornan Woods to chase Reynard, because the country at large is appointed to stop ye all. N.B. We are fully determined to deprive ye of rents and pleasure from henceforth, Hurrah for Parnell and the Land League. We are all united.

---

4 *Irish Times*, 23 Dec. 1880.   5 *Galway Vindicator*, 12 Oct. 1881.   6 The title of 'suspect' was conferred on those arrested and imprisoned under the Protection of Person and Property (Ireland) Act 1881 and it was regarded as a badge of honour by many of them and even the title 'ex-suspect' enjoyed currency for years after their release from jail.   7 *Western News* and *Irish Times*, 24 Dec. 1881; NAI, CSO, RP 1882/1404.

Persse said he had a right to visit his friends and he would insist on doing so. The crowd prevented the opening of the gate and told Persse 'we'll have no hunting till the suspects are released'. At that stage, policemen and a detachment of infantry from Galway arrived under the command of RM William Morris Reade, who told the crowd to disperse within five minutes. The hunting party eventually went to a distant covert where they were not expected and they 'enjoyed a brilliant run of forty-five minutes'.[8] Also on St Stephen's Day, another hunt, organized by John Pollok at Lismany near Eyrecourt, was prevented.[9]

The anger generated by the campaign of interference led to the holding of a meeting of the Galway Blazers in Athenry on 31 December. The chairman was Lord Clonbrock and the attendance included Lord Clanmorris, Sir Henry Grattan Bellew, Colonel John Archer Daly, Burton and Henry Persse, Andrew Comyn, Christopher Ussher and Frank and Giles Lambert. Burton Persse referred to the grave crisis for the hunt and informed the meeting of the events at Kilcornan. He had received several threatening letters stating:

> Honoured Sir, take notice that all the coverts are to be poisoned ... If you run the risk your hounds will be destroyed, as there is as much deadly poison bought for them as would poison all the justices of the peace and hounds in the Co. Galway.

The warnings were linked with the action demanded from magistrates to have the suspects released. Persse was of the opinion that the hostility was not directed personally against him but 'towards one of his class and towards all landlords without distinction'. The decision of the meeting was that fox-hunting should cease for the season.[10] By the end of January, Burton Persse disposed of eleven choicely bred horses at Tattersalls sales. Several of them were sired by famous thoroughbreds of the time, such as Birdcatcher and Lothario. The prices ranged from £47 to £170 per horse and reached a total value of £1,233.[11]

Elsewhere in the country, there were numerous disruptions of hunts between October and December 1881, and the escalation of protests may have been influenced by the marked increase in the number of arrests of suspects during that period. Passions aroused at county conventions in Kildare and Waterford, probably contributed to the general air of militancy. In Waterford, resentment was fuelled by the serving of writs of eviction and may also have been influenced by the fact that Captain Owen R. Slacke, special resident magistrate for Waterford and Tipperary and therefore responsible for the administration of the

---

8 *Western News, Galway Express* and *Freeman's Journal*, 31 Dec. 1881. 9 *Western News*, 31 Dec. 1881. 10 *Galway Vindicator*, 4 Jan. 1882; *Western News*, 7 Jan. 1882. 11 *Galway Vindicator*, 25 Jan. 1882.

PPP (Ireland) Act, was a devoted follower of the hunt.[12] Protests directed at the Curraghmore Hunt on 6 October resulted in its disbandment. Following meetings with landholders, the Kildare Hunt made a similar decision and again the protests were linked with the cause of the suspects. The meeting passed a resolution petitioning the government 'to release the political suspects now detained in prison; and do hereby declare that their incarceration and the act under which this county is proclaimed is no longer necessary for the peace and preservation of property in this county'.[13] Florence Arnold-Forster recorded in her journal that the chief secretary's depression was increased by the action of the Kildare Hunt members.[14] By January 1882, at least twelve hunts had disbanded and many others had suspended hunting temporarily. The Kildare Hunt was responsible for organizing the annual racing festival at Punchestown but, because of the agitation, they were forced to cancel the meeting scheduled for April of that year.

Following the disbandment of the Galway Blazers, protests gradually died out but they were revived again in October 1882 when the Blazers resumed hunting. The recurrence of protests coincided with the resurgence of political agitation following the establishment of the Irish National League. By November, numerous protest meetings had been held at which pledges were given to restart the campaign to stop hunting. On 9 November, the County Galway Hunt met at Eastwell, Kilrickle, the home of the Ussher family. Placards were posted in the area, including one that declared 'Go to Ganty and see what happened there', a reference to the evictions on the Blake estate in October 1882 (see below, pp 129–30). The hunt commenced but a large number of men attacked the dogs and the fox, driving them back to the covert.[15] Several other attempts to start the hunt were foiled by attacking the dogs and groaning at the huntsmen. The hunt decided to reassemble at Cregclare, Ardrahan, on 11 November,[16] but they were confronted by men carrying sticks and throwing stones, one of which hit RM de Vere Pery (Loughrea). The hunt proceeded to Rahasane, where another confrontation occurred with forty to fifty men, resulting in the abandonment of the hunt and the arrest of ten tenant farmers.

The prisoners – Michael Sylver, Thomas Holland, William Coen, Michael Cahill, James Keane, John Fahey, John Ruane, James Howley, Michael Connaire and John Connell – appeared at Ardrahan Petty Sessions on 20 November, charged with forming a riotous assembly and preventing the hunt on their lands. A crowd of hundreds gathered for the court hearing that was held in a room in the local dispensary. A subscription of £30 was collected for the defence of the prisoners and Mr Humphrey McInerney, barrister-at-law, was engaged. Mr William French Henderson prosecuted and RM de Vere Pery, who had been

12 Curtis, 'Stopping the hunt', pp 365–7.   13 *Freeman's Journal*, 5 Dec. 1881.   14 Moody & Hawkins (eds), *Florence Arnold-Forster's Irish journal*, pp 329–30.   15 *Galway Vindicator*, 15 Nov. 1882.   16 Ibid.

injured in the affray, presided. In addition to the charge of riotous assembly, four of the prisoners were also charged with attempting to rescue prisoners from Constable Boland and threatening to slay him. Lieutenant Colonel Mollan RM (Gort) stated that he and nine friends were ordered to leave the field by men with sticks and in response he pulled out his revolver. Mr McInerney asked him if he was afraid and the intrepid Mollan answered 'I was not in dread or fear but the demeanour of the crowd was sufficient to put anyone in dread and fear'. The case was adjourned for two weeks but, following protests from the defence counsel, de Vere Pery agreed to continue the enquiry on 22 November in Galway courthouse.[17]

On that occasion, the court was presided over by Colonel Pearse RM and it commenced with the reading of the evidence of Lieutenant Colonel Mollan, who was not in attendance. His deposition stated that 'he was hunting with ten or twelve men and very suddenly a yelling crowd of about forty persons armed with sticks came up from behind us ... flourishing their sticks in a threatening manner'.[18] Mollan saw the mare of William Persse 'most violently struck' and his own horse was prevented from jumping a fence. The men formed a line and 'being so violent in their gestures that I apprehended a general attack on our party'. Mollan then drew his revolver and while pointing the muzzle towards the ground he announced that 'he would fire if the party were stopped'. He was struck twice on the head by missiles but was unable to state who was responsible. The defence counsel, Mr McInerney, raised objections as to the admissibility of the statement and the fact that Mollan was not present for examination. He also claimed that the court was not properly constituted to hear the case. The objections were dismissed and the case proceeded.

William B. Persse, son of Burton Persse, said a hound died suddenly at Cregclare and the hunt left for Rahasane. When he tried to pass through a gap, he saw three men armed with sticks who said 'no man passes here'. At Carrigan, his mare was struck on the head by a stick five feet long. Persse then aided Lieutenant Andrew Nugie of the 84th Regiment in the arrest of two men, whom he pointed out in court (Connaire and Holland). In cross-examination, Persse was asked 'how he could tell the two persons arrested were part of the crowd?' He replied: 'I kept the crowd all along in view. While jumping the fence I kept my head sideways looking at the crowd'. Lieutenant Nugie referred to the conduct of the crowd as riotous, violent and disorderly and sufficient to inspire terror into any of Her Majesty's subjects, and he rode at them to get through. Lieutenant Bere Ichem of the 12th Suffolk Regiment claimed that 'he heard Mollan say "If any man stops me, I will shoot him", or words to that effect'. He identified James Keane in the mob. McInerney argued that the only testimony against the prisoners was that they were part of the crowd and this was not

17 *Tuam News*, 24 Nov. 1882. 18 Ibid.

enough. There was no evidence that any of the prisoners did anything apart from James Keane, who flourished a stick but did not strike anyone. The argument was not accepted and seven of the prisoners were sent for trial at Galway assizes. Three boys, who had also been arrested, were admitted to bail.[19]

At the winter assizes in Galway, the strong legal team of Sergeant Robinson QC and The McDermot QC acted for the prosecution and John R. Stritch and M. McDonnell Bodkin[20] QC for the defence. The presiding judge was James Lawson. The McDermot for the crown told the jury that

> they were dealing with a number of men who had taken the law into their own hands to put down hunting in the Co. Galway. The object was to deprive the gentry of their legitimate sports and drive them out of the country. There would then be established, no doubt, Land League amusements and Mr Matt Harris would in all probability be lieutenant of the county (laughter).[21]

The evident class bias of the remarks revealed the privileged upbringing of The McDermot and his failure to grasp the nature of the political and social revolution taking place in the country, which within sixteen years would see the administrative duties of the grand jury system transferred to the county council. In charging the jury, the judge referred to the right of farmers 'to tell the hunt to go off their lands but no witness was produced to show that the lands belonged to the members of the mob'. The jury found guilty verdicts and Lawson, addressing the prisoners, said he had no doubt but 'they had acted under the influence of designing people who took these steps to drive every gentleman out of the country and get rid of the landlords'. Lawson said 'Sylver and Keane were the worst' and they were sentenced to eighteen months' imprisonment. The others were sentenced to twelve months with the exception of Holland, who expressed regret and was released. One of the prisoners asked if they would be allowed a reduction of sentence on account of the time they had already spent in jail and the judge replied 'I won't allow one hour'.[22] There were several other revealing comments during the court hearings.[23] John Berwick Sams, agent for Major Surgeon Isidore Bourke, brother of the recently assassinated Walter, said that 'Rahasane was always a happy hunting ground until these savages' (pointing to the prisoners). Lieutenant Nugie could not identify

---

19 *Galway Vindicator*, 25 Nov. 1882. 20 Mathias McDonnell Bodkin QC, a native of Tuam, Co. Galway, admitted to the Bar in 1877. He was editor of *United Ireland* at the time of the 'Parnell split' and was elected MP for Roscommon North in 1892, defeating James J. O'Kelly. He was appointed county court judge for Clare in 1907. He was the author of several historical works and novels, including a biography of *Lord Edward Fitzgerald* (Dublin, n.d.) and *Famous Irish trials* (Dublin, 1918, 1997). 21 *Western News*, 23 Dec. 1882. 22 *Western News*, 23 Dec. 1882. 23 *Tuam News*, 24 Nov. 1882.

Holland or Conaire individually, but said he could do so collectively! Although Judge Lawson did not show any mercy to the prisoners, the intervention of Captain John Nolan and Mitchell Henry, the county MPs, resulted in the release of Coen, Cahill, Fahey and Connell in May 1883 and a promise to release Sylver and Keane in October, when they would have served eleven months of the sentence.[24]

Other incidents reported were the stopping of the hunt in Kilcolgan[25] and a hunt that started at Dalystown and moved to Ballydugan (where it was stopped). During the confrontation with local farmers, RM Paul drew his revolver. This was another example of a resident magistrate taking the law into his own hands.[26] A meeting of farmers from the Eyrecourt-Meelick area resolved that 'we will not allow fox-hunting or harrier hunting over our farms'.[27] Later in the month, the last reported interference with a hunt happened at Ballycrissane, when John Pollok's pack was prevented from entering a farmer's land.[28] Pollok, a commercial farmer from Scotland, was a particular target because of the ruthless clearance of estates that were purchased after the Great Famine.[29]

LAND LEAGUE HUNTS

An interesting feature of the 'Stopping the hunt' campaign was the staging of hunts by Land League members, advertised widely and often proclaimed by the authorities as illegal assemblies. They were commonly referred to as 'People's Hunts' and, in an attempt to avoid police and military interference, the notices advertising them frequently nominated false locations instead of the actual venue. A crowd of five hundred people attended a hunt on the Roxborough demesne of Dudley Persse on 15 January 1881. The organizers advertised the event widely but changed the time to deceive the authorities and the hunt took place by moonlight. A successful hunt was reported and several deer, hares and rabbits were killed. Many hours later, twenty policemen and a detachment of the 28th Regiment arrived at the demesne but found that the hunt had already taken place and they had to depart empty-handed. On the same day, another hunt took place in Cappataggle.[30] Bogus advertisements were posted for a Land League hunt at Oatfield on 22 January that attracted a force of forty police and a detachment of the 28th Regiment under the command of RM Paul. They found no evidence of hunting but their attention focused on a number of men in Carra bog, some distance away. The police and soldiers deployed across the boggy

---

24 *Tuam News*, 29 June 1883. 25 *Tuam News*, 23 Nov. 1882. 26 *Tuam News*, 29 Nov. 1882. 27 *Tuam News*, 1 Dec. 1882. 28 *Western News*, 30 Dec. 1882. 29 Padraig Lane, 'The social impact of the encumbered estates court on counties Galway and Mayo, 1849–58' (MA, UCD, 1969). 30 *Western News*, 21 Jan. 1882

terrain and surrounded the men who were innocently engaged in digging a drain.[31]

As well as disruption to the activities of the East Galway Hunt, a poaching raid took place on John Pollok's property at Lismany on 23 December 1881.[32] Elsewhere in Galway, a crowd of eight hundred attended a hunt on the Gunning estate near Headford on 8 January 1881 and paraded in military order afterwards, bearing their booty. A shot was discharged at the police during the arrest of three of the men.[33]

In January 1882, a Land League hunt meeting in Derryoober, Woodford, was attended by several hundred people while a large force of police and military were miles distant at the publicly advertised venue. However, the police arrived as the crowd dispersed and they arrested sixteen men. They were taken to Loughrea Bridewell which they entered whistling 'God Save Ireland' and Mrs John Sweeny provided refreshments for them.[34] Also in January 1882, poaching hunts were reported at Peterswell and Ardrahan.[35]

For a time, the anti-hunting campaign had an important role in the agitation against landlordism and, although the games of cat and mouse only lasted for a few months, they placed an extra demand on police and military forces that were already under severe strain. During the winter of 1881–2, it provided a rallying call for those local activists who had not already been arrested under the Coercion Act, and it focused attention on the plight of the interned suspects and provided support for their families. However, the severe penalties meted out in the Rahasane case and the provisions of the Prevention of Crime Act to outlaw illegal assemblies and arrest the ringleaders led to the cessation of protests by early 1883. The campaign united many elements within the Land League, medium and small farmers, labourers and townspeople. Only the large farmers were not supportive because many of them hunted and were in sympathy with the gentry. The campaign promoted the politicization of the nationalist community and the taunt that the huntsmen had no right to enter their lands echoed the traditional claim that foreigners had usurped the land in the first place. Servility to landlords was no longer a social or political option.

---

31 *Tuam News*, 27 Jan. 1882. 32 NAI CSO RP 1881/46236. 33 *Irish Times*, 10 Jan. 1881.
34 *Tuam News*, 14 Jan. 1882. 35 NAI CSO RP 1882/747 and 748.

5 Rent, evictions and outrages

FAIR RENT AND THE GRIFFITH'S VALUATION

Rents and land tenure reform were a dominant concern of people throughout the Land War. In his review of the matter, Philip Bull reaches the conclusion that 'The demand for a "fair rent" lay at the bottom of almost all aspects of the land tenure system'. In addition, 'It was the total failure of the 1870 Act to recognise its importance which doomed that legislation to ineffectiveness'. As far as the tenant farmers were concerned, 'the only fair rent would be no rent, for there was no acceptance of the legitimacy of the institution of landlordism nor recognition of the landlords' right to extract an income from land which they had acquired by confiscation'.[1]

The negotiations relating to the payment of rent in two estates, those of Lord Dunsandle in Gurteen and Kiltulla and Lord Huntington in Killeenadeema, illustrate the Land League policies in operation at the end of 1880. Lord Dunsandle's tenants assembled at Martin O'Halloran's house on 9 December and marched to Dunsandle in military order, each village having its own commander. O'Halloran acted as spokesman and informed William Daly that in compliance with the rules of the Land League the tenants would pay the Griffith's valuation and no more. Daly, son of Lord Dunsandle and agent for his estate of thirty-four thousand acres, replied that he had instructions authorizing a liberal reduction of rent but not at Griffith's valuation. He hoped that the government might soon settle the land question on a basis satisfactory to both landlord and tenant. O'Halloran advised the tenants to lodge the rent money in the bank and wait until the landlords would be glad to take it. Later that evening, a tenant went to Dunsandle House to pay the full rent but Daly refused to take it, warning the tenant about retaliation if the other tenants became aware of his payment.[2] On the same day, Mr Fitzgerald, Lord Huntington's agent, attended at Nevin's Hotel, Loughrea, to receive rents. The tenants' leader, Michael Cunningham, informed Fitzgerald that they could not pay rent above Griffith's valuation, claiming that the rules of the Land League compelled them to adopt this course. The agent agreed to accept the rent at that level.[3] However, despite the assertions relating to Griffith's valuation as being the appropriate rent, there were other views. Revd Carroll CC, Loughrea, one of the more militant supporters of the Land League, argued in a speech at Mullagh that tenants should fix their own rents and not mind Griffith's valuation because, in his opinion, Griffith's valuation was usually too high.[4]

1 Philip Bull, *Land, politics and nationalism* (Dublin, 1996), p. 78. 2 *Irish Times*, 10 Dec. 1880. 3 Ibid. 4 *Western News*, 15 Jan. 1881.

According to W.E. Vaughan, the landlords 'had continued to extract a large surplus from agriculture, about £340 million between 1850 and 1879, a sum far greater than that collected by any other agency in Ireland'. Despite their considerable incomes, the landlords were very slow to invest in their estates and housing for tenants. Vaughan calculated that only 4 or 5 per cent of rental income was invested annually. He concluded that 'even after paying taxes and interest on mortgages, landlords were still as a group enormously rich'.[5] Therefore, it is not surprising that, because of the obvious disparity in wealth between the landlords and their tenants, there was a widespread perception among Land League members that rack-renting was a common occurrence. Historians writing from a nationalist perspective also defend this position, but more recent historical analysis challenges these beliefs. Donnelly, using records of Cork estate rentals, found that, while two landlords – Thomas L. Cave and Sir John Benn-Walsh – raised rents considerably, in the other Cork estates examined, 'rent increases ranged from 20 to 30 per cent and were therefore well within the limits of the price and production increments of the time'. He also found that rents could vary substantially, even within the same estate.[6]

Barbara Solow concludes that, while Griffith's valuation gave a fairly accurate reflection of real rental values in the period 1848–52, by 1875–80 it was 25 to 30 per cent below value.[7] In addition, Ball Greene, in evidence to two royal commissions, advised that Griffith's valuation was 33 per cent below the letting value in 1876. However, the Land Commission favoured a reduction of rents and in the period 1882–91 they recommended an average reduction of 22.6 per cent.[8]

Solow refers to the remarks of Prof. Thomas Baldwin, assistant commissioner of the Richmond Commission in Ireland. He claimed that 'I never could find from my own experience any instance of bad treatment by the old landlords ... But then ... supposing one of these land jobbers is in a county, he may drive terror into the rest of the tenants'.[9] However, at a later date, Baldwin made a contradictory statement to the Cairns Commission that he 'was surprised at the amount of rack-renting he encountered as a sub-commissioner under the Land Act of 1881'.[10]

Although there were many landlords who treated their tenants fairly and enjoyed good relationships with tenants on their estates, there were enough instances of harsh dealing by landlords to engender a widespread perception of

---

5 W.E. Vaughan, *Landlords and tenants in mid-Victorian Ireland* (Oxford, 1994), pp 217–20 and Appendix 13. 6 Donnelly, *The land and the people of nineteenth-century Cork*, pp 190–4. 7 Barbara Solow, *The land question and the Irish economy, 1870–1903* (Cambridge, MA, 1971), pp 66–7. 8 Solow, *The land question and the Irish economy*, pp 66–7. 9 HC 1881 [C.2778], xv, p. 139. Richmond Commission 1881, Preliminary report from Her Majesty's commissioners on agriculture, 14 Jan. 1881. 10 Solow, *The land question and the Irish economy*, pp 66–7 and HC 1883 (204), Third report from the Select Committee of the House of Lords on Land Law (Ireland), p. 114.

excessive levels of rent. There is also no doubt that in many parts of the impoverished west and south-west of Ireland, rent on poor tillage lands was excessive and any rent became unaffordable in times of crisis such as 1879–80. Although many landlords offered rent reductions of 10 to 20 per cent at that time, Dooley argues that this may not have produced any marked reduction of their rental income because the decreases 'did not necessarily apply to all tenants, or to all administrative units of a landlord's estate'. The refusal of tenants to pay rents and to allow arrears to accumulate had a much greater effect on landlords' incomes.[11] According to Vaughan,

> the significance of the agricultural crisis that began in the late 1870s was not a mere aberration or pause in a period of prosperity, like that of the early 1860s. It was in fact the beginning of a long period of economic difficulty, for some agricultural prices never again reached their 1876 level until 1914.[12]

The extensive agitation promoted by the Land League and the disturbed state of the country undoubtedly influenced Gladstone's thinking on the land problem that resulted in the passage of the 1881 Land Act. Several years later, in an address to the House of Commons, he said 'I think it is generally and deeply felt that without the agitation the Land Act of 1881 would not have been passed'.[13] The act essentially delivered the '3 Fs' and the Land Commission established by the act played its part by reducing rents by 22.6 per cent, thereby approximating the level of Griffith's valuation.

EVICTIONS

The memory of the very large number of evictions during the Great Famine and immediately afterwards had a profound influence on the political attitudes of the next generation of Irish people. The families of Michael Davitt and Mark Ryan had both experienced eviction followed by emigration. The memory of the clearance of estates purchased by commercial farmers such as John Pollok (see below, p. 82) was still vivid during the Land War and the evictions at Knockatogher in 1847 by Lord Dunsandle were recalled by speakers at the Riverville meeting and greeted with groans by the audience. P.G. Lane records a notable example for June 1850 when 236 families and 1,467 individuals were evicted in Galway West Riding. During the same month, in Galway East Riding,

11 Terence A.M. Dooley, 'Landlords and the land question, 1879–1909' in King, *Famine, land and culture in Ireland* (2000), p. 120.   12 Vaughan, *Landlords and tenants in mid-Victorian Ireland*, pp 226–7.   13 Hansard's parliamentary debates, third series, vol. 341, 1686–7.

178 families and 813 individuals suffered the same fate. In the months March to December 1851, 4,793 occupiers in Co. Galway and 5,696 in Co. Mayo were evicted.[14] It is no surprise that people attending Land League meetings a mere thirty years later could readily recall these events.

There has been considerable variation in the estimates made by historians of the number of evictions that took place during the Great Famine. Vaughan's analysis of the constabulary reports from 1846–9 yields a figure of 37,286 and between 1850 and 1855 the number was 35,665 evictions without readmission. This represents a total of 72,951 families and 291,804 individuals. In his study based on court records, O'Neill concludes that between 1846 and 1854 144,759 families, comprising 579,036 individuals, were evicted. As in Vaughan's analysis, the extensive clearances that occurred immediately after the Great Famine are included and both estimates indicate the scale of the social disaster of that period.

Solow[15] concludes that after the Great Famine evictions were few and far between. Based on a calculation of six hundred thousand tenants in 1855, and excluding those readmitted as tenants and caretakers, she decides that only 17,775 evictions took place, giving an eviction rate of 3 per cent. O'Neill claims that the reasons for Solow's underestimate are her failure to take into account police under-recording of evictions, illegal evictions and the problem of cottiers who could be evicted without recourse to the courts.[16]

There was a marked reduction in the number of evictions and between 1865 and 1877, a time of relative prosperity, there were 6,336. The families who were evicted but readmitted as caretakers remained in a perilous state because they had no legal rights and they lived with the constant fear of being evicted again. The social and emotional impact of ejectment orders has been minimized by Solow and others, showing no appreciation of the depths of despair engendered among vulnerable people eking out an existence on poor land. The threat of eviction was often used to force the payment of rent but it could become a routine ploy, as in the case of Lord Leitrim, who 'served all his tenants annually with notices to quit and kept them in a permanent state of insecurity'.[17]

The official statistics demonstrate an increase in the incidence of evictions of 91 per cent between 1879 and 1882, with the numbers of families evicted in Ireland in the peak years of 1881 and 1882 being 3,415 and 5,201 respectively. In Co. Galway in 1881, 131 families were evicted and in 1882 the total was 541. Table 6 (p. 54) shows the number of families evicted and the number readmitted as caretakers or tenants during the years 1877–82 in Ireland, Connacht and the East and West Ridings of Galway.

14 Padraig G. Lane, 'The tedious business of unwanted tenants: Galway and Mayo in the 1850s', *Journal of Galway Archaeological and Historical Society*, 60 (2008), 126–35. 15 Solow, *The land question and the Irish economy*, pp 54–7. 16 Tim P. O'Neill, 'Famine evictions' in King (ed.), *Famine, land and culture in Ireland* (2000), pp 29–70. 17 Vaughan, *Landlords and tenants in mid-Victorian Ireland*, p. 32.

Table 6 Numbers of families evicted and readmitted as caretakers or tenants, 1877–82 (sources: HC 1880 (254), lx, 361, HC 1881 (2), lxxvii, 713, HC 1881 (185), lxxvii, 746, HC 1882 (9), lv, 229 and HC 1883 [C.3465], lvi, 99).

1877	Families evicted	Re-admitted	% re-admitted	1878	Families evicted	Re-admitted	% re-admitted
Ireland	463	57	12	Ireland	980	146	15
Connacht	118	16	14	Connacht	365	37	10
Galway E	8	0	0	Galway E	27	9	33
Galway W	37	5	14	Galway W	192	17	9

1879	Families evicted	Re-admitted	% re-admitted	1880	Families evicted	Re-admitted	% re-admitted
Ireland	1,238	140	11	Ireland	2,110	217	10
Connacht	313	45	14	Connacht	387	22	6
Galway E	22	0	0	Galway E	21	4	19
Galway W	46	0	0	Galway W	74	10	14

1881	Families evicted	Re-admitted	% re-admitted	1882	Families evicted	Re-admitted	% re-admitted
Ireland	3,415	1,880	45	Ireland	5,201	2,529	49
Connacht	784	397	51	Connacht	1,457	794	54
Galway E	34	18	53	Galway E	70	42	60
Galway W	97	27	28	Galway W	471	194	41

Table 7 Evictions without readmission as caretakers or tenants during 1881 and 1882 (sources: HC 1880 (254), lx, 361, HC 1881 (2), lxxvii, 713, HC 1881 (185), lxxvii, 746, HC 1882 (9), lv. 229 and HC 1883 [C.3465], lvi, 99).

	Families evicted			
	Ireland	Connacht	Galway East	Galway West
1881				
1st quarter	350	47	2	2
2nd quarter	1,065	268	9	40
3rd quarter	1,282	303	19	48
4th quarter	718	166	4	7
1882				
1st quarter	1,317	354	35	98
2nd quarter	1,732	583	23	288
3rd quarter	1,443	323	6	49
4th quarter	709	197	6	36

Nationally, the rate of evictions varied considerably and Vaughan's ranking of counties most affected during the Land War places Longford, Kerry and Leitrim in the leading positions and Antrim and Down as the least affected.[18] Variations also occurred within counties and there is a notable disparity in the number of evictions in the two Galway ridings throughout the period. The marked increase in the number of evictions in Galway West during 1881–2 and particularly during the second quarter of 1882 is noteworthy. This probably indicates the difficulties of tenants in the more impoverished West Riding and the zeal of new landlords, who had recently acquired properties, to rid themselves of tenants who were badly in arrears. The period with most evictions extended from April 1881 to September 1882, with the peak occurring between January and June 1882 (see table 7, above).

In June 1881, a force of two hundred police and military accompanied the sub sheriff and five bailiffs to evict thirteen families in Carraroe, Belleek and Derrygimley in Galway West Riding. A report in January 1882 claimed that already thirty-two families had been evicted on the Berridge estate (formerly the Martin estate).[19] Further extensive evictions were reported in April and May on the properties of Mrs Kirwan (Blindwell), Mr Eyre (Clifden Castle), Mr Blake (Towerhill) and Mrs Wall (Errislannon). More than 150 families were evicted.[20] The re-admission rate was only 21 per cent and one of the results was the emigration, in May 1882, of fifty-five families (three hundred persons) from Galway to Quebec, which was arranged by the Quaker philanthropist, J.H. Tuke.[21]

18 Ibid., Appendix 4, pp 235–6. 19 *Galway Vindicator*, 6 May 1882. 20 *Galway Vindicator*, 17 May 1882. 21 *Galway Vindicator*, 6 May 1882.

Even if evictions were not numerous in many areas, the sufferings of families like the Fallons of Moneen, Ardrahan, created an atmosphere of anger and contempt for the evictors – in this case the Persse family of Roxborough House. The townland of Moneen contained a dozen houses and Mike Fallon's holding comprised a house and nine acres of land. During the late 1870s, when the harvests were poor, he became indebted to shopkeepers and was unable to pay rent. As a result, his mare and foal were seized to pay his debts. He suffered further misfortune when his cow died and through ill health he was unable to till the farm. He approached the Persses and asked for payment for the work he had done at Roxborough House, but was refused. At that stage, he owed two years' rent, a sum of £18. The eviction saga commenced in September 1880, when Algernon Persse evicted Fallon and his family of five children, including an infant. For the occasion, Sub Sheriff Mr Redington and large numbers of police accompanied Persse. Kitchen utensils and furniture were removed from the house and the family remained in the open air and fasting until the workhouse car brought them to Loughrea Workhouse. They returned to their home on 19 September and the following day Persse offered to give Fallon permission to return as caretaker but he refused. Fallon said that 'he meant to keep a firm grip with the support of the Land League' and he told Persse that the 'day when bad landlords could do as they pleased is past and the Land League will support me against your tyranny'. Persse threatened prosecution and Fallon responded with a reference to the clearances carried out by the Persses in 'black 47. If the people had the pluck they have now you and your father would not have a demesne wall around Roxborough sheltering rabbits and pheasants where the people should be living'.[22] Two days later, Persse ordered the removal of Fallon's crop of oats. On 19 September 1880, at the land meeting in Riverville, Matthew Harris nominated Fallon to preside over the proceedings and he took the chair to a rousing reception. Between March 1881 and June 1883, he appeared at the petty sessions on thirty-four occasions charged with trespass and on each charge he was usually fined ten shillings or, in default of payment, a sentence of one week in jail was applied. In fact, the total amount of the fines would have exceeded the amount owed in rent.

In January 1882, forty suspects in Galway Jail went on prison diet to show support for Fallon who, at that time, along with his wife, was in his fourth term of imprisonment. The prisoners placed their weekly allowance from the Ladies' Land League in a fund for the Fallons and Miss Mary Barrett, president of the Craughwell Ladies' Land League (see below, chapter 9, p. 112), presented a sum of £35 to the family.[23] In February, another conviction did not result in imprisonment because Revd Considine and others subscribed the £2 fine. When Mrs Fallon was jailed, she always brought her youngest child with her, while the

22 *Tuam News*, 25 Sept. 1880. 23 *Tuam News*, 27 Jan. 1882 and 10 Mar. 1882.

Ladies' Land League supported the rest of the family. During March 1882, it was reported that a large crowd assembled in a field in Ballymana that had been bought for the Fallons by the Craughwell Ladies' Land League and sowed an acre of potatoes for the family.[24] In May, the *Tuam News* reported that Algernon Persse evicted Fallon again and levelled the walls of the house and fields.[25] During October, Persse, accompanied by 'Emergency Men' and a guard of soldiers, carried off the hay that had been saved on the holding, thereby removing the winter-feeding for the stock purchased with the money subscribed by the suspects in Galway Jail.[26]

The saga continued into 1883 and in January, at Ardrahan Petty Sessions, Fallon was sentenced to seven weeks in prison and his wife to two weeks. In June, Fallon applied to the Loughrea Poor Law Board of Guardians for outdoor relief and was granted five shillings to support the seven family members for seven days. When the application was discussed by the board, Algernon Persse objected to the granting of outdoor relief on the grounds that Fallon had money. Patrick Cawley (Craughwell), also a member of the PLG board, roundly berated Persse for his heartless behaviour.[27] In the same month, Fallon was back in Ardrahan court, where he was fined £2 with the alternative of four weeks in jail if he failed to pay the fine.[28] He was sent to Galway Jail and, while he was there, SRM Clifford Lloyd ordered the arrest of Mrs Fallon, who was charged at Galway assizes and found guilty of forcible entry and confined in Galway Jail. On a visit to Loughrea in August 1883, Robert Hayden, an American journalist, interviewed John Fallon, aged thirteen. The young boy said 'he was determined to stay in the holding, sleeping in the house except when it rained, when they sheltered in a neighbour's house. His sister cooks for them and looks after the baby'.[29] Fallon was released from jail on 13 August but his wife remained incarcerated.

On a visit to Loughrea, Michael Davitt addressed a large crowd and also visited the Fallon children in Moneen. Davitt gave £6 to the Loughrea journalist, Thomas Cunningham, to purchase clothes for the family, saying 'they shall not want for anything as long as I live'.[30] In December 1883, Mrs Fallon pleaded guilty at Sligo assizes and was discharged by Judge William O'Brien,[31] on condition that the holding would be given up.[32] She was released from jail on 8 January 1884 and on her return to the locality she was greeted with bonfires and illuminations in Ardrahan and Craughwell, and an indignation meeting was held in Labane at which Matthew Harris spoke.[33] In a later report on the sad affair, Divisional Magistrate Andrew Reed stated that, since her liberation, Mrs

24 *Tuam News*, 24 Mar. 1882.   25 *Tuam News*, 26 May 1882.   26 *Tuam News*, 13 Oct. 1882.
27 *Tuam News*, 15 June 1883.   28 *Tuam News*, 29 June 1883.   29 *Western News*, 4 Aug. 1883.
30 *Tuam News*, 17 Aug. 1883.   31 William O'Brien (1832–99), Justice of Common Pleas Division, 1882. See F.E. Ball, *The judges in Ireland, ii: 1221–1921* (London, 1926), p. 374.
32 *Tuam News*, 28 Dec. 1883.   33 *Tuam News*, 11 Jan. 1884.

Fallon returned on only one occasion to the family home and was living in a neighbour's house.[34]

AGRARIAN OUTRAGES

Agrarian incidents, referred to as outrages in official communications, were commonplace in Ireland throughout the nineteenth century. In order to qualify as agrarian, an outrage had to be shown to arise from agrarian discontent and to be directly connected to a specific motive related to land. Evictions were an important cause of discontent, as were land grabbing, rack-renting and disputes over land between tenants and also within families. It is noteworthy that the greatest prevalence of outrages was associated with social and political upheavals such as the Tithe War in the 1830s, the Great Famine in the 1840s and the Land War of 1879–82. A total of twenty-eight coercion acts were passed between 1847 and 1875; these included the suspension of habeas corpus from 1848 to 1849 and from 1866 to 1869, and those prolonging the various crime and outrage acts. In 1871, the lord lieutenant was given power to order internment without trial in Co. Westmeath and parts of Co. Meath and King's County (Offaly). An inevitable outcome of the disturbances and the response to them was the large number of police supported by military required to maintain order.

In his remarkably indulgent review of the matter, Vaughan suggests that

> too much should not be made of the coercive legislation. It is true that the suspension of habeas corpus deprived Ireland of one of the most cherished liberties of the British subject. On the other hand, the very mass of coercive legislation between 1847 and 1875 was misleading: most of the twenty-eight acts were renewals of the acts of 1847 and 1856 ... Their temporary character suggests not only a solicitude for the freedom of the subject, but also a curious optimism that regarded Irish disorder as recurrent rather than endemic and permanent.

Vaughan goes on to state that

> The coercive legislation at its most severe was hardly draconian except by the remarkably liberal standards of mid-nineteenth-century Britain. ... A more secretive and arbitrary regime would have dealt with its *mauvais sujets*[35] more discreetly, and a country where public houses could be closed only by a special warrant from the highest official in the land was hardly groaning under oppression.[36]

34 NAI, CSO, RP 1884/2262, Reed to under secretary, 28 Jan. 1884. 35 Bad or disloyal subjects. 36 Vaughan, *Landlords and tenants in mid-Victorian Ireland*, pp 140–1.

Table 8 National outrage statistics, 1879–83 (sources: HC 1881 (5), lxxvii, 793, HC 1882 (7), lv, 615, HC 1883 (6), lvii, 1047, HC 1883 (6), [C.3511], lv, 13, HC 1883 [C.3566], lvi, 17, HC 1883 [C.3608], lvi, 21, HC 1883 [C.3664], lvi, 25, HC 1883 [C.3681], lvi, 29, HC 1883 [C.3743], lvi, 33 and HC 1884 [C.3894], lxiv, 13).

	Jan.	Feb.	Mar.	Apr.	May	June	July	Aug.	Sept.	Oct.	Nov.	Dec.	Total
1879	33	31	35	57	76	64	45	45	65	110	167	135	863
1880	114	97	83	67	88	90	84	103	168	269	561	866	2,590
1881	448	170	151	308	351	332	271	373	416	511	534	574	4,439
1882	495	410	542	465	401	284	231	176	139	112	93	85	3,433
1883	58	54	83	73	92	67	61	58	78	53	54	46	777

While there is no doubt that individuals guilty of serious crime were interned without trial under the PPP (Ireland) Act of 1881, many innocent persons were also deprived of their liberty for pursuing legitimate political aims.

The national outrage statistics for 1879–83 are shown in table 8, above, and the outrage statistics for the same period in Galway East and West Ridings in table 9 (see below, p. 60).

The national figures show a low prevalence during the early part of 1879 and a gradual increase with the developing agricultural crisis during the autumn and winter of 1879–80. The worsening of the national picture between October 1880 and January 1881, with a total of 2,144 outrages, had a major influence on Chief Secretary Forster's decision to introduce repressive legislation in March 1881. However, the arrest of suspects under the PPP (Ireland) Act had no immediate effect, with a continuing high level of agrarian crime from April 1881 onwards. The peak was reached in the winter of 1881–2 and after May 1882 the numbers reported decreased, especially after the introduction of the Prevention of Crime (Ireland) Act in July 1882.

The seriously disturbed nature of the country in those years is evident not only from the fifty-seven homicides but also from the 149 cases of firing at the person, 326 cases of firing into dwellings, 129 armed attacks on dwellings, 306 serious assaults (not including those on police and bailiffs) and 847 incendiary fires.[37]

A relatively small number of outrages had occurred in Co. Galway between 1848 and 1878, but in the period from 1879 to 1882 Galway was ranked third nationally, surpassed only by Kerry and Limerick.[38]

It is notable that the number of outrages in the West Riding in each year exceeded the numbers in the East Riding. There was also a greater number of evictions in the West Riding and this supports the suggestion of a link between

---

37 Ball, 'Policing the Land War', p. 312.   38 Vaughan, *Landlords and tenants in mid-Victorian Ireland*, Appendix 22, pp 285–6.

Table 9 Galway East and West Riding outrages, 1879–83 (sources: HC 1880 (131), lx, 199, HC 1881 (5), lxxvii, 793, HC 1881 (13), lxxvii, 607, HC 1882 (7), lv, 615, HC 1882 (8), lv, 1, HC 1882 (72), lv, 17, HC 1883 (6), lvii, 1047, HC 1883 (12), lvi, 1, HC 1884 [C.3894], lxiv, 13 and HC 1884 [C.3950], lxiv, 1).

Year	East Riding	West Riding	Total
1879	33	147	180
1880	79	323	402
1881	197	281	478
1882	158	181	339
1883	25	31	56

the numbers of evictions and outrages as suggested below (see p. 61). A comparison of Cos Galway and Mayo is of interest because the land agitation in Mayo was less of a force from mid-1880. In Mayo, the peak incidence of outrages occurred between October 1880 and January 1881, whereas in Galway the peak occurred much later, between October 1881 and February 1882.[39]

In 1881 in Galway East Riding, the crimes included three murders, six serious assaults, five of firing into dwellings, eighteen incendiary fires, fifteen episodes of killing or maiming cattle and 139 instances of intimidation.[40] This reflects a typical pattern, with threatening letters and notices constituting the vast majority of reported outrages. Ball's analysis of agrarian and political murders (table 10, below) shows the range of motives involved.

Table 10 Analysis of agrarian and political murders, 1880–2 (source: Stephen A. Ball, '"Policing the Land War": official responses to political protest and agrarian crime in Ireland, 1879–91' (PhD, U London, 2000), p. 312).

Motive	Number of victims	Percentage
Police informer	9	16
Working for boycotted landlord	9	16
Paying rent	3	5
Land grabbing	8	14
Policeman, bailiff, process server	7	12
Political assassination	2	4
Landlord/employee assassination	11	19
Family/neighbour dispute	8	14
Total	57	100

The eight victims of murder in the Athenry and Loughrea police districts during 1881–2 were a landlord and his soldier guard, a land agent and his servant, a policeman and three men accused of land grabbing. Many of the

39 Jordan, *Land and popular politics in Ireland*, p. 234. 40 HC 1882, (7), lv, 615.

Table 11 National statistics of evictions and outrages, 1879–82 (sources: HC 1881 (5), lxxvii, 793, HC 1882 (7), lv, 615, HC 1882 (8), lv, 1, HC 1883 (6), lvii, 1047 and HC 1884 [C.3894], lxiv, 13).

Year	Evictions	Outrages
1879	1,238	863
1880	2,110	2,590
1881	3,415	4,439
1882	5,201	3,433

murders were well organized and the police believed that IRB groups were involved in their planning and execution. All the victims were shot, indicating the ready availability of arms in the community. These murders will be described in detail in chapter 8 (see below, pp 88–102).

The experience of dispossession clearly fuelled resentment and a thirst for revenge, and the often callous disregard for human suffering displayed by landlords and their agents was condemned at the mass Land League meetings and widely publicized in the local press. It is, therefore, not surprising that the prevalence of evictions in a community and the occurrence of outrages were linked. This assessment was widely accepted at the time and Parnell stated in his evidence to the Special Commission that evictions were the root cause of agrarian crime.[41] Support for this contention has been provided by the positive correlation of agrarian outrages and evictions demonstrated by Andrew Orridge.[42] A relationship is also evident from the figures in table 11 (see above) with relatively low levels of both in 1879 and a substantial increase in outrages and evictions in 1880–1. This is particularly true of the second half of 1881, with over 2,000 evictions and 2,679 outrages. In 1882, the increase in evictions continued with an incidence of 5,201, and this probably indicates the desire of the landlords to rid themselves of 'bad' tenants before settlements under the Land Act of 1881 became widespread. The total number of outrages in 1882 was 3,433; of those, 2,597 were committed during the first half of the year and only 836 in the second. This dramatic decrease is related to the decline in agitation and the effect of the measures introduced by the Prevention of Crime (Ireland) Act 1882.

---

[41] NLI, Parnell Special Commission, vol. 7, p. 45. [42] Andrew Orridge, 'Who supported the Land War?: an aggregate data analysis of Irish discontent, 1879–82', *Economic and Social Review*, 12:3 (1981), 203–33.

6 Agrarian secret societies and the Fenian organization

AGRARIAN SECRET SOCIETIES

The long tradition of agrarian secret societies in Co. Galway dates back to a group known as the 'Houghers' in 1711–12, whose activities were concentrated in west Galway. Their origin coincided with the development of commercial farming that resulted in antagonism between graziers and small cultivators.[1] The Whiteboy movement that arose in 1761 mainly affected southern counties and there are no reports of Whiteboy activity in Galway at that time. A later secret society, the Right Boys, was based in Munster but it was also active in Woodford, Gort, Aughrim and Tuam. In the 1790s, the Defenders, a Catholic secret society, were based in Cos Louth, Monaghan and Cavan but they also had some influence in the Loughrea district.[2] The economic prosperity associated with the Napoleonic Wars (1803–15) rapidly declined after 1815, and poverty and grievances led to agrarian disturbances; these were attributed to Whiteboyism, which became prevalent in 1819–20 in Oranmore and parts of east Galway, where it was linked to the Pastorini cult.[3] The disturbed nature of Co. Galway at that time is evident from the comment of the sheriff that, whenever his sub sheriff distrained goods of the peasantry without an armed guard, he was lucky to escape with his life.[4] In January 1819, Chief Magistrate Pendleton was sent to four baronies in east Galway to maintain order. In addition, the murder of a local magistrate, Edward Browne, led to a raucous meeting of gentry at Loughrea, where the government was asked to proclaim nine additional baronies. Despite the influx of military personnel, outrages continued through the winter and spring of 1820 and further meetings in Athenry and Loughrea censured Dublin Castle for not reviving one of the earlier coercion acts, the Insurrection Act, which had lapsed in 1818. The local population showed considerable hostility to the crown forces, and patrols and outstations came under frequent attack. Nevertheless, Pendleton secured twenty-eight felony convictions (including seven capital sentences and four life transportations) and order was restored by April 1820.[5] The most famous local individual is Anthony Daly, who was

---

1 S.J. Connolly, 'The Houghers' in Philpin (ed.), *Nationalism and popular protest in Ireland* (1987), pp 139–62. 2 David Ryan, 'Disaffection and rebellious conspiracy in the Loughrea area, 1791–1804' in Joseph Forde, Christina Cassidy, Paul Manzor and David Ryan (eds), *The district of Loughrea, i: history, 1791–1918* (Loughrea, 2003), pp 3–6. 3 James S. Donnelly, 'Pastorini and Captain Rock' in Clark and Donnelly (eds), *Irish peasants* (1983), pp 102–39. Pastorini predicted the destruction of Protestantism in 1825. 4 S.H. Palmer, *Police and protest in England and Ireland, 1780–1850* (Cambridge, 1988), p. 265. 5 Ibid., pp 219–20.

regarded as the leader of the Whiteboys in the area. Following attacks on Roxborough House, Raford House and St Clerans in early 1820, Daly was arrested, convicted and executed at Seefin between Loughrea and Craughwell.[6] The poet Antoine Raifterí, who was very familiar with south Galway at that period, commemorated Daly in his poem *Antoine Ó Dálaigh* and he also referred to Whiteboy activity in poems entitled *Na Buachailli Bána*.[7]

A similar pattern of agrarian incidents continued in the 1830s, and in 1831–2 the Connacht police district (which included Co. Clare) reported a total of 125 homicides.[8] In 1836, G. Cornewell Lewis commented that the people administering oaths to individuals in Clare came from south Galway.[9] At the same time, there were reports of peasants sleeping in the fields to avoid recruiting visits by activists from Galway.[10] The Terry Alt secret societies were prevalent in Co. Clare in the 1830s, and also in the Gort area. There were reports that threatening notices were displayed and that arms were stolen from the houses of gentry.[11]

The police and local magistrates strongly believed in the existence of secret societies, but often they were unable to provide accurate estimates of the number of people involved and the exact composition of them. The role of agricultural labourers in such societies has received particular attention.[12] Between the Great Famine and 1881, a marked reduction occurred in the number of labourers. In 1841, they constituted 56 per cent of the labour force, decreasing to 38 per cent by 1881. In the same period, the proportion of farmers increased from 28 to 40 per cent and farmers' sons from 14 to 20 per cent. Multiple factors account for these changes. Clearances during and after the Great Famine hastened the change of farming practice from tillage to pasturage. The increased use of machinery on farms decreased the available work for labourers and resulted in a high emigration rate. Discontent among labourers was fostered by their failure to benefit from the relative prosperity enjoyed by farmers during the 1870s, a prosperity generated by the increase in prices for stock and agricultural produce. Other grievances included payments in kind rather than wages and this, combined with the lamentable standard of housing, reduced many labourers to a precarious level of subsistence. It is noteworthy that the crowds besieging Poor

---

6 David Ryan, 'The trial and execution of Anthony Daly' in Joseph Forde, Christina Cassidy, Paul Manzor and David Ryan (eds), *The district of Loughrea, i: history, 1791–1918* (Loughrea, 2003), p. 99.   7 Antoine Raifterí (1784–1835), born in Killeadan, Co. Mayo; buried in Killeeneen, Co. Galway.   8 Cited in Palmer, *Police and protest in England and Ireland*, p. 326.
9 G. Cornewell Lewis, *On local disturbances in Ireland* (London, 1836), pp 194–5.   10 Michael Beames, *Peasants and power: the Whiteboy movements and their control in pre-famine Ireland* (Brighton, 1983), p. 53.   11 Marguerite Grey (ed.), *Gort Inse Guaire* (Gort, 2000), p. 176.
12 Padraig G. Lane, 'Agricultural labourers and rural violence, 1850–1914', *Studia Hibernica*, 27 (1993), 77–87; John W. Boyle, 'A marginal figure: the Irish rural laborer' in Samuel Clark & James S. Donnelly Junior (eds), *Irish peasants: violence and political unrest, 1780–1914* (Manchester, 1983), pp 311–38; Samuel Clark, *Social origins of the Irish Land War* (Princeton, NJ, 1979), pp 249–52.

Law Guardian board meetings and Bishop Duggan's residence in 1880 consisted mainly of landless labourers and the urban poor. The founding of the Land League increased the expectations of labourers that they would share in the benefits of land reform, but disillusionment set in when it became apparent that the Land League was not promoting their interests, unlike its strong advocacy of the farmers' cause. This contrasted with the situation earlier in the nineteenth century, when there was a greater degree of compatibility between the interests of labourers and farmers. The Select Committee on Outrages of 1852 confirmed 'that Ribbonism's rank and file were the labourers and that they cooperated with the tenant leadership of the movement'.[13]

Despite possible conflicting interests and the overall reduction in their numbers, it is very likely that the labourers were a source of recruitment into secret societies and there is evidence that this occurred in relation to both labourers and herds.[14] Lane refers to constabulary reports of 1883 and 1885 that acknowledged the fears of farmers regarding the large number of labourers in secret societies.[15] There is also support for this opinion in the pattern of arrests under the ordinary law for nocturnal attacks between June 1880 and June 1882, when eighty-two farmers, forty-six farmers' sons and fifty-four labourers were arrested.[16] Another factor favouring the participation of labourers in secret societies was the seasonal nature of their employment, which was concentrated in the spring and autumn months. Readily available forces during the winter months probably explain the preponderance of outrages reported when the longer hours of darkness facilitated acts of intimidation and violence.

Secret societies seem to have formed in a spontaneous manner in response to local crises such as the issuing of ejectment notices and evictions, and the acts of violence were a reaction to such events. During the Land War, the increased level of political activity, the agricultural crisis and the difficult relationships with landlords in south Galway provided the necessary stimulus for the reactivation of secret societies. It is probable that armed and well-organized groups of IRB members melded with local agrarian formations and that individual Land League members belonged to both, even though the Land League executive condemned this association. Revd Michael O'Donovan, PP of Corofin, Co. Clare, later observed that 'all the moonlighters were not Fenian. There seemed to be wheels within wheels'.[17] The societies flourished despite the Catholic Church's long-standing distrust of secret political movements and regular

13 Lane, 'Agricultural labourers and rural violence, 1850–1914', pp 80–1. 14 John Cunningham, 'A spirit of self-preservation: herdsmen around Loughrea in the late 19th century' in Joseph Forde, Christina Cassidy, Paul Manzor and David Ryan (eds), *The district of Loughrea, i: history, 1791–1918* (Loughrea, 2003), pp 457–80; Jarlath Waldron, *Maamtrasna: the murders and the mystery* (Dublin, 1992), pp 17, 312–13; John W. Boyle, 'A marginal figure: the Irish rural laborer' in Clark & Donnelly (eds), *Irish peasants* (1983), pp 311–37. 15 Cited in Lane, 'Agricultural labourers and rural violence', p. 82. 16 HC 1882 (403), lv, 609. 17 NLI, Parnell Special Commission, vol. 8, p. 21.

denunciations by Catholic clergy. The existence of secret societies and their responsibility for the killings in Galway was the subject of many police reports, and local activists belonging to both IRB circles and agrarian secret societies may have formed units to carry out the more serious acts of violence.[18]

THE FENIAN ORGANIZATION[19]

After the abortive Fenian rising of 1867, the organizers of the Fenians in Galway were Matthew Harris, John O'Connor Power and Mark Ryan. Griffin estimates the Fenian membership as follows: Galway City 501–1,000; Ballinasloe 101–500; Tuam 31–100; Athenry 10–30; and Loughrea, Gort and Kilchreest 1–9. In his memoirs,[20] Mark Ryan refers to his attendance at secret meetings in different parts of Co. Galway, including Athenry, where drilling took place, and he indicates that the Fenian Centre for Loughrea was Joseph O'Flaherty. When Ryan returned to England, he became actively engaged in the exportation to Ireland of arms that were purchased in Liverpool from a gunsmith named Robert Jones. In 1873, Ryan dispatched six revolvers to John Scanlon, a general merchant in Loughrea. However, when the police discovered the arms, Scanlon denied all knowledge of them and the person who sent them. During the following year, Ryan wrote to John Sweeny, Loughrea, requesting the balance of payments due for arms. The method of payment involved the sending of half notes with the order and the remaining halves on receipt of the arms and ammunition.[21] Ryan also sent consignments of arms to Portumna and Woodford. In evidence to the Parnell Special Commission, Matthew Harris said he was aware of arms importation between 1867 and 1879. Arms were sent directly to him and others in considerable numbers and each man who had paid and was a member got a rifle and a sword bayonet.[22]

In the early 1870s, the war office had decided to dispose of surplus arms and many of those weapons were bought and sent to Ireland.[23] A letter to *The Independent* from Edward M. Richards referred to the 'most serious error of Lord Beaconsfield's government in allowing the discarded Enfield rifles to find their way to Ireland'.[24] A great many of the imported arms went to farmers, reflecting the changed composition of the Fenian movement from the earlier urban-based organization to one with a substantial membership of tenant farmers and labourers. The change in composition may also indicate the expectation

---

18 Ball, 'Policing the Land War', p. 144 and Fergus Campbell, *Land and revolution* (Oxford, 2005), p. 147.   19 A comprehensive account of the Fenian movement in Connacht is contained in the unpublished MA thesis by Brian Griffin: 'The IRB in Connacht and Leinster, 1858–78' (Maynooth, 1983).   20 Mark Ryan, *Fenian memories* (Dublin, 1946), p. 37.   21 NAI, Fenian A files, A 567.   22 NLI, Parnell Special Commission, vol. 10, p. 171.   23 Hansard's parliamentary debates, third series, vol. 271, col. 24 (22 June 1882).   24 NAI CSO RP 1880/20598.

among small farmers that the redistribution of land would occur if the Land League agitation proved successful.

Fears of renewed Fenian agitation, including attacks on landlords, were expressed in April 1878 and reference was made to the importation of arms, principally revolvers.[25] In June 1879, the under secretary, Thomas H. Burke, writing to the solicitor general, Hugh Holmes,[26] referred to 'armed parties going about at night ... and outrages are in some instances committed on tenants who have paid their rents'.[27] Police reports prepared in 1878 referred to the spread in parts of Co. Galway of secret societies that 'combined agrarianism with Fenianism', particularly in the Dunmore area. In Clonbern, a man called Barrett was killed and Head Constable O'Connor and petty sessions clerk James McDonogh were wounded. The report commented that 'there is no doubt whatever that these outrages are the results of the Secret Society, nearly all the members are known to the police and kept under strict surveillance'.[28] Deputy inspector general of the RIC, Robert Bruce, visited north Galway and south Mayo in late June 1879, at the time the land agitation was gaining momentum. Bruce recommended 'constant and watchful patrolling by police, especially at night, and the establishment of special stations ... where any outrages of a serious nature have been committed. The costs to be levied on the immediate districts'.[29]

In April 1879, John Devoy undertook an extensive tour of Ireland at the request of the IRB supreme council. He reported his views on the membership and its state of organization to the Clan na Gael leadership in August.[30] During his tour, he attended many meetings of local and county circles and found in Connacht that most of the members were farmers and farmers' sons and he estimated the membership at twenty-four thousand. In the rural districts, he found 'a great want of system' and advised that much more was needed to sustain a great political movement than a 'mere willingness to risk life and liberty'. With the financial support of Clan na Gael, Devoy arranged for the importation of arms at a cost to members of £1, and before his departure for America provision had been made for the purchase and storage of ten thousand guns. John O'Connor, P.N. Fitzgerald and William Mackey Lomasney, a Fenian veteran and now a member of Clan na Gael, were in charge of the importation of arms and they were quickly successful in importing large quantities of arms and ammunition.[31] In a letter to Devoy, Davitt stated that he had 'visited the

---

25 NAI CSO RP 1878/7008, RM H.A. Blake to chief secretary, 15 Apr. 1878. 26 Hugh Holmes (1840–1916), born in Dungannon, Co. Tyrone, law adviser 1877, solicitor general Dec. 1878. Elected MP for Dublin University 1885, attorney general 1885–87; when he resigned he became a judge of the high court. 27 NAI CSO RP 1879/9785 in 1879/10612. 28 NAI CSO RP 1879/10269. 29 NAI, CSO, RP 1879/10881, DI G. Bruce to IG Hillier, 27 June 1878. 30 NAI, Fenian A files, A 612, copy of report. 31 Owen McGee, *The IRB* (Dublin, 2005), pp 80–1.

districts where disturbances arose some few weeks ago and found a great and general desire among people to become possessed of material [arms]. Several of the successful attacks were prompted by him'.³² Writing to Devoy in February 1880, James J. O'Kelly asked for 'credit of $7,000 with which to purchase 500 short [revolvers] at £2 and 1,000 long [rifles] old pattern at about 5 or 6 shillings'.³³ In October 1880, RM Paul stated that in Galway East Riding large quantities of arms were sold publicly and secretly. RM Franks (Gort) stated that there was no trade in arms but they could be easily purchased in neighbouring towns.³⁴ In the Loughrea area, in the summer of 1880, Joseph Huban claimed to have distributed arms to farmers.³⁵

It is noteworthy that Dr Leonard, who performed the post-mortem examinations on Peter Dempsey and Peter Doherty, stated that the fatal bullet was conical, similar to those used in Snider rifles (see pp 90, 95). These rifles were commonly imported by the Fenians and John F. Taylor claimed that they were for sale in the country for five or six shillings.³⁶ In Tuam, rifles and revolvers were offered for sale openly and the principal purchasers were shop men, farmers' sons and labourers. Despite the reported availability, the arms and ammunition were well concealed because five searches for arms in Galway East Riding during 1881 yielded no results.³⁷

Resident magistrates in other parts of the country were also making the links between the Fenians and the Land League. RM Captain A.S. Butler claimed that the Ribbon and Fenian societies in the midlands and north-east appeared to be amalgamating.³⁸ RM Traill (Mayo) considered that the Land League 'is carried on secretly but it is generally combined with some other secret society'. He thought that the IRB, Fenianism and Ribbonism 'are very general among all young men in the Division'.³⁹ In 1880, Under Secretary Burke articulated the Irish executive's concerns about arms and links with the Fenians: 'there can be little doubt that some members of the Land League are acting in concert with the Fenians here and in America and that arms are surreptitiously smuggled into this country'.⁴⁰ At the same time, a circular from the executive body of Clan na Gael stated that 'Clan na Gael as an organization has never gone into the Land League, but its members have been from the first the most active workers in that movement and have contributed heavily to its support'. Clan na Gael expressed the fear that the Land League was actively fostering hostility to the Fenian organization.⁴¹ P.J.P. Tynan, writing about the Invincibles, claimed that

---

32 O'Brien & Ryan (eds), *Devoy's post bag*, i, 6 Feb. 1880, Davitt to Devoy, pp 482–3. 33 O'Brien & Ryan (eds), *Devoy's post bag*, i, 11 Feb. 1880, pp 489–90. 34 BL, Spencer papers, 77317. Reports of resident magistrates. 35 NAI, ILL and INL documents, carton 2. 36 *Tuam News*, 18 July 1884. 37 NAI CSO RP 1882/449, return by IG Hillier, 28 Feb. 1881. 38 NAI CSO RP 1882/34012, RM Butler to under secretary. 39 NAI CSO RP 1882/34013, RM Traill to under secretary. 40 BL Spencer Papers, 77316A, memo of Mr Burke for cabinet. 41 O'Brien & Ryan (eds), *Devoy's post bag*, ii, p. 106.

'although the IRB organization remained intact ... several of its leading spirits joined the new movement [Land League] and among those who joined were some of the officers of the IRB'.[42]

The Land League executive appointed two secretaries, Michael Davitt and Thomas Brennan, an assistant secretary, M.M. O'Sullivan, and a treasurer, Patrick Egan; all were past or current IRB members. Other IRB members were the organizers Matthew Harris (a supreme council member until 1880), Michael Boyton and P.J. Sheridan. Harris later said that the reason for his departure from the supreme council was the passage of a resolution in the summer of 1880, 'prohibiting any man belonging to the organization, above an ordinary rank and file man, from connecting himself with the Land League'.[43] In retrospect, Davitt was in no doubt about the importance of the link with the IRB, stating that 'from the very beginning at Irishtown, known IRB members such as P.W. Nally, John O'Connor Power, John O'Keane and Thomas Brennan were prominently associated with the Land League'.[44] The police believed that when Davitt visited Mayo in early 1879, he was given the names of IRB members by the County Centres.[45] Later, Parnell and Davitt, the two leaders of the Land League, expressed opposing views on the relationship between the Land League and the Fenians. Parnell claimed in evidence to the Special Commission that the 'physical force organization has been consistently hostile to us since 1880'.[46] Davitt, on the other hand, stated that 'the great majority of those who believed in the final objects of the revolutionary movement were more or less in full sympathy with the league and its objects'.[47]

The Fenian leaders Kickham and John O'Leary were both opposed to the Land League, mainly because of the associated prevalence of agrarian outrages as well as their traditional distrust of constitutional politics. Davitt believed the Fenian organization was fully supportive of the Land League. While this may have been true of individual members, the IRB supreme council, especially after the departure of Davitt and Harris, was opposed and P.W. Nally, one of the organizers of the Irishtown meeting (see above, p. 17), who replaced Harris on the supreme council, became critical of the Land League and withdrew from its activities. Thereafter, Nally devoted himself to the IRB organization and an informant, T. Smyth, claimed that Nally was given arms by commercial travellers and distributed them:

> By some arrangement he has, he can carry six or seven revolvers under an apparently tight-fitting suit without the slightest suspicion being created by his appearance. An immense deal of arms are concealed in the

42 P.J.P. Tynan, *The Irish National Invincibles and their times* (London, 1894), p. 432. 43 NLI, Parnell Special Commission, vol. 10, p. 225. 44 Davitt, *The fall of feudalism*, p. 147. 45 PRO CO 904/box 16/reel 7. 46 NLI, Parnell Special Commission, vol. 7, p. 88. 47 Davitt, *The fall of feudalism*, p. 245.

bogs of Mayo and Galway and I have seen a few that were taken from such a place and they were quite worthless.[48]

One of the problems for the government in their dealings with the Fenians/IRB and illegal secret societies was the undeveloped state of the intelligence service. It was formed in 1865 when Samuel Lee Anderson, crown solicitor for Waterford and Kilkenny, was appointed to advise Dublin Castle. In June 1872, SI James Ellis French from Belfast was appointed as detective director of constabulary. He was given a staff of three plain-clothes men and an office in the Phoenix Park Depot. Over the next seven years, systematic reporting of Fenianism/Ribbonism was established, but with resources that were totally inadequate for the purpose of countrywide surveillance. Superintendent John Mallon[49] of the Dublin Metropolitan Police became the dominant figure in relation to Fenian matters, not only in the Dublin area but throughout the country. In the aftermath of the Phoenix Park murders in May 1882, the new lord lieutenant, Earl Spencer,[50] gave serious consideration to the circumstances surrounding the killing of Lord Cavendish and Thomas Burke. The inspector general of the RIC, George Hillier, retired and Colonel Henry Brackenbury[51] was appointed as assistant under secretary for police and crime. Brackenbury produced a plan for a new system of secret intelligence work. He proposed the recruitment of agents to infiltrate the secret societies and he also sought the right to select his own agents from the ranks of the RIC and the DMP. He requested a budget of £20,000 per annum and suggested that informers he recruited would be guaranteed immunity from prosecution. The cabinet demurred about immunity from legal proceedings and Gladstone agreed to a budget of just £25,000 over two years. There was still a quite prevalent view that somehow spying was ungentlemanly behaviour and indeed Spencer regarded informers as a detestable necessity. Nevertheless, by January 1884, £2,725 had been allocated to reward and assist emigration of witnesses and informers. A sum of £2,915 had been paid to police and resident magistrates and £6,500 for information.[52] Brackenbury received the whole-hearted support of Earl Spencer and Under Secretary Sir Robert G.C. Hamilton and Spencer was deeply hurt when Brackenbury abruptly resigned the post in July 1882 in order to rejoin his regiment for the war in Egypt.

In a report prepared in 1882, County Inspector Andrew Reed referred to

---

48 NAI, Fenian B files, B 99, letter from T. Smyth. 49 John Mallon, in 1858, became a clerk in the office of Sir Henry Lake, chief commissioner of police; he was appointed inspector in the detective department and superintendent in 1874. 50 John Poyntz Spencer (1835–1910), 5th Earl Spencer, lord lieutenant of Ireland, 1868–74 and 1882–5. 51 Formerly chief commandant of police in Cyprus, private secretary to viceroy of India and military attaché in Paris. 52 E.G. Jenkinson to Lord Spencer, 15 Jan. 1884 in Peter Gordon (ed.), *The Red Earl* (Northampton, 1981), p. 262.

Ribbonism being absorbed into the Fenian and other secret societies and he claimed that the moonlight society was identical to that of Fenianism and the IRB: 'the moonlight society principally arranges and carries out house attack outrages and a connection was established with the Land League apparently to the advantage of both'. Reed also commented on the importation of arms (labelled as hardware), often with the connivance of railway officials and stored in turf stacks and underground caves. He went on to claim that 'the Land League availed itself of this more or less organized and armed body to perpetrate outrages on persons obnoxious to their doctrines'.[53] Reed did not provide any names of individuals involved in Ribbonism in Galway but he compiled an incomplete list of Fenians in Galway East Riding that included prominent Land League members such as Matthew Harris, Martin O'Halloran and Peter and John Broderick.

Harris had been a Fenian since 1865 and was also closely linked to the local branches as a Land League organizer. This association led to the promotion of the idea that armed revolution was imminent.[54] A typical example was the alarmist communication of SI Alan Bell, Athenry, in June 1882. He had previously reported to Dublin Castle regarding the relationship of the Land League with secret societies[55] and he now referred to information obtained by Sub Constable Lee from 'a source that cannot be doubted'. He stated that 'the IRB was irresistibly strong and that any moment an organized open movement may be expected'.[56] Previously, shortly after the killing of Peter Doherty (see below, p. 95), Bell had advised Dublin Castle about the existence of the IRB society in the district and that its strength had increased.[57] Mallon produced an estimate of IRB strength in February 1882, which suggested that the total for the country was thirty-six thousand members with six thousand in Connacht. Mallon also claimed that Connacht and Munster were wonderfully well armed with rifles.[58]

Mallon established a network of contacts throughout the country. His persistence resulted in the acquisition of information leading to the convictions of the Invincibles involved in the Phoenix Park murders. In June 1882, Superintendent Mallon accompanied P.J. Quinn, a prominent member of the Land League, on a journey from Enniskillen, Co. Fermanagh, to Kilmainham Jail. Quinn had been arrested in October 1881 after the proclamation of the Land League. Mallon claimed that, in the course of their conversation, Quinn stated that the officers of the central executive were not responsible for the outrages and that 'it was the executive officers of the country branches that devised boycotting and other activities as a means to an end'. Quinn also acknowledged that most of the

---

53 NAI, Fenian B files, B 134, CI Reed to Jenkinson, 4 Oct. 1882. 54 Anne B. Finnegan, 'The Land War in south-east Galway, 1879–1890' (MA, UCG, 1974). 55 NAI CSO RP 1881/41971. 56 NAI, Fenian B files, B 27. 57 NAI CSO RP 1881/41971, 28 Nov. 1881. 58 NAI, Fenian B files, B 251, report of John Mallon, 23 Feb. 1883.

executive officers in the country had at one time been Fenians.[59] Based on his conversation with Quinn, Mallon reported in late 1881 that in

> almost every district, Fenians and Ribbonmen as the case may be were Leaguers, and it required great efforts to restrain them but [Patrick] Egan kept their pent up passions as a reserve and when it suited him he gave out the word in effect, there's your game, select it and do as you please. Although the assassination of resident magistrates such as Clifford Lloyd was proposed several times, it was not listened to by the executive or such men as Tim Healy, John Redmond, Thomas Sexton, T.P. O'Connor and Edmund Leamy.[60]

Mallon also referred to Patrick Egan and Thomas Brennan, respectively treasurer and secretary of the Land League, fraternizing with the Fenians in Dublin.[61] In addition, Mallon claimed 'that the extreme nationalists have been given complete control of the organization'. He said he was aware of eight secret organizers of the 'Land League conspiracy' who always travelled in disguise and under assumed names. One of those, a man called Butterfield, had 'proceeded to the west, no sooner had he arrived ... outrages followed on his path'.[62] Mallon was of the opinion that IRB members gave arms to individuals in agrarian secret societies who were not Fenians.[63] It is believed that P.J. Sheridan, who was described both as a Land League and a Fenian organizer, was expelled from the Fenian movement for this reason.[64]

Tynan, in his history of the Invincibles, claimed that branches of the Invincibles existed in all four provinces and that P.J. Sheridan was involved in their organization in Ulster, Connacht and Munster.[65] It is of interest that Sheridan's activities were also referred to by the informer John Moran, who claimed that Sheridan formed an Invincible circle in Tubbercurry, Co. Sligo. Moran also alleged that the Craughwell prisoners claimed to know that Sheridan was a Fenian organizer in their area.[66]

The relationship between the Fenians and the Land League was not necessarily harmonious and Mallon observed jealousies among the officers of both organizations and 'moderate men were every day taunted about the absurdity of constitutional agitation'.[67] It is impossible to decide on the reliability of Mallon's reports, but it does seem likely that IRB members formed a militant core in the Land League with a considerable crossover of the membership of the two

---

59 NAI, Fenian B files, B 2, Mallon to Talbot, 15 June 1882. 60 NAI, Fenian B files, B 267, Mallon to Talbot, 28 Nov. 1881. 61 Ibid. 62 NAI, ILL and INL documents, carton 9, Mallon to Talbot, 24 Nov. 1881. 63 NAI, Fenian A files, A 639, Mallon to Talbot, 20 Dec. 1880. 64 McGee, *The IRB*, p. 78. 65 Tynan, *The Irish National Invincibles and their times*, p. 443. 66 NAI CSO RP 1884/15544 in 1885/5161, DI Joyce to Anderson, 29 June 1884. 67 NAI, Fenian B files, B 2, Mallon to Talbot, 15 June 1882.

organizations. Individual witnesses at the Parnell Special Commission, such as James Mannion (Letterfrack) and Michael Hoarty (Shanaglish), admitted that they were members of both organizations.[68] DM Andrew Reed believed that in Loughrea and other branches in east Galway an inner circle of the Land League tried to further the objects of both associations.[69]

The police authorities monitored the local membership of the IRB and they relied heavily on informers as well as on routine surveillance. Policemen mingled with crowds at fairs, and the drafting in of extra police gave greater opportunities to the regular police to continue with detection duties. In Galway, the intelligence activities were intensified after the appointment of SRM Clifford Lloyd in July 1882. Existing records of payments to informers date from the late 1880s but, at that time, the IRB membership in the Loughrea area was essentially the same as in the earlier period. A man referred to as 'Fee' was described as an ordinary IRB member who was paid £4 for information in 1889. An individual called Joe Duro was reputed to be an inner circle member and he was paid £15 in 1889 for information on the organization and the movements of suspects. Two other ordinary IRB members were paid £19 and £10 respectively for information on the state of the district, plots to assassinate and contemplated outrages.[70]

In an earlier record of Fenian members, there are no names listed for the Loughrea area, while six were included for Athenry.[71] The list is incomplete because even the acknowledged Centre for the Loughrea area, Joseph O'Flaherty, is not mentioned. In October 1882, Andrew Reed furnished a memorandum to Dublin Castle that contained information from all previous reports on membership of the Fenians. Five individuals from the Athenry area were included: Michael Shaughnessy, Peter and John Broderick, John Lynskey and John J. Kelly. This list of names was certainly incomplete, as only John Kelly and James Connell were recorded from Loughrea.[72] Other police reports indicate that the more militant Land League members in the Loughrea area were also Fenians; they included John Sweeny, John McCarthy, Thomas Cunningham, John Farrell and John O'Loughlin.[73] The veteran Fenian Matthew Harris worked closely with all the Galway branches and a report by RM Andrew Reed had identified Harris as 'an agent of a secret society having revolution as its object'.[74] The police named John McCarthy as the County Centre for Galway until 1885 and

> a leading member of the Land League and Irish National League, which he joined for the purpose of facilitating his work of organizing the IRB.

68 NLI, Parnell Special Commission, vol. 2, pp 32, 64. 69 NAI CSO RP 1885/1279, Reed to Jenkinson, 4 Dec. 1884. 70 PRO CO 904/box 18/reel 8. 71 NAI, IRB index of names, 1866–71. 72 NAI, Fenian B files, B 134, Reed to Jenkinson, 4 Oct. 1882. 73 NAI CSO RP 1883/153; PRO CO 904/box 18/reel 8. 74 NAI CSO RP 1880/34686, report of RM Reed, 31 Oct. 1879.

He is an old organizer of secret societies and is well known as such in Galway, Clare and Tipperary, as well as in Dublin. He has frequently admitted to the police that he was a Fenian of extreme views.[75]

His job as a commercial traveller facilitated freedom of movement around the country. He was arrested twice in 1882 under the PPP (Ireland) Act of 1881 and was later charged with the murder of Constable Linton (see below, p. 93). In relation to John Sweeny, secretary of the Loughrea branch of the Land League, the police believed that he held high rank in the IRB and was an associate of all the well-known IRB leaders in the west and south of Ireland.[76] He was imprisoned as a suspect from 15 June 1881 until August 1882 (see below, appendix 1). He later became an active member of the Irish National League and played a prominent part in the Plan of Campaign in south Galway. He was convicted at Wicklow assizes in October 1888 and sentenced to six months in prison.[77] Joseph Huban was another leading suspect arrested under the PPP (Ireland) Act and the police believed that he had sold arms to local farmers (see above, p. 67). John Farrell, a carrier, was suspected of conveying arms to Loughrea for the use of the secret society. He was imprisoned twice in 1882 and again in 1888, when he was sentenced to six months' imprisonment for conspiracy and larceny of hay from an evicted farm.[78] Thomas Cunningham, a tailor and the Loughrea correspondent for the *Tuam News* and Dublin and London papers, was imprisoned as a suspect and was believed to be an active organizer of an illegal secret society.[79]

The Fenians played a very active part in the early years of the Gaelic Athletic Association.[80] On 15 August 1884, Michael Cusack attended a meeting in John Sweeny's house and held discussions on its foundation (fig. 1). Following the meeting, a deputation requested Bishop Patrick Duggan to become the first patron of the organization. However, he declined on grounds of age and suggested that they approach Thomas Croke, archbishop of Cashel. Michael Cusack did so and the GAA was officially founded in Thurles, Co. Tipperary, on 1 November 1884, with Archbishop Croke as patron.[81] The interest of the IRB in the new movement is clear from the fact that many of those present at the Loughrea meeting were IRB members. As well as Sweeny, they included James Lynam (Eyrecourt), believed by the police to hold high rank in the IRB,[82] William J. (Willy) Duffy, later an MP, Michael Glennon (Kilchreest), John McCarthy, County Head Centre of the IRB, and Peter Kelly of Grangepark, Loughrea, who admitted to membership of a secret society and was also named

75 PRO CO 904/box 18/reel 8. 76 Ibid. 77 NAI CBS/1892/5528/S. 78 PRO CO 904/box 18/reel 8. 79 NAI CSO RP 1883/153. 80 W.F. Mandle, *The Gaelic Athletic Association and Irish nationalist politics, 1884–1924* (London & Dublin, 1987), pp 8–9. 81 Marcus De Búrca, *History of the GAA* (Dublin, 1980), pp 49–50, 69. 82 PRO CO 904/box 18/reel 8.

1 A number of those present at the Loughrea meeting, 15 August 1884: Peter Kelly, William Duffy, John Sweeny and John McCarthy (sources: Croke Park GAA Museum, private possession of the present author and Norman Morgan).

Agrarian secret societies and the Fenian organization

in police reports.[83] In 1889, Kelly became the second president of the GAA in succession to Maurice Davin and he served until 1895. During his period in office, members of the IRB dominated the executive and used the organization to further its aims.

---

83 PRO CO 904/box 18/reel 8.

7 The Land War and the response of the government

INTRODUCTION

In April 1880, an early problem for the newly elected government of Gladstone was whether or not to renew the Peace Preservation (Ireland) Act of 1875, which was due to expire in June 1880. Chief Secretary Forster and Under Secretary Thomas Burke prepared memos to inform the discussions in cabinet. Forster recorded the desire expressed in December 1879 by all the resident magistrates for renewal of the act. He noted the increase in agrarian outrages from 301 in 1878 to 863 in 1879, and referred to the action of the previous government that increased the military force in Ireland by four regiments because of the land agitation in Galway and Mayo. Burke advised that restrictions on the possession of arms were effectual in preventing armed bodies assembling and parading for unlawful purposes. He referred to the 'unsatisfactory' condition of the west of Ireland, the organized conspiracy against the lawful rights of property and the need for police escorts for the serving of eviction notices. Burke was also concerned about the smuggling of arms into the country and their use at evictions.[1] However, the government decided not to renew the Peace Preservation Act and Forster and Lord Cowper, the lord lieutenant, agreed to govern the country under the ordinary law.

The year 1880 saw a marked increase in agitation between September and December.[2] It is not surprising that alarm was spreading among the landlords, typified by a letter to the *Irish Times* from a 'Western Landlord'.[3] The letter claimed that 'murder is the object of the present land agitation' and called for 'the repeal of habeas corpus and stern repression'. Correspondence to Dublin Castle also gave ample testimony to the landlords' concerns. The earl of Kenmare said 'all our trouble here is caused by the Land League, otherwise everything would be peaceful and quiet'. He claimed that he was warned that his life was in danger. Lord O'Hagan wrote to Forster, enclosing a letter from Charles Kelly, the county judge at Ennis, who wrote that Galway was in

> a most frightful state ... We are living under a reign of terror, governed not by the laws of the state but by those of the Land League, to which we all submit. Any outrage can be committed with perfect impunity. The gentlemen never go out at night, and seldom in the daytime, unless they are armed and in company with some of their family and servants.[4]

1 BL, Spencer papers, 77316A, memorandum of Under Secretary Thomas Burke for cabinet, May 1880. 2 HC 1882 (7), lv, 615. 3 *Irish Times*, 1 Oct. 1880. 4 BL, Spencer papers,

In early October 1880, Forster's thoughts were already turning to the suspension of habeas corpus and the arrest and detention of men on suspicion, but he wished to delay until the existing law was given a fair trial and the leaders of the agitation were prosecuted.[5] However, the landlords were becoming increasingly anxious and on 7 October Cowper and Forster met a deputation of more than sixty landlords, chiefly drawn from disturbed districts. On 8 October, Forster stated in a letter to Gladstone that the landlords 'were in a state of great but suppressed excitement ... and calling upon us to give them protection'[6] and by 25 October Forster informed Gladstone that 'I do not believe any bill would be of real use short of suspension of habeas corpus'.[7] Cowper was also clearly influenced by the deputation of landlords and he advised cabinet in a memorandum dated 8 November that the suspension of habeas corpus was the proper remedy.[8] In a memo to cabinet on 15 November, Forster expressed concerns about the increase in agrarian outrages and the high concentration of police and military in Galway. At that time, there was one policeman for every forty-seven adult males and a soldier for every ninety-seven, 'and yet no man in Galway can safely take an evicted farm'. He also noted that a large proportion of the outrages were threatening letters and that 'in districts where the law breakers were stronger than the law, the letters have a real meaning and effect'.[9]

Nationally, outrages continued unabated, numbering 268 in October 1880 compared with 107 in September. The administration claimed that the outrages were caused by the passions generated at Land League meetings but there does not appear to be a direct causal link. Between January and August 1880, there were eight meetings and 727 agrarian crimes whereas in the period September to December there were 468 meetings and 1,803 outrages.[10] Therefore, while the number of meetings increased nearly sixty-fold, the number of outrages increased by less than three-fold.

LAND LEAGUE ACTIVITIES IN EARLY 1881 AND
THE RESPONSE OF THE GOVERNMENT

The first large public meeting of 1881 was held on 1 January at Cappataggle and it was notable for the show of strength by some sixty police under the command of SI Alan Bell from Athenry.[11] The following day, many thousands attended a meeting in a four-acre field on Athenry Road, Loughrea. Nineteen clergymen were on the platform, including the chairman, Revd Egan (Loughrea), Revd Considine (Ardrahan) and Revd Geoghegan (Craughwell). The chairman made several references to the expected introduction of coercive laws that he asserted

77316A. **5** Wemyss Reid, *Life of Forster*, ii, p. 255. **6** Ibid., p. 258. **7** Ibid., p. 261. **8** BL, Spencer papers, 77316A. **9** Ibid., Forster to cabinet, 15 Nov. 1880. **10** HC 1881 (5), lxxvii, 793. **11** *Western News*, 8 Jan. 1881.

would be ineffectual in the face of the policy of passive resistance now exercised by a united people. The Loughrea Town Commissioners presented an address of welcome to Davitt and Parnell, although only Davitt was present. John Sweeny read a letter to the meeting from Bishop Duggan, in which he recalled the recent actions of charitable organizations and asserted that 'it is high time the rattle of the begging box should cease, and that an end be put for ever to this mendicancy which, ... is a standing reproach to our British rulers'. He also stated that

> until the farmer is rooted in the soil on terms that will enable him to live in decent comfort, free from the apprehension of starvation in those periodical famines which have become normal in our social condition, there cannot be ... contentment in Ireland.[12]

Revd J. Cunningham CC referred to the display of military power to frighten them and a coercion bill to silence them, which would be opposed by the organized strength of the Land League. Davitt, in an emotional speech, spoke disparagingly of Lord 'Clanrackrent' (Clanricarde) 'taking £30,000 annually from the country without giving one shilling abatement of rent'. He condemned Clanricarde's failure to support the provision of a railway for Loughrea and his refusal to provide a site for a new cathedral. He also commented on the transformation that had taken place in the country since the previous January and 'he read the death knell of landlordism in their ringing cheers'.[13] Davitt advised that no rent should be paid if a coercion act was passed that imprisoned the agitators. Joseph Huban spoke of the importance of seizing power at the elections for boards of guardians and town commissioners, and Davitt, agreeing, called on those present to 'put out the ex-officio chairmen and banish the shoneens from their local boards'.[14]

At a land meeting in Gort on 9 January, Revd Considine stated that no justice would be done to Ireland until there was a parliament in College Green. Stephen J. Meany, a member of the executive council of the Land League in New York, addressed the meeting and claimed that he had been arrested in Gort in 1848 and spent thirteen months in jail. He nominated his own version of the '3 Fs': 'Freedom, Faith and Fatherland'.[15]

At this time, increased police activity targeting Land League members became obvious. The police prohibited a meeting scheduled for 20 January in Kiltulla but the assembled crowd crossed the bog to Gloves and proceeded with the meeting there.[16] Constable Linton in Loughrea was alert to subversion when he arrested a ballad singer called Moran. The crime committed was the singing

12 Ibid. 13 Ibid. 14 Ibid. 15 NAI, Parnell Special Commission, box 3. 16 *Irish Times*, 20 Jan. 1881.

of a ballad entitled *Davitt's advice to his country*. The magistrates released Moran on bail on condition that 'he is of good behaviour, give up all his ballads and leave town immediately'.[17]

THE RESPONSE OF THE LANDLORDS

The landlords' alarm at the developing agitation and violence led to the formation of two organizations in opposition to the Land League – the Property Defence Association (PDA) and the Orange Emergency Committee. The PDA asked for the public's support for the rights of property and both organizations served writs in areas where local process servers refused, bought property at sheriff's auctions and provided labourers, who became known as 'Emergency Men', to work on boycotted farms.

In April 1881, Mr Redington, the sub sheriff, auctioned a number of properties on the Clanricarde estate. The existing tenants purchased two of the farms, paying the full amount of debts and costs. John Henry Blake, Clanricarde's agent, bought three properties.[18] On 19 April, Redington attended at Loughrea to sell the interest in five holdings on the estate of Mrs Hannah Lewis, Ballinagar. Two weeks previously, an abortive attempt at a seizure had been made but the stock and effects had all been removed beforehand. A Mr Kennedy, Gort, had been asked to conduct the sale but declined because, he said, he was intimidated, so Redington acted as auctioneer instead. Representatives from the PDA were present and entered briskly into competition as each holding was auctioned. The farms were eventually knocked down to a representative of the tenants, the holdings realizing the full amount of the rent claimed and all costs.[19] On 3 May, a similar sale took place in Ballinasloe, where John Ross Mahon was bidder against the tenants who again purchased the holdings.[20] On 23 May, Redington sold eight farms, four on the estate of Dean Augustus West, Roveagh, which were knocked down to his agent at a cost of £5 each, and four on Walter Bourke's estate. Bourke purchased three of those farms, also for £5 each. For the fourth farm there was a vigorous competition between the landlord and the tenant. The debt and costs on the farm amounted to £160 but Bourke bid up to £350 to secure the farm.[21]

In August, members of the Orange Emergency Committee and the PDA, who had already purchased several farms, attended sales in Galway where Revd P.J. McPhilpin, vice president of the Athenry Land League, made a successful bid on a farm belonging to Patrick Callanan, Kilrickle.[22] On other occasions, the Land League prevented the sale of farms vacated because of non-payment of

17 *Irish Times*, 22 Jan. 1881. 18 *Galway Vindicator*, 8 Apr. 1881. 19 *Galway Vindicator*, 20 Apr. 1881. 20 *Galway Vindicator*, 4 May 1881. 21 *Galway Vindicator*, 24 May 1881. 22 *Galway Vindicator*, 20 Aug. 1881.

rent and also the sale of stock and crops seized by bailiffs. Throughout the spring and summer of 1881, however, this type of financial burden was to prove increasingly costly for the Land League, and the policy of letting the farms go became common. This resulted in successful purchases of farms by 'Emergency Men', but because of the prevalence of boycotting it was often impossible to find new tenants willing to take the farms.

THE PROTECTION OF PERSON AND PROPERTY BILL

The introduction of the PPP (Ireland) Bill was delayed by dissension in cabinet until early January 1881. Joseph Chamberlain MP and John Bright MP expressed strong views against the introduction of coercion. Forster linked this bill with another to amend the law relating to the carrying and possession of arms. By that time, the state trial of Parnell, John Dillon, Patrick Egan and eleven others, including Matthew Harris and M.M. O'Sullivan, had commenced in Dublin. They were charged with

> conspiracy to prevent the payment of rent, defeating legal processes for the enforcement of rent, prevention of the letting of farms from which tenants had been evicted and the creation of ill-will between different classes of Her Majesty's subjects.[23]

The prosecuting counsel included the attorney general, Hugh Law, and James Murphy QC. There was drama at the opening of the trial when Lord Chief Justice May was forced to withdraw because of prejudicial remarks he had made about the defendants. On the fifth day of the trial, evidence was given regarding the speeches at Riverville in September 1880, particularly the speeches of Huban, Harris and O'Sullivan. Huban had urged those present 'to combine openly and legally'. Harris had condemned the clearances by Lord Dunsandle and advised the crowd to organize in opposition to tyranny. O'Sullivan had advocated the establishment of a branch of the Land League in the area. The evidence from the speeches could not have led to a verdict of guilty on the charges and there was no surprise when the trial ended with the failure of the jury to agree on a verdict. Parnell and his parliamentary colleagues had already shown their contempt for the court proceedings by absenting themselves to attend parliament and join the debates on the PPP (Ireland) Bill. The passage of the bill was characterized by stormy debates and eloquent speeches, particularly by Parnell and Thomas Sexton. Furthermore, the tactic of parliamentary obstruction was used, with one sitting of the House of Commons lasting twenty-two hours and another forty-one hours.

23 *Freeman's Journal*, 29 Dec. 1880.

THE PROTECTION OF PERSON AND PROPERTY (IRELAND) ACT 1881

The PPP (Ireland) Act, popularly known as the Coercion Act, finally became law on 2 March 1881. It was quickly followed, on 21 March, by the Peace Preservation (Ireland) Act that prohibited the possession of arms in proclaimed districts and restricted the sale of arms. The principal aims of the Coercion Act were the disruption of the Land League organization and the suppression of agrarian crime. It was to have a major effect on the Land League, the country in general and the lives of the many individuals arrested under its provisions, and on their families. The act provided for the detention without trial of persons 'reasonably suspected' of treasonable activity and agrarian crimes such as intimidation, incitement to violence, injury to persons and damage to property.

The decisions regarding arrests were made by a group of senior officials at Dublin Castle that often included the lord lieutenant. Decisions regarding the issuing of warrants for arrest were based on the advice of resident magistrates and senior police officers. The procedure was criticized by SRM Clifford Lloyd, on the grounds that it was overused by the police in order to take suspects out of circulation and therefore resulted in police officers neglecting their duty to find evidence of criminal offences.[24] The case of each prisoner was considered at three-monthly intervals and decisions about release were made following recommendations from local police and magistrates that were scrutinized by the lord lieutenant and law advisers. In a letter to Gladstone, Spencer complained about the burden of work placed upon him by such decisions:

> I am rather distressed at not making more way with the suspects. I have ordered the release of about forty or fifty but that implies a great deal more work as I put by for later consideration, cases where the suspects have been concerned in crime. However, I do not well see how I can get any faster. I have a box always near me with cases ready for consideration, and when I have a pause in other work I look at the cases, besides giving one or two hours continuous work to them.[25]

Even before the act became law, Michael Davitt had been arrested on 3 February by the action of a magistrate who revoked his licence for release and Davitt spent the next fifteen months in Portland Prison. Not surprisingly, the passage of the act was greeted with a storm of protest at meetings throughout the country. Ten counties, including Galway, Mayo and Clare, were initially proclaimed and five people from Galway were among the first to be arrested, including Martin O'Halloran of Kiltulla. He had been identified as a suspect by

---

24 NAI CSO RP 1882/12743. 25 BL, Spencer papers, 76854, Spencer to Gladstone, 8 May 1882.

the resident magistrate and local police and was accused of denouncing Lord Dunsandle in the most virulent way. The resident magistrate believed that O'Halloran had created the ill feeling that existed towards Dunsandle and William Daly, his son and agent. He was also believed to have held secret meetings and a land court at his house.[26] O'Halloran was arrested in Loughrea, where he had gone to attend a meeting called for the purpose of giving instructions to the local Land League branches regarding actions to be adopted under the Coercion Act. After the arrest, Revd Egan (Loughrea) addressed the meeting and said that the first blow had been struck against the Land League. He pledged the support of the priests of Loughrea and urged the members to carry on the agitation until victory crowned their efforts.[27] A meeting was held in Woodford on 23 March to condemn the introduction of the Coercion Act and to urge the continuation of the Land League even if the executive members were arrested. In his speech, John Dillon MP reiterated the policies of the Land League in relation to land grabbing, evictions, boycotting and the payment of a fair rent. He said that the principles were printed on the 250,000 membership cards issued by the Land League, the cards being displayed on the hats of those present at the meeting.[28]

The arrest of Matthew Harris followed on 16 April and the resident magistrate referred to his long association with Fenianism and his speech in Galway during which Harris said he would not object to the shooting of landlords like partridges. John Pollok, one of the commercial farmers who had bought land in east Galway and cleared it of tenants after the Great Famine, had employed Harris. It was alleged that Harris had held Pollok up to public odium and for this reason Pollok dismissed him. The resident magistrate was unable to link him directly with any outrage.[29] At the time of his arrest, Harris pledged that 'if every leader in Ireland were arrested, the movement would go on notwithstanding'.[30]

Political activities continued without interruption in the three months after the passing of the PPP (Ireland) Act. The Land Convention held on 22 April in the Rotunda in Dublin adopted unanimously a resolution that 'the peasantry of Ireland would be satisfied with nothing less than the abolition of landlordism'. However, the tactical outcome favoured Parnell's desire to seek amendments on arrears of rent and other aspects of the land bill.[31] A resumption of mass land meetings followed and speakers urged aggressive action and a general strike against payment of rent was advocated by Thomas Brennan at Maryborough and Andrew Kettle at Strokestown on 15 May[32] and at many public meetings on 22 May.[33] Shortly afterwards, both Brennan and Kettle were arrested and by

26 NAI CSO RP 1880/34686. 27 *Western News*, 12 Mar. 1881. 28 *Western News*, 26 Mar. 1881. 29 NAI, Protection of Person and Property (Ireland) Act 1881. List of all persons arrested, carton 1. 30 *Freeman's Journal*, 18 Apr. 1881. 31 *Freeman's Journal*, 23 Apr. 1881. 32 *Freeman's Journal*, 16 May 1881. 33 *Freeman's Journal*, 23 May 1881.

early June other leaders such as Michael Boyton, P.J. Sheridan, Jasper Tully, Patrick J. Gordon, John Dillon and Timothy Harrington had been jailed. Clifford Lloyd had taken a vigorous stand in Co. Limerick, resulting in a riot at New Pallas and the arrest, on 20 May, of Revd Eugene Sheehy, the militant Land League member from Kilmallock. The arrest of a clergyman provoked a countrywide protest and indignation meetings were held in Athenry, Loughrea, Kilrickle and Ballinasloe.[34] In July, the American reporter James Redpath noted that land meetings were fewer and less violent. 'Not one of the conspicuous leaders of last autumn is in the field today. Those who are not in parliament are in prison'. Redpath went on to claim that the spirit of the people was more defiant than ever and that there were 1,800 branches of the Land League and 440 branches of the Ladies' Land League in operation. He thought it especially significant that priests were joining the movement in increasing numbers.[35]

The attrition of local leaders was also dramatic, with the arrest of prominent Land League members such as John Sweeny, John Hazel (Gort) and Edward Barrett (Craughwell), and of Michael Glennon (Kilchreest), an elected member of the board of Loughrea PLU. The grounds for Glennon's arrest on 9 July were the posting of threatening notices and the incitement of persons to leave certain employments. When he was being escorted from his home, his mother wished him 'Godspeed' and said she was proud of his arrest as a suspect.[36] There was a marked reduction of arrests in August 1881, when only ten suspects were detained, and there were no arrests during September.

PRISON CONDITIONS OF SUSPECTS ARRESTED UNDER THE
PROTECTION OF PERSON AND PROPERTY (IRELAND) ACT 1881

The PPP (Ireland) Act provided that those detained were not treated as convicts. Their families were eligible for outdoor relief at a rate of £1 per week and their continued detention was reviewed every three months. Many of those arrested were politicians of local and national importance who were free to correspond with relatives and the newspapers and they could, therefore, expose any adverse prison conditions to public scrutiny. The prisoners were allowed to wear their own clothes and the Land League, and later the Ladies' Land League, provided food, books and items of furnishing for the cells. A financial subsidy of £1 per week to the families supplemented the outdoor relief. The prisoners could associate for six hours daily but were confined to their cells from 5.10pm until 7.30am.

On 9 November 1881, SI Alan Bell arrested Peter Broderick, secretary of the

---

34 Ibid. 35 *Connaught Telegraph*, 30 July 1881; Norman Dunbar Palmer, *The Irish Land League crisis* (New Haven, CT, 1940), p. 280. 36 *Irish Times*, 23 July 1881

Athenry branch of the Land League, and Patrick C. Kelly. In justifying these arrests, CI Leighton admitted that he was unable to connect either man with any outrages in the Athenry district but he claimed that, 'in consequence of Broderick's teaching, outrages have been committed'. He alleged that Broderick 'had strong Fenian proclivities and was looked on as a leader here in that line'.[37] A vivid account of the conditions in Galway Jail is contained in Broderick's handwritten diary covering the period from his arrest to March 1882.[38] Arriving in his cell on the evening of his arrest, 'the repeated banging of doors, clinking of keys and martial tread of office-bearers made me then believe I was in prison'. He made an inventory of his cell and found it measured sixteen feet long and five and a half feet wide; it had a boarded floor, a groined ceiling and a semi-circular window six feet from the floor. The window was guarded by ten vertical bars and three horizontal bars, all about two inches thick. On the bed were a straw mattress, a fibre mattress, two sheets, two blankets and a quilt. There was a deal table, an oak chair, a little mirror, a washing basin and a container for slops. Displayed above the table, in bold relief, was a copy of the eighteen rules made by the lord lieutenant under the Coercion Act. The door of the cell was two inches thick and it was lined inside with sheet iron. There was a spy hole near the top. On his first night in jail, Broderick retired to bed and 'a sleepless night wore away and then came the morrow'. In the morning, when he entered the exercise yard, he was greeted on all sides by friends who congratulated him on his arrival as a suspect. The first person he spoke to was John Sweeny, who by this time had been in jail for five months.

The suspects did not have to exist on the dreary prison fare at all meals. The Ladies' Land League provided funds for a special diet delivered by caterers in the city. A parliamentary report indicated that Mrs Mason, who was the wife of the governor of Galway Jail, was one of those who supplied meals.[39] Breakfast on that first day consisted of two hard-boiled eggs, a cup of tea, and a penny loaf. Dinner was described as of a very good quality and was supplemented by a large bottle of stout. Many of the prisoners would not have fared so well at home. Broderick received regular visits from family members, Revd O'Brien, PP of Athenry, and Mrs Carberry, a member of the Athenry Ladies' Land League branch, who brought him apples. At Mass on Sunday 13 November, all sixty-three suspects were in the back seats of the gallery and the convicted and untried prisoners in the lower seats. Among the suspects, Broderick recognized Thomas Cunniffe and Patrick and Thomas Morrissey from Carrigan, imprisoned in relation to the Doherty killing (see below, p. 95). Broderick described Sunday 20 November as a very fine day and 'the tolling of the church bells seeming to mock us in our lonely cages'. The following day, Dr Kinkead, Professor of Queen's College and medical officer to the jail, visited the exercise yard and Matthew

37 NAI CSO RP 1880/34686.   38 James Hardiman Library, NUIG, Special Collections.
39 HC 1882 (276), lv, 661.

Harris made a request that the shed be sheeted on the sides for protection from the elements. Broderick had been elected to the Loughrea Board of Guardians and on 22 November he received a letter containing a resolution of sympathy that was unanimously agreed. He regarded this as 'a most unprecedented honour from that aristocratic body'. The association rooms were the venue for many happy gatherings and, on the evening of that day, an impromptu concert took place with contributions of a patriotic nature such as Pat Kelly (Athenry) singing *Rising of the moon*, Martin Spellman (Craughwell), *Our land shall be free*, Michael Connolly (Brusk), *The Fenian men of war*, Timothy Harrington (Tralee) reciting *The fall of Poland*, Michael Noud (Roscommon), *Ode to victory*, John Sweeny, *The vagrants of Erin* and *Lord Dunsandle*, and Joseph Huban (Loughrea) completing the entertainment 'telling lies to any amount'. Before retiring to bed, Broderick wrote to Revd O'Brien, PP of Athenry, enclosing a copy of the Board of Guardians' resolution and he gave advice regarding the proposed sewerage scheme for Athenry. A few chapters of Charles Kickham's *Knocknagow* completed a happy occasion.

An attempt by the Land League leadership to reduce the level of financial support and the frequency of meals was a matter for much debate on 21 December. The figure suggested by Parnell and John Dillon was fifteen shillings per week and one meal daily from outside. A vote was taken and the decision reached was to demand the continuation of three meals daily as well as the financial award.

For Broderick, Christmas Eve brought a mixture of sadness and joy and regret that he was in prison and unable to celebrate the occasion at home with his family and friends. His thoughts turned to his mother: 'I miss her sweet face, who was ever beaming with love and smiles, her placid countenance is fresh before my mind as she lay in the sleep of death last summer'. He contemplated mutiny but decided the obstacles were too great, so, instead, he looked forward to smuggled literature.

During 1881, the regime in Galway Jail under Governor Gildea was more benign than in other prisons and the warders also showed sympathy and undoubtedly connived at the smuggling. Broderick's prize possession was a *Resurgam United Ireland* dated 24 December 1881, one week after its suppression. John Sweeny contributed copies of *The Nation* and the *Weekly News* and also two bottles of whiskey that would have been procured from his public house in Loughrea. After supper, Broderick boiled a saucepan of water over the gas jet and got sugar to make a good tumbler, and with *United Ireland* in one hand and John Jameson's best in the other, 'I thought to drown grief'. He was woken by the pealing of bells at midnight and

> when their brazen tongues were proclaiming *Peace on Earth to men of goodwill*, how hard it was for me with the shadow of my prison bars on

my ceiling and the general aspect of my abode, one of hardship and torture and to act in accordance with that injunction.

Breakfast on Christmas morning was a poor repast, a dry loaf and a sausage, even though he was able to share a portion of turkey with John Sweeny and Pat Kelly. Sweeny was again successful in obtaining supplies of alcohol and generously distributed refreshments during the day. On 28 December, Broderick received news from home: 'a great collection for priests of £90, hunts stopped and a lot of other cheering material'. The following day, he reported two new arrivals – Patrick Corbett and John Keane from Killeeneen, who 'brought funny accounts about the Kilcornan hunt and it afforded general pleasure'[40] (see above, p. 43).

On 30 December, a telegram was received from John Dillon in Kilmainham, stating his inability to do anything in connection with their dietary arrangements. Timothy Harrington responded by writing to the Ladies' Land League, indicating the intention of the suspects to go on prison fare at once. Several newspapers at that time carried complaints about the prison conditions in Kilmainham and Galway jails. A letter in the *Galway Vindicator* commented on the conditions in Galway Jail. Twelve of the cells were on the ground floor, where the surrounding wall of the prison shut out the light. The three association rooms were too small to accommodate the seventy-four suspects currently incarcerated. Another danger that was highlighted was posed by the gas supply. The control switch was outside the cell and if the light from the jet became extinguished, escaping gas could endanger the prisoners.[41] The correspondent did not blame the Galway prison officials, who treated the suspects with courtesy and consideration. When George Mason became governor in 1882, conditions deteriorated, with many complaints about solitary confinement being used to punish minor infringements and inward and outward communications being delayed unduly.[42] For instance, during January, Mason, without giving a reason, refused to allow the posting of two letters from John Sweeny to J.R. Cox, a suspect in Dundalk Jail.[43] Patrick and Thomas Morrissey from Carrigan were also confined in Dundalk Jail and Patrick said it was a haven for rats and the food was very inferior. Thomas regularly corresponded in a coded fashion, praising the governor and saying that he was a real gentleman, like Lambert. The recipients had no difficulty interpreting what he meant because Lambert was the hated landlord in Aggard House.[44]

Summing up the year's events on 31 December, Broderick found himself

---

40 On St Stephen's Day, a large crowd of protestors confronted the Galway Blazers, led by their master, Burton Persse, at Kilcornan demesne. **41** *Freeman's Journal*, 3 Jan. 1882; *Galway Vindicator*, 4 Jan. 1882. **42** NAI CSO RP 6947 in 1882/14603. **43** Diary of John Sweeny, in possession of the author. **44** Personal communication, Maura Lyons (née Morrissey), Carrigan, Co. Galway.

> a prisoner for not even the semblance of a crime. British supremacy cannot compel that obedience to its law, which is the natural outcome of loyalty, but is it not strange to the student of contemporary history, why this obedience cannot be procured, when he looks around and sees the outrages, the cruelties, the glaring injustice exacted on the people of Ireland in the name of law. Today England shows a political record of twelve months of a liberal administration unequalled by the most despotic tyranny that ever cursed the earth – enough to beget instead of loyalty, undying enmity.

Entering his third month of captivity, Broderick commented that the effect of imprisonment on him and the others was to sustain their spirits and to increase their desire for revenge. He also referred to the fact that Matthew Harris 'looked poorly' after nine months in jail and indeed Harris was released on health grounds on 3 February 1882.

On 19 January 1882, Thomas Cunningham proposed that the prisoners should go on prison fare and that the savings should be placed in a fund for Michael Fallon from Moneen, Ardrahan, who had been evicted in September 1880 (see above, p. 56). The collection raised £35 for the support of Fallon and his family.

Broderick was dismayed when Michael Lardner conveyed the news of his brother Johnny's arrest to him and there was also consternation among the prisoners regarding the multiple arrests in Athenry and Loughrea at the end of January. The prisoners were kept informed of political developments and the voluntary work carried out by neighbours and friends on prisoners' farms, and Thomas Cunningham was able to contribute articles to the *Tuam News*.

Broderick's diary ended in March 1882, but he was not released until 4 May for a parole period of two weeks. On his arrival at Athenry station, he made a spirited speech and SI Alan Bell and RM Paul, on hearing of this breach of parole, strongly opposed his permanent release. He was returned to Galway Jail and remained there until he was released on 23 August 1882.

8 Serious incidents in south Galway, May 1881 to June 1882

INTRODUCTION

Between May 1881 and June 1882, eight individuals were murdered in a triangle bounded by Loughrea, Athenry and Ardrahan, Co. Galway (fig. 2). The victims included a policeman, a landlord and his bodyguard, a land agent and three tenants who had transgressed the Land League prohibition on taking lands deemed to belong to evicted tenants. In addition, there were two non-agrarian murders – those of Michael Gibbons on 17 July 1882 and Mary Kelly on 3 August 1882. After each killing there were widespread consequences for the communities, initially associated with the police and magisterial investigations and preliminary court hearings. Furthermore, the influx of large numbers of police and military contributed to the already heightened tensions in the area and the local community was also faced with a tax levied for the maintenance of the additional security forces.

THE KILLING OF JAMES CONNORS, 13 MAY 1881

The first murder of the year occurred on 13 May, when James Connors, Killariff, Kiltulla, was shot at Forge Hill, Bookeen, while returning with his wife from a family funeral. Connors was a small farmer with a holding of fourteen acres on the Dunsandle estate. In addition, he worked as a bog ranger or gamekeeper on the estate. This position had been held previously by a man called James Keogh who had been ordered to resign by the Kiltulla Land League. When Connors took the job he was immediately boycotted. Food had to be supplied to the family by the police and he was abused as a land grabber.[1] The post-mortem conducted by Dr Leonard (Athenry) revealed that death was caused by a bullet that passed through the left lung.[2]

Soon after the killing, three members of the Kiltulla Land League were arrested – Timothy Dolan, Patrick Keogh (son of the previous bog ranger) and Edward Fahey. A meeting of the branch held that evening denounced the killing.[3] The magisterial inquiry was held in Loughrea courthouse and SI Dominick Barry stated that, because he received no cooperation from the local people, he was unable to produce any material evidence. He added that the

---

1 NLI, Parnell Special Commission, vol. 1, p. 473. 2 *Irish Times*, 16 May 1881. 3 *Galway Vindicator*, 14 June 1881.

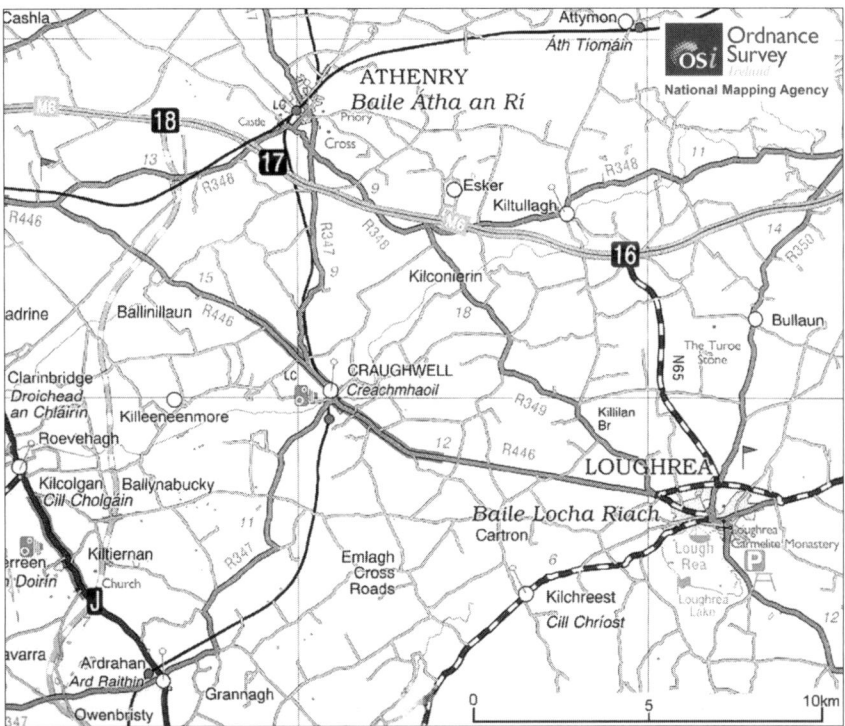

2 Map of the murder triangle: Loughrea–Athenry–Ardrahan (after: *Official road atlas Ireland, 2012–13* (Dublin & Belfast, 2011), Ordnance Survey Ireland permit 8956 © Ordnance Survey Ireland/Government of Ireland).

'temper and disposition of the neighbours is remarkable and none of them attended the funeral'. In fact, the only evidence against Fahey was that Constable R. Hughes had found a band in a field near the crime scene that fitted a hat found in Fahey's house. The evidence against Dolan was that soon after the killing he was strolling near his residence, one mile from the scene of the crime, while under the influence of drink. The only reason given for the arrest of Keogh was that he was the son of the former bog ranger. He was asleep in bed when the police went to his house on the morning of the killing.[4]

Following several remands, the prisoners appeared in court on 4 June, when SI Barry could produce no evidence linking the suspects with the killing. The prisoners' solicitor, Frank Sheppard, demanded their release and the magistrates consented. However, as they left Loughrea courthouse, Mr Townsend of the detective department in Belfast served the accused men with warrants for their arrest under the PPP (Ireland) Act on the grounds that they were suspected of

4 *Irish Times*, 20 May 1881.

murder. The suspects were escorted to cars under a guard of three hundred armed policemen.[5] This was probably the first instance of the Coercion Act being used in this arbitrary manner. The three suspects along with another man, John Ryan, who had been arrested on 16 June 1881, remained in jail until the general release of suspects in August 1882. Eventually, Patrick Keogh and John Ryan were brought to trial in 1883 at the summer assizes in Sligo before Judge James Murphy. The court was told of conflicting evidence given by Mrs Julia Connors on different occasions. At the inquest into her husband's death, she said that she could not recognize any of the attackers.[6] When Mrs Connors applied for compensation in November 1882, she declared that Patrick Keogh and John Ryan were members of the shooting party. Subsequently, in an investigation before Justice of the Peace Peter H. Dolphin, she stated that she had no knowledge of the men engaged in the crime. Judge Murphy charged in favour of Keogh's acquittal and the crown then entered a plea of *nolle prosequi* in relation to John Ryan.[7]

On their return to Kiltulla, the prisoners were 'greeted by bonfires, wisps were lighted and cheers rent the air'.[8] An interesting comment on the case appeared later in a report by SI Alan Bell in which he stated that Revd J. Pelly, the local parish priest, had told him 'if Keogh was found guilty it would be wrong'. Revd Pelly travelled to the trial in Sligo to give Keogh a good character reference but apparently he was unwilling to do the same for Ryan.[9]

THE KILLING OF PETER DEMPSEY, 29 MAY 1881

The farm at Riverville, which had been vacated by Murty Hynes in September 1880, lay vacant until April 1881, when it was taken by Peter Dempsey, who had worked as a gardener for Henry Persse at Glenarde for eighteen years and for his brother, Burton Persse, at Moyode Castle for seven years. Dempsey was boycotted and on 29 May, on his way to Mass in Kilconierin Church, accompanied by two of his children, he was shot dead at Hollypark, quite close to the residence of Peter Blake.[10] At the inquest on 30 May, Dr Leonard gave evidence that a single bullet entered the left arm and left side of the chest, perforated the left lung and spinal column, passed through the right lung and finally lodged in the right arm. He considered that the rifle used was a Snider, the type of rifle that had been imported by the Fenians.

Martin Bermingham, the evicted tenant, was arrested along with his nephew Patrick Glynn. In evidence, SI Barry stated that at the time of the shooting Bermingham was at Mass in Athenry and Glynn was in another part of the

---

5 *Irish Times*, 6 June 1881. 6 *Galway Vindicator*, 14 May 1881. 7 *Tuam News*, 4 Aug. 1883.
8 *Western News*, 4 Aug. 1883. 9 NAI CSO RP 1884/18360. 10 *Irish Times*, 31 May 1881.

country.[11] They were released but again the Coercion Act was used to re-arrest Bermingham on 16 June.[12] He was never brought to trial but nevertheless remained in Dundalk Jail as a suspect until August 1882. Local knowledge suggests that the killing of Dempsey was carried out by members of a Craughwell secret society and that the Joyce brothers, Thomas and Dominick of Grenage, Craughwell, were selected by lot to shoot Dempsey.

On 15 and 17 June, four more arrests were made under the Coercion Act – John Sweeny, Thomas Cunningham, Joseph Huban and John Darcy.[13] The list of suspects, prepared by SI Barry, described Sweeny as a carpenter and publican, aged thirty-four and secretary of the Loughrea Land League. His public house was claimed to be the resort of prominent members of the League and it was believed that secret meetings and a land court had been held there. He was described as a man of very disloyal tendencies. Sweeny's notebook gives a graphic description of the manner of his arrest and removal to Dundalk Jail (see below, appendix 1). Thomas Cunningham was described as an active and mischievous organizer and the suspected author of threatening notices posted around Loughrea. Joseph Huban was referred to as a Land League organizer and the author of 'violent speeches that had very seriously disturbed relations between landlord and tenant'.[14] Huban was arrested in Ballinasloe, where he had gone to give a talk on the 'Bards and music of Ireland'.[15]

An unsigned police report of a later date contained a statement that on the day Peter Dempsey was shot, a number of persons emerged from John Sweeny's house, carrying green branches and cheering.[16] The three suspects (Sweeny, Cunningham and Huban), who were arrested as accessories to the murder of James Connors and Peter Dempsey, were never brought to trial and no evidence was presented linking them with the murders. Nevertheless, they remained in jail for fourteen months until August 1882.[17]

THE SHOOTING AT JOHN W. LAMBERT, 20 JUNE 1881

The next significant incident was the shooting at John W. Lambert of Aggard House, who owned 3,410 acres. Relationships with his tenants were fraught and he had recently evicted Thomas Corbett, Ballyglass, for non-payment of rent. After Corbett had re-entered the property, he was arrested and was awaiting trial in Galway Jail when the shooting took place.

On the afternoon of 20 June, Lambert and his son were driving in the direction of Ardrahan when four shots were fired at them from behind a hedge. A

11 *Galway Vindicator*, 11 June 1881. 12 *Irish Times*, 11 June 1881. 13 *Irish Times*, 16 June 1881; *Galway Vindicator*, 18 June 1881. 14 NAI, Protection of Person and Property (Ireland) Act 1881, vol. 1. 15 *Western News*, 18 June 1881. 16 NAI, Parnell Special Commission, box 7. 17 NAI, Protection of Person and Property (Ireland) Act 1881, vol. 1.

bullet went through Lambert's hat, grazed his head and knocked him off the car.[18] Three men had been seen loitering near the scene prior to the shooting.

RM John W. Byrne, SI Barry (Loughrea) and SI Bell (Athenry), accompanied by a strong force of police, carried out the investigations. No clues to the identity of the assailants were found at the scene and no arrests were made. A local man, John (Soldier) Morrissey, later claimed that his uncle, Thomas Morrissey from Carrigan, was present at the shooting and that one of the guns used in the attack belonged to his grandfather.[19]

Lambert was placed under police protection, but his relations with the local community remained hostile and the boycott already in force was intensified.[20]

THE KILLING OF CONSTABLE JAMES LINTON, 24 JULY 1881

Constable Linton, a native of Co. Down, aged forty-two years, had been stationed in Loughrea for twenty years and had gained a reputation for discharging his duties with great diligence. He had incurred the enmity of many local citizens because of his vigilance regarding breaches of the licensing laws. Linton's duties also included note-taking at meetings and supervision of prominent Land League members and other suspected persons. During the state trials of Parnell and others in early January 1881, he had given detailed evidence regarding speeches made at the Riverville meeting (see above, p. 36). It was believed that he concealed himself in barrels outside houses where meetings were taking place in an attempt to overhear the conversations. He was also reputed to adopt disguises, such as dressing as a woman, in order to spy on suspects. In addition, the fact that he gave evidence at the state trials did not endear him to local Land League activists. Linton's superior officer, SI Dominick Barry, had advised him not to leave the barracks at night unless he was accompanied, because of the hostility displayed towards him. However, Linton preferred to go out alone.[21]

At 10pm on Sunday 24 July, while returning to barracks for roll call, Linton was fired at and mortally wounded outside the Protestant church in Church Street. Bleeding profusely, he went along the pathway towards Main Street and was helped into Scanlon's Hotel, where he died shortly afterwards. One witness, John Burke, said he heard a shot and then a cry of 'murder, I am shot'.[22] The post-mortem was performed by Dr Burke, who found that a bullet entered below the right groin and penetrated the femoral artery. In his opinion, Linton was shot from behind and the bullet was fired from a large revolver. Later, a revolver

18 *Galway Vindicator*, 22 June 1881.   19 Letter written by John (Soldier) Morrissey in possession of Maura Lyons (née Morrissey).   20 *Irish Times*, 25 June 1881.   21 NLI, Parnell Special Commission, vol. 1, p. 507.   22 *Galway Vindicator*, 27 July 1881.

from which one shot had been fired was found on the lands of J. O'Toole (Mount Pleasant).[23]

On the night of the killing, two suspects were arrested – Michael Dilleen, a licensed publican, whose premises had been searched by Linton on the day of the shooting, and Patrick Hynes. They were released the following day.[24]

At the weekly meeting of the Loughrea Land League, the members gave public expression to the regret and abhorrence at the recent appalling assassination of Constable Linton. A formal resolution was passed stating that

> adhering to the principles enunciated by Davitt, and constantly followed by the Land League we ... condemn the employment of threats and violence, for we cannot but see that crime and outrage, no matter by whom or for what motive committed, furnish a weapon unscrupulously used by able and influential enemies to asperse and discredit our columns and organization.[25]

The next person arrested was John McCarthy, who was charged with possession of an old flint pistol without a licence. At the trial, McCarthy requested an adjournment for the purposes of obtaining a solicitor to represent him. Mr W. French Henderson, who prosecuted, made a lengthy statement about the murder and said that 'Linton got no adjournment'. RM Byrne, in delivering his judgment, spoke at great length of 'the awful crime that was committed in their midst', and said that 'no man was safe in such a town'. No evidence was produced to link McCarthy with the killing and, given the evidence about the size of the bullet that caused death, it could not have been fired by the flint pistol. RM Byrne claimed that 'McCarthy's premises would not be searched if there was not strong suspicion that he had some connection with the horrid crime' and he considered it his 'bounden duty to commit the defendant to Galway Jail for two months with hard labour'.[26]

McCarthy was released from Galway Jail on 11 October 1881 and his homecoming was celebrated by the Loughrea Brass Band playing *Harvey Duff*.[27] He was carried shoulder-high to his house on Main Street and Revd Egan read an address of welcome. The gathering was watched over by a 'formidable array of police', but there were no violent confrontations.[28]

Michael Clarke and his wife, Mary Anne, were arrested on 5 August and brought before Galway spring assizes in March 1882.[29] In evidence, Edward Kennedy said that he saw two people coming from Church Street after the

23 *Galway Vindicator*, 23 Aug. 1881. 24 *Galway Vindicator*, 27 July 1881. 25 *Galway Vindicator*, 3 Aug. 1881. 26 *Freeman's Journal*, 13 Aug. 1881. 27 Harvey Duff was a police agent disguised as a peasant named Keach in the popular play 'The Shaughraun' in *Selected plays of Dion Boucicault* (Gerrards Cross, 1987). 28 *Galway Vindicator*, 15 Oct. 1881. 29 *Galway Vindicator*, 29 Mar. 1882.

shooting; one was Linton and the other man was not Clarke but Michael Dilleen. During his charge to the jury, Chief Justice May directed that Mrs Clarke could not be convicted on the evidence. After a short deliberation, the jury returned a verdict of not guilty in relation to both prisoners.

From the beginning, Dilleen was a chief suspect. In January 1881, he had been arrested under the Coercion Act on a warrant citing intimidation against rent. Released in June, he was re-arrested the following month when a large number of arrests were made in the aftermath of the killing of John Henry Blake (see below, p. 98). Released once more in August 1882, he was again arrested in February 1883 and charged with the killing of Constable Linton. Also re-arrested on the same day was John McCarthy. The trial of Dilleen took place in December 1883 at the winter assizes in Sligo. The legal teams are of interest because the solicitor for the crown was Thomas D. O'Farrell, while his son J.C. O'Farrell represented Dilleen. O'Farrell Senior defended this practice by explaining that there was no collusion between them because one office was in Loughrea and the other in Galway.[30] This was not the first time that the father and his son had appeared on opposite sides in court and CI Byrne had expressed grave concern regarding the propriety of the practice.

Sergeant Robinson QC, presenting the case for the crown, claimed that 'Loughrea was notorious for crime'. In evidence, there was reference to Dilleen's public house having been searched by Constable Linton on the morning of the killing. Edward Kennedy said that, at the time of the killing, he saw a mist and the discharge of a gun and 'in the midst a man in a green suit – the prisoner'. He heard Linton say twice 'stop the murderer'. Another witness said he met Linton who 'cried out "Dilleen shot me"'. In the previous trial of Michael and Mary Anne Clarke, Kennedy had given evidence that he saw only one other man in the street, but in this trial he swore that a number of men could have escaped from the lane before he went up to it. At this point, Sergeant Robinson stated that he would not go on with the case and entered a plea of *nolle prosequi*. The judge concurred and said that 'out of the graves of time true evidence would arise'. It never did and there were no further prosecutions.[31]

On 13 December, a rumour spread that Dilleen would return to Loughrea that evening. A large crowd and the Loughrea Brass Band gathered to welcome him, and police under the command of SI Chambers confronted them. The crowd was assaulted by the police at the gate of Mount Carmel Convent and later on Main Street. When two mounted policemen attempted to disperse the crowd, there were protests to CI Byrne and he ordered the police to return to barracks. The following evening, when Dilleen had arrived in Loughrea, the crowd gathered again and they were baton-charged by the police. Dilleen

30 NAI CSO RP 1883/24152, letter of Detective Inspector John D. Phillips to SRM Clifford Lloyd, 20 Aug. 1883. 31 *Tuam News*, 28 Dec. 1883.

addressed the crowd from a window of his residence and thanked them for their welcome and support. An indignation meeting was held and a committee composed a memorial to Earl Spencer, the lord lieutenant. The memorial requested a 'searching and impartial sworn inquiry into the action of the constabulary'. An acknowledgment was received from the under secretary but no action was taken.[32]

THE KILLING OF PETER DOHERTY, 2 NOVEMBER 1881

On the night of 2 November 1881, Peter Doherty was shot dead at Carrigan, which is close to Rahasane House and a few kilometres from Craughwell village. The killing resulted from a dispute over land and was preceded by the boycotting and intimidation of the Doherty family. At the inquest on the victim, Dr P.R. Dalton (Oranmore) stated that the fatal bullet was conical and resembled those used in Snider rifles. He had made a similar comment on the bullet used in the killing of Peter Dempsey (see above, p. 90).[33]

THE KILLING OF WALTER BOURKE AND CORPORAL WALLACE, 8 JUNE 1882

Although there had been no mass public meetings and no killings in south Galway since November 1881, there was evidence of continuing agrarian unrest, and in June 1882 four murders occurred. On the afternoon of 8 June, Walter Bourke was returning from Gort to Rahasane House when he and his guard, Corporal Robert Wallace of the Royal Dragoon Guards, were ambushed at Castletaylor and shot dead.[34] Bourke had an estate of two thousand acres at Rahasane and he also had extensive holdings near Claremorris in Co. Mayo. On the day of the killing, Bourke had attended the Gort Petty Sessions to obtain orders to evict his tenants in Carrigan. Wallace had recently arrived in Rahasane and he made a special request to travel with Bourke that day. Bourke was armed with an eighteen-chamber Winchester rifle and Wallace had a carbine. After the killings, the assailants took possession of their guns and escaped through the fields in the direction of Craughwell, meeting Mr Shawe-Taylor, the landlord of Castletaylor, along the way. Three arrests were made near the scene of the killing, but RM Franks discharged the men because of lack of evidence.[35]

On the day following the shooting, thirty soldiers of the 88th Connaught

---

[32] Ibid. [33] The details of the killing, the police and magisterial investigations and the trials and sentencing to death of two innocent men are presented in Finnegan, *The case of the Craughwell prisoners.* [34] *Western News*, 10 June 1882. [35] *Irish Times*, 10 June 1882.

Rangers and ninety of the 84th York and Lancaster Regiment joined police and military from Loughrea, Gort and Athenry, giving a combined force of approximately three hundred. They searched 'every ditch, dike and wall for miles around'; three old guns were found but none were serviceable.[36] The inquest was held at Rahasane House[37] and Mr Shawe-Taylor gave evidence that he heard five or six shots in succession and saw five or six armed men. He noticed one of the men carrying two guns but he said that he was unable to identify any of the men. He thought they were poachers until he found Wallace lying in a pool of blood and Bourke lying against the wheel of the trap. Dr Dalton performed the post-mortem examination on Walter Bourke and found that two bullets had penetrated the brain and in his opinion death was instantaneous. Dr Charles Blake Lewis of the Army Medical Department made the examination on Robert Wallace. He found that the fatal bullet had caused laceration of the brain.[38] Walter Bourke was buried on 13 June in the family vault at Barnacarroll, Co. Mayo, and Corporal Wallace was interred with full military honours at the military cemetery at Arbor Hill, Dublin.[39]

A proclamation published on 9 June in the *Dublin Gazette* offered a reward of £2,000 and a further reward of £1,000 for private information leading to conviction. A free pardon and the protection of the crown were promised to anyone who knew about the murders other than those who actually committed them.[40]

There was considerable speculation regarding the identity of the killers, and Superintendent Mallon suspected that people from Mayo were involved. Following a conversation he held with P.J. Quinn, he concluded that Quinn knew 'a good deal about the murder of Bourke and the Dragoon'.[41] Police reports claim that a branch of the Invincibles was formed by tradesmen from Dublin working at Tullira Castle and Tyrone House,[42] and P.J.P. Tynan attributed the 'suppression' of Walter Bourke to the actions of the Invincibles.[43] Notwithstanding these speculations, local knowledge indicates that men from Craughwell and Ballymana were responsible for the killings. It is alleged that four of the men emigrated to America shortly afterwards and money was collected locally to pay for their passage. That the local IRB was involved in the killings is supported by a witness statement by Martin Newell, son of John Newell, the Fenian Centre for the barony of Dunkellin. He claimed that his father knew about the plan and while conversing with Bourke on the day prior to his death he had the bullets used in the killing in his pocket.[44] It is believed that the guns used in the attack and the weapons of the victims were buried in a bog near Rahasane and it has been claimed that Wallace's gun was used again

36 *Galway Express*, 10 June 1882. 37 *Irish Times*, 10 June 1882. 38 Ibid. 39 *Galway Vindicator*, 14 June 1882. 40 *Dublin Gazette*, 9 June 1882. 41 NAI, Fenian B files, B 2, Mallon to Talbot 15 June 1882. 42 PRO CO 904/12, precis of information and reports on secret societies, May 1910. 43 Tynan, *The Irish National Invincibles and their times*, p. 487. 44 Military Archives, Bureau of Military History, WS 1,562, Martin Newell witness statement.

during the Easter Rising.⁴⁵ Even though a large number of arrests were made in the Craughwell area under the Coercion Act in July 1882, none of those arrested was charged with the killing of Bourke and Wallace.

THE KILLING OF JOHN H. BLAKE AND THADY RUANE, 29 JUNE 1882

At the end of June, evictions in Piggott's Lane, Loughrea, resulted in the clearing of the whole street, including fifteen cabins and a three-storey house accommodating eight families. John Henry Blake, Lord Clanricarde's agent, ordered the evictions and by the time the newspaper account appeared he and his driver had been shot dead.⁴⁶ On 29 June, on the outskirts of Loughrea, Blake and his servant, Thady Ruane, were killed and Blake's wife was wounded. Blake lived at Rathville House, Kiltulla, and was appointed agent to Lord Clanricarde in 1860. He was regarded as an unsympathetic individual, who, in carrying out the harsh instructions of Clanricarde, incurred the enmity of tenants. However, there is evidence that he tried to moderate the intransigent attitudes of Clanricarde by keeping him informed about the more lenient behaviour of other landlords in the area. He had apparently submitted a letter of resignation from the post of agent in January 1882,⁴⁷ but his involvement in the Loughrea evictions indicates that he was still employed by Clanricarde at the time of the killing.

Blake, with his wife and driver, left home at 11am to travel to Loughrea to attend Mass on a church holiday. Within a mile of the town, from behind a wall a shot was fired that struck Blake, knocking him from the car. Ruane tried to escape but he was also hit and died instantly. Blake's wife, Henrietta Frances, a daughter of Dr Francis Lynch of Mount Pleasant, Loughrea, was shot in the thigh. Examination of the scene revealed that stones had been removed from the wall to make loopholes for the guns.⁴⁸ Drs O'Donohue, Leonard and Burke carried out the post-mortem examinations and the inquest was held at Clanricarde's agency office. The examinations revealed that Blake was killed by a bullet that passed through the brain and a similar bullet wound caused the death of Ruane, who was survived by his widow, six sons and five daughters.⁴⁹

On the day of the killing, three men, Michael Sweeney, Michael Connolly and Thomas Cahill, who happened to be in the vicinity of the shooting, were arrested and on the following day Patrick Rafferty and John Halloran were also taken into custody.⁵⁰ The five individuals were soon released because of a lack of any evidence that they were involved in the killings. On the day that Blake's

45 Campbell, *Land and revolution*, p. 219; *Connaught Tribune*, 12 Apr. 1947. 46 *Tuam News*, 30 June 1882. 47 Catherine Kelly Desmond, 'John Henry Blake: villain or victim' in Jordan (ed.), *Kiltullagh Killimordaly* (2000). 48 *Freeman's Journal*, 30 June 1882. 49 *Freeman's Journal*, 1 July 1882. 50 *Western News*, 8 July 1882.

funeral cortege left Loughrea, Clifford Lloyd, the newly appointed special resident magistrate for Galway, made a dramatic entrance into Loughrea, preceded by two mounted police and two carloads of police as bodyguards. Clifford Lloyd stayed at Scanlon's Hotel and held immediate consultations with the resident magistrates and CI Byrne.[51]

As in the case of the killing of Constable Linton, the two main suspects were John McCarthy and Michael Dilleen, who had been arrested as suspects under the Coercion Act in January 1882 and released in June. This prompted the comment of Chief Secretary George Otto Trevelyan that the early release of suspects could be linked with subsequent killings, as alleged by the land agent Samuel Hussey in relation to a murder in Kerry.[52] A police report on McCarthy indicated that he had left Loughrea and travelled to Dublin before the killing. He returned on 1 July and, en route, had a long conversation with Matthew Harris in Ballinasloe.[53] Clifford Lloyd believed that McCarthy had gone to Dublin to get money and that, on his return, he went to the country at 2am to hand over the money to a man suspected of carrying out the murder.[54] McCarthy and Dilleen were among twenty-three people arrested on 4 July in Loughrea, suspected of involvement in the killing of Blake and Ruane. All the arrests were on charges of being accessories to murder or of conspiracy to murder.

Spencer described in a letter to Trevelyan, how Clifford Lloyd, his energy undiminished by an attack of gout, arrived at the Viceregal Lodge at 5.15pm on 3 July, to meet with him and the attorney general, John Naish.[55] Spencer referred to Clifford Lloyd's statements being so

> strong and it was almost inconceivable that so widespread a conspiring to assassination could exist among so many people. Put this as ghastly proof of the existence of the conspiracy, not only in the two double murders 1) Bourke and Wallace, 2) Blake and his man but also of Linton, Dempsey and Connors within a short time in the same neighbourhood.

Spencer also indicated that 'the information received by the police came from two advanced Land Leaguers and one policeman'.[56] They carefully went through Clifford Lloyd's recommendations for arrests and the warrants for arrest were prepared and copied in time for Clifford Lloyd to leave by the 7.30pm train. Therefore, the deprivation of the liberty of twenty-three people could be decided in the space of just over two hours. This hardly represents 'a scrupulous legal procedure for assessing prominence and culpability', as

---

51 *Freeman's Journal*, 1 July 1882. 52 BL, Spencer papers, 76946, Trevelyan to Spencer, 29 June 1882. 53 NAI, Crime Branch Special, 1892/5528/S. 54 BL, Spencer papers, 77080, Lloyd to Spencer, 14 July 1882. 55 John Naish (1841–90), law adviser 1880–3, solicitor general Jan.–Dec. 1883, attorney general Dec. 1883–5, lord chancellor 1885–6, lord justice of appeal 1885 and 1886–90. 56 BL, Spencer papers, 76946, Spencer to Trevelyan, 5 July 1882.

Margaret O'Callaghan claims, although she acknowledges that the lord lieutenant, Cowper, confirmed that 'they prevailed upon themselves to be less scrupulous'.[57] Writing to Assistant Under Secretary E.G. Jenkinson,[58] Clifford Lloyd stated

> I acted on fresh warrants for being accessory to murder and a clearer case than that I presented to his excellency could not be. We are only beginning and his excellency must be prepared to sign more warrants. If the men arrested are in for a couple of months I shall not fear to then let them out. Loughrea, however, is a den of infamy and must be made to pay under the new act.[59]

On 15 July, in a letter to Earl Spencer, Clifford Lloyd referred to the twenty-three men arrested as 'the members of the central organization at Loughrea of the Assassination Society. Their arrest will, I believe, secure the lives of many persons whose fates were decreed'.[60] Spencer had earlier complained to Gladstone of the great burden of work placed on him having to decide about the release of suspects.[61] It would appear that their arrest could be decided more expeditiously, however, considering the brevity of Clifford Lloyd's visit to the Viceregal Lodge on 3 July.

Three of the suspects – Thomas O'Brien, Andrew McEntee and William O'Flynn – were members of the Loughrea Town Commissioners, and on the night before their arrest they had attended a meeting of the town commissioners that unanimously passed a vote of sympathy on the death of Blake.

The local belief is that members of an agrarian secret society and IRB members based in Rathruddy, not far from the murder scene, were responsible for the killings. The transfer of one of the weapons used was observed to take place between two women at the West Bridge in Loughrea.[62]

COMMUNITIES UNDER SIEGE AND FINANCIAL DURESS

The murders committed between May 1881 and June 1882 in the Athenry and Loughrea police districts had profound effects on the local communities. The number of murders in the area exceeded that in any other region of the country and resulted in the concentration of large numbers of police and military in an attempt to restore order.

57 Margaret O'Callaghan, *British high politics and a nationalist Ireland* (Cork, 1994), p. 85. 58 BL, Spencer papers, Lloyd to Jenkinson, 7 July 1882. 59 Prevention of Crime (Ireland) Act 1882. 60 BL, Spencer papers, 77080, Lloyd to Spencer, 15 July 1882. 61 BL, Spencer papers, 76854, Spencer to Gladstone, 21 July 1882. 62 Personal communication, Christy Martyn.

The choice of victims was influenced by the unpopularity of the landlord and the land agent and resulted in the collateral killing of their bodyguard and servant. The policeman, Constable Linton, had acquired a degree of notoriety and his habit of patrolling the town on his own made him an easy target. The remaining targets were the victims of disputes over land and the consequent social ostracism that continued in relation to the families after the event.

It is noteworthy that the police were accorded no cooperation from the local communities in their investigations and this undoubtedly explains their failure to obtain convictions in all but one instance. In the case of the Doherty killing, the conviction of two innocent men was achieved only by means of the perjured testimony of two informers. The large number of arrests meant that rank and file members of the Land League were also at risk of arrest, even though they had no connection with the IRB or other illegal societies.

The financial costs of the increased numbers of police and military were levied on the area and in the baronies of Athenry and Loughrea this amounted to £11,000. There is no doubt that these penalties generated considerable hostility towards the authorities and this may explain the exclusion of such provisions when the Prevention of Crime (Ireland) Act of 1882 was renewed in 1887.

COMPENSATION HEARINGS

The Prevention of Crime (Ireland) Act 1882 provided for compensation to be paid to victims of crimes that were agrarian or the result of actions by an unlawful society. The hearings in relation to seven of the eight killings were held in Galway record court before Mr J. Alexander Byrne QC in November 1882.[63] At the later hearing on the compensation claim for Walter Bourke, Byrne stated that he 'was not only to investigate ... the motives of the alleged crime, but also to consider how far the inhabitants of the district connived or participated in it; or withheld information respecting it'.[64]

James Connors
The first claim was that of Julia Connors, the mother of five children and widow of James Connors (Killariff). She said that her late husband rented a farm of twenty acres from Lord Dunsandle. In addition, he earned between £20 and £30 per year by burning lime. The McDermot QC outlined the circumstances of the killing and said that the people of the country were not satisfied with the murder of her husband but they also boycotted her farm and she had to rely on Lord

---

63 *Galway Vindicator*, 2 Dec. 1882. 64 *Galway Express*, 2 Dec. 1882.

Dunsandle's agent to have the land ploughed and tilled. Since her husband's death, she had been unable to obtain any kind of assistance from her neighbours to help with the farm. The hearing was not completed, probably because the trial of those arrested for the killing had not yet taken place. However, she later received a sum of £800.[65]

Peter Dempsey

The claim of Mrs Mary Dempsey (Riverville), widow of Peter Dempsey, was heard next and The McDermot QC, introducing the case, referred to the fact that she had been boycotted since the killing. Lord Dunsandle's son and agent, William Daly, stated that Dempsey had requested to rent the disputed land and that he had advised against it because of the boycott. However, Dempsey decided to take it on 5 March 1881. Two weeks before his murder, he had been fired at but thought that the shot was intended for someone else. Mary Dempsey said that she had been married for ten years and had four children, the oldest being eight years and the youngest fourteen months. Since the murder, she was under police protection and a workman she had hired also needed protection. None of her neighbours would help her and she could not hire a car to take her from Craughwell to Athenry. She had decided that she would have to give up the farm. The sum awarded to her was £800.[66]

Constable James Linton

John Linton of Annalong, Co. Down, claimed compensation for the murder of his brother James, who had joined the RIC in 1861. Over a twenty-year period, his brother had visited him on three occasions and during one visit had given him £5. Evidence was given that Constable Linton received an annual salary of £72 16s. 6d. and would have been eligible for a full pension after thirty years. SI Barry said that he had received help from only one local person in the investigation of the killing and that his colleague SI Jones had 'met with every opposition'. There is no record that any compensation was awarded.

Peter Doherty

The next claim was that of Peter Doherty (Senior) in relation to the killing of his son Peter in Carrigan in November 1881.[67] He said that Peter Junior was his only son and that he had two daughters, Kate and Mary Anne. Prior to taking the boycotted land, he had a farm of twelve acres with five cattle, twenty sheep and two horses. His son took extra land – four acres for meadow and oats and conacre for potatoes. When he and his cousin took the disputed land, stones were thrown through the windows, the horse's tail was cut and thirty yards of a stone wall

---

65 HC 1884 (80), lxiii, 529. 66 Ibid. 67 Finnegan, *The case of the Craughwell prisoners.*

were broken down. After the killing, he gave up the disputed land (known as the boycott to this day) and was unable to get anyone to help with his own holding. Local blacksmiths refused to shoe the horse and he had to go to Athenry to have it shod. The judge thought that a sum sufficient for the good fortunes for the two girls should be provided and the award amounted to £600.

Corporal Robert Wallace
Mrs Fanny Wallace claimed compensation for the death of her husband, Corporal Robert Wallace, who at the age of twenty-five was shot, with Walter Bourke, at Castletaylor. They were married in 1879 in Colchester and she had a two-year-old daughter. She would not receive a pension because her husband had not been in the army sufficiently long to qualify. An award of £300 was made.

Walter Bourke
The claim for compensation for the killing of Walter Bourke was heard in Claremorris courthouse in November 1882, shortly after his brother and heir, Dr Isidore Bourke, had evicted 170 people on his Mayo estate.[68] Bourke claimed that his brother was on good terms with his tenants in Mayo until 1879, when relationships deteriorated and he feared for his life. A similar problem developed with his Rahasane tenants in early 1882. John Berwick Sams, agent on that estate, gave instances of hostility shown towards Walter Bourke and himself in Gort, Ardrahan, Craughwell and Loughrea. It was revealed that there were nearly two hundred tenants on the Curraleigh estate at Claremorris and the rental income was £1,700 per annum. There was a mortgage of £25,000 on the property. On the Rahasane estate, there were forty-five tenants and the rental income was £16,000.[69] Isidore Bourke, who earned £1,500 per annum from his surgical practice in London, claimed that he suffered severe financial loss because of frequent visits to Ireland since the death of his brother. He also itemized the poor income from the encumbered estates and claimed compensation of £20,000.[70] The award made was £1,500, to be paid in three instalments.[71]

John Henry Blake and Thady Ruane
An award of £3,000 was made to Blake's widow in relation to the death of her husband and £1,200 in compensation for her own injuries sustained in the shooting. In stark contrast to these generous awards, Thady Ruane's widow and her eleven children were awarded £400.

---

68 *Tuam News*, 8 Dec. 1882. 69 Ibid. 70 *Galway Express*, 2 Dec. 1882. 71 HC 1884 (80), lxiii, 529.

9 Suppression of the Land League

THE LAND LAW (IRELAND) ACT 1881 AND
THE RESPONSE OF THE LAND LEAGUE

After the general election of 1880, a commission was set up to examine the working of the Land Act of 1870. The earl of Bessborough chaired the commission and its report and proposals for legislation were published on 4 January 1881.[1] It advocated reform of the system of land tenure on the basis of the '3 Fs', namely fair rent, security of tenure and the right of tenants to sell the interest in their holdings, but also looked forward to the creation of peasant proprietors. Among those who gave evidence to the commission was John Henry Blake. Speaking on 22 October 1880, he agreed that the previous three years had been very bad and the tenants had lost a good deal of their stock. However, he thought part of the problem was that 'There was extravagance in the way of living and in the clothing. The women ... were very expensive in their habits of clothing. They idled a great deal of their time. They buy everything in the shops'.[2] Blake also considered that the tenants were losing a great deal of their respect and allegiance towards agents and landlords. He said that the daily wages of an unskilled labourer were 1s. 6d. at harvest time and in the spring the wage increased to 2s. and 2s. 6d. He opposed the idea of providing government funding for the purchase of land. He also believed that 'a good system of emigration' would benefit those left behind and those sent away.

Burton Persse of Moyode, owner of 6,769 Irish acres with a rental of £7,791, claimed that only one eviction had been carried out on his property during the previous twenty years and hardly any ejectment notices had been served.[3] He shared Blake's views on the idleness of tenants and thought that the creation of peasant proprietors would be 'the worst thing that would happen to the country'. William Daly of Dunsandle thought that a peasant proprietary would be decidedly injurious to the country but if it was granted to some tenants it would make them 'more loyal and peaceable'. He told the commission that the rents on the Dunsandle estate were 25 per cent above the Griffith's valuation and the only eviction in sixteen years was that of Martin Bermingham at Riverville.[4] Colonel John Archer Daly (Raford) had an estate of twelve thousand acres. He claimed that the only increase of rent occurred after the Galway election of 1872 because the tenants 'did not vote the right way'. In his opinion, peasant proprietary on a large scale 'would be fatal to the country'.[5]

The Land Law (Ireland) Act 1881 granted the '3 Fs'. It established a system

---

1 HC 1881 [C.2779], xviii, 1.   2 HC 1881 [C.2779], xviii, 597.   3 HC 1881 [C.2779], xviii, 600.   4 HC 1881 [C.2779], xviii, 604.   5 HC 1881 [C.2779], xviii, 626.

of dual ownership by landlords and tenants, rather than the peasant proprietary demanded by the Land League, and a land commission to supervise the application of the act. A land court had the duty of fixing a fair rent and registering rents agreed by tenant and landlord. An important amendment, known as the Healy clause,[6] stated that 'No rent should be made payable in respect of improvements made by the tenant' and provided a considerable strengthening of the bill's provisions in favour of the tenants. However, tenants in arrears and lease-holders were excluded from its provisions and left exposed to the danger of mass evictions. In 1881, more than 100,000 tenants, one third of tenants in the country, were in arrears of up to three years. Following the Kilmainham agreement, a new act, the Arrears of Rent (Ireland) Act of 1882,[7] was to provide for the abolition of £1.76 million of arrears. Those tenants affected were then able to apply to the land courts to have their rents fixed. Lease-holders received the same benefit in the land act of 1887.

The Irish Parliamentary Party was divided on the appropriate response to the Land Act and on 15 September 1881 held a convention that was attended by 1,200 delegates. The delegates representing Galway were Revd P.J. McPhilpin and Peter Broderick from Athenry, James Kilmartin (Ballinasloe), Henry Pilkington (Killeenadeema), Thomas Flatley (Tuam), James Neely (Gort) and Patrick Nolan (Tynagh). During the prolonged debate, many of the delegates indicated that the act did not achieve the important demand of the Land League that landlordism should be abolished and a peasant proprietary established. American opinion was firmly opposed to the act and the *Irish World* urged the convention 'to unfurl the banner of No Rent'. The third resolution of the meeting stated that the Land Act 'cannot be accepted as a just and wise, and still less a final, settlement'. Parnell agreed, claiming that 'as far as it works, it can only help the farmer'. The fourth resolution determined the official policy of the Land League:

> That in order to ascertain precisely and speedily the true effect of the Land Act upon the rental of Ireland, while at the same time preserving the unity and maintaining the strength of the National Land League, the executive be authorized to select at their discretion test cases upon estates in various parts of Ireland, and cause those cases to be brought before the court.

Although many delegates spoke in favour of a contrary view, the majority clearly supported this resolution and also the proposal that tenants would not enter into agreements to pay rent for any period longer than twelve months.[8]

The response of local Land League members to the political events is illus-

---

6 Named after its author, Tim Healy, MP for Wexford Town (1880–3), and various other Irish constituencies until 1918. First governor general of the Irish Free State, 1922–8. 7 Arrears of Rent (Ireland) Act, 45 & 46 Vict., c. 47. 8 *Freeman's Journal*, 16, 17 and 19 Sept. 1881.

trated by the outcome of a meeting of the Craughwell branch and the events at a meeting in Killeenadeema. On 2 October, the Craughwell branch held a meeting attended by Revd Geoghegan (chairman), J. Cuniffe (secretary), Patrick Cawley (treasurer), J. Benn and two hundred tenant farmers. The outcome of their deliberations was an instruction to the secretary to write to the landlords in the locality 'with a view to fixing the rents that the tenants were to pay hereafter'.[9] Therefore, they approved of the act and were prepared to cooperate with its implementation.

The attitude of the authorities had shifted significantly, with a new determination to strongly oppose the holding of mass meetings in the hope of reducing their effect in the turbulent political atmosphere. This more militant response to land meetings was evident in Killeenadeema, where the authorities proclaimed a meeting scheduled for 19 October 1881. The Land League branch reacted by holding the meeting at an earlier hour than advertised and outside the townland of Killeenadeema. At 10am, two hundred policemen under the command of CI Byrne were joined by soldiers from the 28th, 84th, 88th and 94th regiments and RM Byrne was in overall charge of police and military. When the Ballymana group arrived, they were ordered to disperse and the police took the names of those displaying Land League membership cards on their hats. SI Barry and fifty policemen halted a contingent from Kiltulla, en route to the meeting, at the West Bridge in Loughrea. They were ordered to return home and, after an address from Revd J. Cunningham CC, they did so. For the rest of the day, patrols of ten to twenty police marched through the town.

At the meeting, the recent arrest of Parnell was condemned and the resolutions of the Dublin convention were adopted. Henry Pilkington, secretary of the Killeenadeema branch, read an interesting letter from Bishop Duggan to the meeting. Bishop Duggan stated that

> a substantial instalment of justice is foreshadowed in the Land Act, it must also be admitted that any beneficial results to be anticipated from its operations are overhung with a cloud of uncertainty. At the best, the number of tenants in a position to avail of its provisions is very limited.

He regretted the failure of the government to accept the amendments proposed in the House of Commons because then

> the Land Act would have gone far towards tearing up the cancer of feudalism and securing a permanent settlement of the question. Hence the act ... is now only on trial to be tested under the supervision of the organization to which it owes its existence.[10]

Bishop Duggan was evidently accepting the Parnell tactic of testing the act.

9 *Western News*, 8 Oct. 1881.   10 *Galway Vindicator*, 19 Oct. 1881.

THE IMPLEMENTATION OF THE LAND LAW (IRELAND) ACT 1881

In the four years from September 1881 to 21 August 1885, 84,408 rents were fixed by the Land Commission and the civil bills court and 84,230 by agreements between tenants and landlords and lodged with the courts. In 1881 in Co. Galway, 5,942 rents were fixed in court and 3,979 by agreement. By August 1885, there remained 150,000 tenants who were entitled to avail themselves of the provisions of the act but had not yet done so. The average reduction of rents fixed in court was 19.5 per cent and by agreement 16.7 per cent. In Co. Galway, the reductions were slightly greater: 21 per cent for rents fixed in court and 19.2 per cent for those fixed by agreement.[11] K. Buckley comments that the rent reductions were not overgenerous because they were fixed in the expectation that agricultural prices would rise, but this expectation was not realized. Sir W.H. Gregory of Coole Park and Christopher Redington of Kilcornan fixed all their rents by agreement and none in court. Edward Martyn of Tullira met his tenants, many of whom owed two or three years' rent, in Loughrea. He agreed to accept Griffith's valuation as the judicial rent for the next fifteen years.[12] W.P. Lambert of Castle Ellen fixed fifty-four rents by agreement and five in court. In contrast, the intransigent attitude of Lord Clanricarde is indicated by the fact that between 1881 and 1903 the rents of 541 holdings were all fixed in court and none by agreement with the landlord.

RIGOROUS ENFORCEMENT OF THE PROTECTION OF PERSON AND PROPERTY (IRELAND) ACT 1881

The rigorous enforcement of the PPP (Ireland) Act from early October 1881 to April 1882 left the Land League without national and local leaders, causing a progressive dismantling of the organization of the Land League, thus achieving one of the principal aims of the act.

As early as 26 September 1881, Forster had written to Gladstone suggesting that Parnell should be arrested. Gladstone agreed, provided that the law officers of the crown thought he had been guilty of treasonable practices.[13] Large public demonstrations in support of Parnell in Cork[14] and Dublin and the reception accorded Revd Eugene Sheehy following his release from Kilmainham on 27 September increased Forster's apprehensions regarding further disturbances during the autumn and winter. Political tensions were considerably raised by Gladstone's speech in Leeds on 7 October, when he stated that 'There is still to

---

11 K. Buckley, 'The fixing of rents by agreement in Co. Galway, 1881–85', *Irish Historical Studies*, 7:27 (1951), 160. 12 *Galway Vindicator*, 21 Jan. 1882. 13 Wemyss Reid, *Life of Forster*, ii, p. 339. 14 *Freeman's Journal*, 3 Oct. 1881.

be fought a final conflict between law on one side and sheer lawlessness on the other ... the resources of civilization against its enemies are not yet exhausted'.[15] Parnell responded in a provocative manner at Wexford on 9 October, referring to Gladstone as 'the greatest coercionist' and to his 'unscrupulous and dishonest speech'.[16] The scene was now set for the arrest of Parnell on 13 October, along with the other national leaders who were still free, James J. O'Kelly MP, Thomas Sexton MP, John Dillon MP, William O'Brien and Patrick J. Quinn. The Land League responded with hastily convened protest meetings held in Dublin and throughout the country, including in Galway and Ballinasloe.

NO RENT MANIFESTO

At the Land League executive meeting on 18 October, the No Rent manifesto was read. It referred to Parnell's arrest, which it conceded might have been attributable to personal malice, but 'the seizure ... of the chief officials of the League ... put it beyond all possibility of doubt that the British government ... has resolved to destroy the whole machinery of the central League'. It went on to state that

> the executive of the national Land League feels bound to advise the tenant farmers of Ireland from this forth to pay no rents under any circumstances to their landlords until the government relinquishes the existing system of terrorism and restores the constitutional rights of the people.[17]

In order to promote the No Rent policy, financial support from the Land League was promised to anyone evicted in the course of the struggle. The manifesto was signed by Parnell, Kettle, Brennan, Dillon and Sexton and also bore the names of Davitt, who was in Portland Prison, and Egan, who was in Paris. A circular was issued to every Land League branch, instructing them to call an immediate meeting in order to read the manifesto, and also to have it posted in the neighbourhood. Two days later, Forster proclaimed the Land League as 'an unlawful and criminal association that had sought to effect its purposes by an organized system of intimidation, attempting to obstruct process serving and the execution of the queen's writs'.[18] The nationalist press and Archbishop Croke condemned the proclamation, but Croke also opposed the No Rent manifesto, which he had read with 'absolute dismay'.[19] Davitt, writing in 1903, voiced the opinion that 'the no rent shell fired from Kilmainham would only demoralize and could not

15 *Galway Vindicator*, 12 Oct. 1881. 16 Ibid. 17 *Galway Vindicator*, 22 Oct. 1881. 18 HC 1882 [C.3125], lv, 275. Proclamation by the lord lieutenant of Ireland dated 20 Oct. 1881. 19 *Freeman's Journal*, 19 Oct. 1881.

explode. Its fuse had fallen off'.[20] Instead of adhering to the No Rent policy, tenants began to patronize the land court, accept the benefits of rent reduction and preserve the rights to their rented property.

LADIES' LAND LEAGUE IN SOUTH GALWAY

The vacuum created by the proclamation of the Land League and the arrest of the leading national and local figures was in part compensated by the activities of the Ladies' Land League, led by Anna Parnell and Clara Stritch. They had access to the funds of the Land League and were able to provide assistance in various ways. They helped evicted tenants financially and by the provision of prefabricated wooden huts. Assistance was also given to suspects and their families. A meeting of the Loughrea Ladies' Land League in October 1881 acknowledged receipt of £55 for the support of the families of suspects and evicted families.[21] The Craughwell and Ballymana branch had been founded in March 1881 and as many as seventy members attended its meetings. In early 1882, the greater demands placed on the branch led to an increase in the frequency of meetings from monthly to weekly. The first meeting of the year was held on 1 January and it did not escape the attentions of the police. As the members were preparing to leave, constables Judge and Morris arrived with orders to disperse the meeting. The police also informed the members that they had orders to prosecute but after a brief confrontation the police left without taking further action.[22] The officers of the Craughwell and Ballymana branch at the next meeting on 8 January 1882 were Miss Mary Barrett (president), Mrs Benn (vice president), Miss Mary Fahy (treasurer) and Miss Anna Maria Morrissey (honorary secretary). The committee was composed of Misses Forde, Cloonan, Greaney, Moloney and Mary Morrissey and there were sixty members.[23] The president read a letter from Miss Stritch of the central executive that contained instructions for the branch, and the members agreed to make weekly collections for what was known as the Prisoners' Sustentation Fund. The Craughwell and Ballymana branch was particularly active in the support of evicted tenants such as the Fallon family of Moneen and those evicted in Roveagh. Other branches in the area were formed in Loughrea, Gort and Shanaglish. Between October 1881 and the end of May 1882, a total of £70,000 was spent by the Ladies' Land League for the support of prisoners and their families and the victims of eviction.[24]

---

20 Davitt, *The fall of feudalism*, p. 338.   21 *Western News*, 8 Oct. 1881.   22 *Tuam News*, 6 Jan. 1882.   23 *Tuam News*, 13 Jan. 1882.   24 Davitt, *The fall of feudalism*, pp 344–5.

SPECIAL RESIDENT MAGISTRATES, THE ADMINISTRATION OF THE LAW,
FURTHER ARRESTS OF SUSPECTS AND COMMUNITY SUPPORT FOR THEM

In an attempt to improve the administration of the law, Chief Secretary Forster had decided in December 1881 to appoint special resident magistrates. The first appointments were those of Captain T.O. Plunkett,[25] H.A. Blake[26] and C.D. Clifford Lloyd. Blake was initially assigned to Galway until it was placed under Clifford Lloyd's jurisdiction in late June 1882. The special resident magistrates were in charge of groups of resident magistrates' districts and their greater authority was expected to improve the coordination of the efforts of the magistrates, military and police. Difficulties had arisen, with the war office regarding the legality of the employment of soldiers in aid of the police and also the question as to who was in overall control of soldiers in this role.[27] The appointments led to a significant degree of friction, with many RMs resenting what they perceived as a diminution of their power and influence.

That the introduction of martial law was under discussion in Dublin Castle at the end of 1881 is indicated by a letter initialled by Under Secretary Burke to RM J.W. Byrne (Loughrea), asking 'what provisions of martial law he would advise'. Byrne replied on 19 December 1881, stating that he 'had given the subject long and careful consideration'. He thought a very good system of patrols was kept up by the police, 'but they were quite unable to cope with the perfect and the widespread organization which prevails not alone in the neighbourhood of these two outrages[28] but all through my district'. The erection of a police hut (figs 3 & 4, p. 121) would provide protection for the two families who were attacked,

> but it will have no material effect upon the peace of the district and the existing laws and the repressive measures which have recently been put so actively in force, by government, are not sufficient ... to meet or rather to crush out the lawless and desperate system which now dominates thro' this district.

Byrne concluded by saying that the necessity to proclaim martial law was a matter for 'very fair consideration'.[29] Within a few weeks, the existing powers of the Coercion Act were used to make multiple arrests in Killeenadeema. Persons arrested included Henry Pilkington, Peter Kelly PLG, John Keane, Denis and

---

25 Thomas Oliver Plunkett (1838–89), son of Baron Louth, appointed RM in 1866. 26 Henry Arthur Blake, later knighted and became governor of the Bahamas. 27 NAI CSO RP 1883/2214, Ross of Bladenburg's memorandum on the military in aid of the civil power in Ireland, 1881–2, and Richard Hawkins, 'An army on police work, 1881–2', *Irish Sword*, 11 (1973). 28 The shooting into and burning of two houses in the Killeenadeema area. 29 NAI CSO RP 1881/43949 in 1882/23334, Byrne to under secretary, 19 Dec. 1881.

Thomas Cunningham, Thomas Duggan, Martin Mullavel, Michael Calligy and Michael Furlong.

SRM Henry Arthur Blake held a meeting with the landowners of east Galway on 4 January 1882. His purpose was to solicit their support for a vigorous assault on the activities of secret agrarian societies by concentrating large forces of police and military in disturbed areas. The landlords agreed to serve writs on tenants and proceed against them in the courts.[30]

RM John W. Byrne was in charge of a major police and military operation in the Loughrea and Athenry areas on 27 January 1882 that resulted in the arrest of twenty persons. SRM Blake and SI Alan Bell were in charge of the operation in Athenry and eleven arrests were made. G. Shaw Lefevre (Baron Eversley), a member of the Gladstone government, was visiting the area at the time and had recently dined with John Henry Blake. When he heard of the police and military action, he expressed surprise that 'such proceedings should take place in any part of the United Kingdom, that they should be submitted to without disturbance, and that no notice should be taken of them by the English press impressed me not a little'.[31]

On the same day in Loughrea, a combined force of police and military surrounded the town resulting in the arrest of nine suspects. Those arrested were the leading members of the Land League who were still at liberty. Among them was Peter Sweeny, who had become secretary of the local branch following the arrest of his brother John in June 1881. Also arrested were John McCarthy and John Farrell.[32] Others arrested were Bernard Coyle, Martin Greene, Martin Huban (a national school teacher) and Nicholas Barrett, post office employee and reporter for several Dublin and London papers. Prior to their departure for prisons in Naas, Monaghan and Omagh, the Loughrea prisoners, undaunted by their predicament, gave an impromptu concert on the platform of Woodlawn station. Nicholas Barrett sang *My own land*, Bernard Coyle, *Who fears to speak of '98*, Peter Sweeny, *Which shall be the fairest land*, John Farrell, *God save Ireland*, Martin Huban, *The bonny bunch of roses* and John McCarthy, *Goodbye Molly*.[33] RM Byrne reported that on the day of the arrests there was no excitement or disturbance initially, but later the shutters were put up on every shop in the town, 'no doubt intended to convey the regret of the owners at the arrests'. Byrne believed that the more respectable shopkeepers did so 'because they were afraid to incur unpopularity'. He concluded his report by referring to the search carried out on eighty-four houses in the town without finding any arms.[34] The house of John Sweeny was inevitably one of those searched and a tongue-in-cheek newspaper account related that a baby was asleep in its cradle when five sub constables burst in and approached the cradle with fixed bayonets. The baby

---

30 NLI, Clonbrock papers, MS 19,678, quoted in Ball, *Policing the Land War*, p. 164.   31 G. Shaw Lefevre, *Incidents of coercion in Ireland* (London, 1889), p. 11.   32 PRO CO 904, vol. 15, pt 1, 9301/S.   33 *Tuam News*, 27 Jan. 1882.   34 NAI CSO RP 1882/4706.

put up a spirited defence while the cot was searched and the bed ripped with bayonets but no guns were found.[35] Strong resolutions of condemnation of the arrests were adopted at meetings of the Ladies' Land League in Loughrea, Craughwell and Killeenadeema.[36]

Six of the Athenry suspects came from the Kiltulla/Kilconierin area and they were charged with being 'active members of an illegal secret society, the object of which is to prevent the payment of rent by intimidation'.[37] The decision to recommend their arrests was considered at a meeting in Dublin Castle on 24 January attended by Chief Secretary W.E. Forster, John Naish, the law adviser, Under Secretary Thomas Burke, Assistant Under Secretary Samuel Anderson, who had special responsibility for administering the Coercion Act, RM Byrne, SI Dominick Barry (Loughrea) and Constable Murtagh (Craughwell). The involvement of Earl Spencer in the operation of the Coercion Act is evident from the case of one of those arrested that day, Thomas Finnigan, whose release was under consideration in May 1882. SI Paine (Ballinasloe) conferred with RM Beresford and the recommendation was that Finnigan could not be released without 'danger to the peace of the district. His father is herd for Mr Peter Blake at Hollypark and the Blakes look with suspicion on Thomas'. Earl Spencer asked if there was any marked distinction between Finnigan's case and those arrested with him, who had already been released. SRM Blake replied that 'this man was a member of an illegal secret society, and the release of IRB members was undesirable until the Prevention of Crime Bill became law'. Nevertheless, on 5 June John Naish signed the order for Finnigan's release and Earl Spencer appended his initial.[38]

The secretary of the Gurteen branch, Thomas G. Griffin, was one of the leading Land League members and was identified by CI Leighton, along with his brother, as 'men who have excited the people in their district to resist the laws'.[39] SI Bell recommended his arrest in spring 1881 on grounds of intimidation against rent but this did not occur until 11 November. His release was considered in due course, but Bell opposed it because of his participation in a Land League court and his use of violent language. Bell also alleged that Griffin was constantly out at night and that he was involved in the drilling of Land League members. In May 1882, RM Paul wrote to the under secretary protesting against Griffin's release, referring to him as 'a leading and active member of a secret society who does no work but lives on the commission of crime'.[40] Despite this protest, Griffin was released on 18 May 1882, earlier than many of the other Galway suspects.

Threatening notices posted in Loughrea and Craughwell contained denunciations of government policy and appeals to not pay rent. They warned that those

35 *Tuam News*, 27 Jan. 1882. 36 *Tuam News*, 10 Feb. 1882. 37 NAI CSO RP 1883/2141. 38 NAI CSO RP 1882/24132 in 1882/25792. 39 NAI CSO RP 1880/34686, Leighton to inspector general of the RIC. 40 NAI CSO RP 1881/39556 in 1882/24340.

who paid rent should 'remember Doherty and Dempsey' and expect the same fate. The notices probably had a bearing on the fact that not a single tenant farmer from the Loughrea district appeared at the sitting of the land court in the town on 6 February.[41] By the middle of February, eighty policemen and a hundred soldiers were stationed in Loughrea and throughout the month there were numerous arrests under the Coercion Act in the Loughrea and Athenry police districts, mainly for posting threatening notices and intimidation against rent.

Jack Moran, a tailor from Killeeneen who was to play a fateful role in subsequent events, was arrested under the Coercion Act on 27 February 1882.[42] He was charged with intimidation against paying rent and a neighbour had claimed that he would have paid his rent but he was afraid Moran would find out. The record of his arrest stated that he held meetings at his house and took command of parties on their way to meetings. The police believed that he was also involved in drilling groups of men, using the experience of his army career. He was detained in Monaghan Jail until August 1882, and in April 1883 he was to make a dramatic intervention in the Doherty case.[43]

On 28 February, James and Thomas Coane (Clough), and John McGann and Patrick Gilligan (Tiaquin) were arrested in the Athenry area. All the suspects were believed to be members of an illegal secret society.[44] Gilligan wrote to his wife on 2 March to assure her that he and the other prisoners were being very well treated in Monaghan Jail.

A highly controversial case was that of Revd Peter J. McPhilpin CC (Athenry), vice president of the Athenry Land League. The authorities were obviously reluctant to arrest a clergyman, particularly in view of the outraged local and national reaction following the arrest of Revd Eugene Sheehy in May 1881.[45] The decision regarding his possible arrest was postponed and the papers were sent to the Irish office in London for further consideration.[46] Revd McPhilpin was an outspoken activist and during the intensive police activities on 27 January 1882 the police had searched his house. He was summoned to appear at the petty sessions court on 4 April 1882, charged with 'using language to his congregation tending to excite ill-will between the people and the RIC and to deter Her Majesty's subjects from enlisting in the forces'. The vicinity of the court was crowded and a large number of RIC had been drafted in from country stations. In addition, detachments of the 28th Regiment and the 18th Hussars were in attendance. The magistrates were RM Byrne (chairman), SRM Henry Arthur Blake and Colonel John Nolan MP. The prosecution claimed that Revd McPhilpin spoke after Mass while the RIC were in the church and claimed that

41 *Tuam News*, 17 Feb. 1882. 42 NAI, Irish Crimes Records, no. 686. 43 For a detailed account of Moran's role in the Doherty case, see Finnegan, *The case of the Craughwell prisoners*. 44 NAI CSO RP 1883/2141. 45 *Freeman's Journal*, 23 May 1881. 46 NAI CSO RP 1883/2141.

'there were no outrages in Athenry except those committed by the government and the RIC'. A majority verdict found him guilty, with Colonel Nolan MP dissenting, and Revd McPhilpin was bound over to keep the peace.[47]

Community support for the suspects was very strong and the arrival of *meitheals*[48] to work on suspects' farms was often an occasion of great excitement. The first occasion was in December 1881 at Clostoken when a crowd of three hundred men and sixty horses, led by the Clostoken Fife and Drum Band, arrived to plough the lands of Peter Plower, John Glennon, John Connaughton, James Noakley and Patrick Tuohill.[49] On 6 January 1882, sixty horses and carts led by the Killeenadeema Fife and Drum Band drew home the turf of Peter Kelly.[50] In February 1882, a large crowd from the Athenry area ploughed twelve acres belonging to John Melia who had been arrested on 27 January and was currently in Omagh Jail.[51] Other instances included the ploughing of the lands of Peter Broderick, Andrew Keary, Thomas Coyne,[52] and Anthony and Thomas G. Griffin.[53] During May, large crowds assembled in Clostoken for the cultivation of crops for John Connaughton, who had been arrested on 16 December 1881.[54]

In addition, a number of charitable funds contributed to the support of the families of the suspects. The Prisoners' Sustentation Fund received weekly subscriptions from branches of the Ladies' Land League. A concert was held in Loughrea to raise funds and it was reported that members of the local RIC tried to prevent people attending by 'dressing as beggars, jostling and behaving in a coarse and vulgar manner'.[55] A St Patrick's Day ball, organized by the Ladies' Land League, was held in Athenry and the Craughwell branch proposed to hold a ball in Ballymore House on Easter Monday. J. Benn rented this property from Lord Clanricarde and when Clanricarde's bailiff informed the police of the plan, the threat of prosecution forced cancellation of the ball.[56]

In summary, the Bessborough Commission advised the granting of the '3 Fs', resulting in a system of dual ownership by landlords and tenants. It did not recommend a peasant proprietary, which had been vigorously condemned by the landlords. The main defects of the legislation were the failure to include tenants in arrears and lease-holders in the provisions. The response of Parnell was to test the act with selected cases but large numbers accepted its terms and achieved an average reduction in rent of 20 per cent in Co. Galway. The arrest of Parnell and other national leaders was quickly followed by the proclamation of the Land League and the intensification of efforts to suppress it. Multiple arrests took place and the suspects were generously supported by their families, the community and the Ladies' Land League.

47 *Freeman's Journal*, 5 Apr. 1882. 48 Volunteer workers. 49 *Irish Times*, 31 Dec. 1881.
50 *Tuam News*, 13 Jan. 1882. 51 *Tuam News*, 17 Feb. 1882. 52 *Tuam News*, 26 Jan. 1882.
53 *Western News*, 11 Feb. 1882. 54 *Tuam News*, 19 May 1882. 55 *Tuam News*, 17 Feb. 1882.
56 *Tuam News*, 24 Mar. 1882.

10 Analysis of arrests of suspects in Co. Galway

The disturbed nature of the Loughrea and Athenry police districts during 1881–2 is evident from the large number of persons arrested during the period (see table 12, below).

Table 12 Number of persons arrested in the Loughrea and Athenry police districts in 1881 and 1882 under the PPP (Ireland) Act 1881 (source: NAI, PPP (Ireland) Act 1881, carton 1).

	Loughrea	Athenry	Total
1881	31	11	42
1882	53	16	69
Total	84	27	111

The total for the two districts was 111 (11 per cent of the national total), of which eighty-four came from Loughrea and twenty-seven from Athenry. The total number of persons arrested in Co. Galway was 166 (17 per cent of the national total). On 27 January 1882, thirteen arrests were made in Loughrea and seven in Athenry and on 4 July twenty-three men were arrested in Loughrea, including three town commissioners. The July arrests took place in connection with the killing of John Henry Blake and Thady Ruane. Eight individuals arrested in Loughrea in January 1882 for intimidation against rent and subsequently released were re-arrested in July as murder accessories. Most of those arrested outside the Loughrea and Athenry police districts came from Clonbur (14), Ballinasloe (9), Clifden (7), the Aran Islands (6) and Gort (5). The high total for Clonbur is due to the large number of suspects arrested in connection with the killing of Joseph Huddy and his grandson. Three of them – Patrick and Thomas Higgins and Michael Flynn – were subsequently convicted of the crime and executed in Galway Jail in January 1883.

The occupation of arrested suspects under the Coercion Act has been analysed previously by Samuel Clark[1] and Donald Jordan, who did a similar analysis on the Mayo suspects.[2] Jordan's study is difficult to compare with Clark's or the present study because only fourteen suspects were arrested in Mayo.

A complete listing of persons arrested in the Loughrea and Athenry police districts is presented in appendix 2. The occupational analysis of the 166 persons arrested in Co. Galway is presented in table 13 (p. 115).

---

[1] Clark, *Social origins of the Irish Land War*, ch. 8. [2] Jordan, *Land and popular politics in Ireland*, pp 193–6.

Table 13 Occupations of persons arrested in Co. Galway under the PPP (Ireland) Act 1881 (sources: NAI, PPP (Ireland) Act 1881, carton 1; Samuel Clark, *Social origins of the Irish Land War*, p. 250).

Occupations	Number	% of suspects	% of national labour force	% of Galway labour force
Agricultural sector	102	61	66	72
Farmers	62	37	24	
Farmers' sons	27	16	12	
Agricultural labourers	10	6	13	
Herds	3	2	0.4	
Commercial and industrial sector	46	28	23	16
Traders, business proprietors, shopworkers	20	12	12	
Publicans	7	4	0.4	
Artisans	19	11	10	
Professional sector	6	4	4	4
Clergy	0	–	–	
Teachers	4	2	0.5	
Newspaper correspondents	2	1	0.02	
No occupation	5	3	–	
No occupation recorded	7	4	–	
Total	166			

The results of Clark's study and the present study are broadly similar. In Co. Galway, 61 per cent of the suspects belonged to the agricultural sector, slightly less than the 66 per cent in the national labour force and below the 72 per cent expected in Co. Galway on the basis of an occupational analysis of census figures.[3] The breakdown in the agricultural sector is also comparable with Clark's results (see table 14, p. 116), and both farmers and their sons are significantly over-represented compared with the national figures. The proportion of agricultural labourers in Co. Galway is 6 per cent, compared with 7 per cent in Clark's study – both figures less than the proportion of 13 per cent in the national labour force. This may be explained by the fact that the majority of the arrests occurred in south and east Galway, where the agricultural economy had seen major changes from tillage to pasturage, with small farmers joining in the production of stock for the commercial market and reducing employment for labourers (see above, p. 63).

In the present study, the commercial and industrial sector accounts for 28 per cent compared with a national figure of 23 per cent. It is of even greater significance in relation to the proportion for Co. Galway (16 per cent). In the Clark

3 HC 1882 [C.3268], lxxix, 1. Census of Ireland 1881, pt i, vol. iv: province of Connaught.

Table 14 Comparison of the percentages of arrests within the agricultural sector between Clark's study, the Co. Galway figures in the present study and the national labour force (sources: HC 1882 [C.3268], lxxix, 1, Census of Ireland 1881, pt 1, vol. iv: province of Connaught; Samuel Clark, *Social origins of the Irish Land War*, p. 250).

	Clark	Co. Galway	National labour force
Farmers	39	37	24
Farmer's sons	16	16	12
Agricultural labourers	7	6	13
Herds	1	2	0.4

Table 15 Comparison of the percentages of arrests between Clark's study, the Co. Galway figures in the present study and the values in the national and Co. Galway labour forces (sources: HC 1882 [C.3268], lxxix, 1, Census of Ireland 1881, pt 1, vol. iv: province of Connaught; Samuel Clark, *Social origins of the Irish Land War*, p. 250).

	Clark	Co. Galway	National labour force	Galway labour force
Agricultural sector	62	61	66	72
Commercial and industrial sector	33	28	23	16
Professional sector	5	4	4	–

study, there is an over-representation of publicans, with a figure of 8 per cent compared with the national labour force figure of 0.4 per cent. In the present study, the proportion is 4 per cent, ten times the national figure. The facilitation of contacts between the urban and rural populations through commercial outlets contributed to the cohesion of the Land League organization. The opportunity of social meetings in public houses would also have helped the discussion of political news, the planning of meetings and protests and the distribution of notices advertising meetings.

Eighty of the suspects arrested in the Loughrea and Athenry police districts were rural-based, but thirty-one were based in towns, confirming the close cooperation of farmers and townspeople in the Land League organization. It is noteworthy that there were no arrests of suspects in Galway city, which would suggest that the largest urban area in the county exercised little or no influence on the Land League organization.

CATEGORIES OF OFFENCES

The various categories of offences in table 16 (p. 117) indicate that nationally, the vast majority of suspects were arrested for relatively minor offences.

Table 16 Categories of the main offences under the PPP (Ireland) Act 1881 (source: NAI, PPP (Ireland) Act 1881, carton 1).

Categories of offences	Number of arrests		
	Loughrea	Athenry	Ireland
Intimidation, issuing threatening notices, preventing rent payment and boycotting	45	20	594
Murder, inciting to murder and murder accessory	48	4	129
Shooting at persons and dwellings	1	4	38
Treason	1	0	23

A detailed analysis compiled by Stephen Ball indicates that of the 987 arrests in the country, 594 were for intimidation, boycotting, the issuing of threatening notices and preventing the payment of rent. These were the activities that would have engaged the prominent organizers of the Land League. A total of 129 arrests were for murder, incitement to murder and accessory to murder.[4] O'Callaghan also emphasizes this pattern with the arrests for relatively minor offences of men who 'had come to prominence through the Land League and deemed to be potentially powerful in the community', while she refers to 'a smattering of individuals genuinely suspected of serious crimes ... cast in with this collection'. She states that 'such specifications as murder, shooting and wounding, and assaulting dwelling houses, appear from the lists to be confined to the south-west, insofar as they existed at all at this time'.[5] Her analysis failed to detect that there was a large number of arrests in the Loughrea and Athenry police districts, with fifty-two in the serious category relating to murder. This figure represents 40 per cent of the national total and is clearly related to the eight murders in the area and the response of the authorities to these events resulting in the arbitrary arrests of Land League activists and suspected members of secret societies. Even though thirty-seven individuals were arrested, only nine were charged in connection with the killings of whom two were acquitted, pleas of *nolle prosequi* were entered in six cases and one was convicted. Therefore, the majority of those arrested were never brought to court.

Reviewing the initial ineffectiveness of the Coercion Act in stopping outrages, Earl Spencer, in a letter to the home secretary, blamed weak administration.[6] This comment probably refers to the relatively small number of arrests during the first six months of the operation of the act (see table 17, p. 118) when 219 were arrested and 77 were released, leaving only 142 in custody at the end of September 1881. The pledge given by Forster to parliament that he would be

---

4 Ball, 'Policing the Land War', p. 373.   5 O'Callaghan, *British high politics and a nationalist Ireland*, p. 82.   6 BL, Spencer papers, 76898, Spencer to Hartington, 9 July 1882.

Table 17 Arrests under the PPP (Ireland) Act 1881 during 1881 and 1882 (source: NAI, PPP (Ireland) Act 1881, carton 1).

	Jan.	Feb.	Mar.	Apr.	May	June	July	Aug.	Sept.	Oct.	Nov.	Dec.	Total
1881				33	20	58	72	26	10	0	111	120	149	599
1882	102	108	80	43	3	5	47	0	0				388

personally responsible for each warrant also delayed the impact of the Coercion Act.[7]

The idea was prevalent at that early stage that the mere arrest of activists and their detention for even a short period, with its inevitable impact on their livelihoods and families, would act as an effective deterrent to involvement in agrarian crime. The proclamation of the Land League was followed by a dramatic increase in agrarian crime, with a peak national figure of 574 outrages in December 1881. This period coincided with a more rigorous enforcement of the act and a sharp increase in the number of arrests, with 149 in December 1881. In the hope of improving the rate of crime detection, a circular was issued to the RIC authorizing the payment of amounts of £20 to £100 for information on outrages.[8] However, the large number of agrarian incidents in the first quarter of 1882 showed that even widespread arrests or the offer of rewards did not have an immediate impact. By the end of March 1882, a total of 889 suspects had been arrested and 563 were still in custody.[9]

The most zealous of the special resident magistrates selected by the chief secretary in December 1881 was undoubtedly Clifford Lloyd. He was born in 1841 in Portsmouth, but his family had strong Irish connections, an uncle and grandfather having been provosts of Trinity College Dublin. He was greatly favoured by Forster and Earl Spencer, with whom he conducted an extensive private and official correspondence. Following his departure from Ireland, Clifford Lloyd wrote a lively account of the Land War.[10]

The manner in which he interpreted and prosecuted his duties ensured that he was never far from controversy. One of the measures he suggested to the home secretary, Sir William Harcourt, was the purchase of bloodhounds to be used for tracking offenders. He justified his request by stating 'the brutal and cowardly assassins must expect that in future every device that human ingenuity can suggest will be used to bring them to justice'.[11] The home secretary did not accede to this request but Earl Spencer quickly agreed to the provision of joint military and police posts to provide intensive surveillance.[12] Clifford Lloyd's

7 Moody & Hawkins (eds), *Florence Arnold-Forster's Irish journal*, p. 84 n. 3.   8 *Irish Times*, 10 Dec. 1881.   9 NAI, Protection of Person and Property (Ireland) Act 1881, carton 1; HC 1882 (156), lv, 635.   10 Charles Dalton Clifford Lloyd, *Ireland under the Land League* (London, 1892).   11 NAI CSO RP 1891/28047, Brackenbury to Trevelyan, 8 July 1882.   12 BL, Spencer papers, 76946, Courtenay Boyle to Trevelyan, 4 July 1882. Boyle was private secretary

vigorous application of the Coercion Act in Cos Limerick, Clare and Galway confirmed his reputation for ruthless action to restore order. He became resident magistrate in Limerick on 12 May 1881 and quickly began to target the local Land League committees, 'the hostile power in occupation'.[13] The arrest of Revd Eugene Sheehy, president of the Killmallock branch, gave rise to considerable local and national anger and a spirited debate in the House of Commons.[14] In September 1881, Forster referred approvingly to his

> cool temperate proceedings as a magistrate – dismissing some cases – committing others for trial, and showing himself apparently quite sufficient master of the situation to account for the ferocious vapourings of the Land League agitators, who object to any strong hand over the people except their own.[15]

Forster's high opinion of Clifford Lloyd had changed by February 1882, however, when he referred to SRM Plunkett as the best for his work. 'With all his vigour, Mr Lloyd is a little too impulsive, too much up and down, and father finds that it does not do to quote him too quickly'.[16] Indeed, volatile mood shifts are evident within the course of a single report.[17]

Forty-five people were arrested in Limerick, eighty-two in Clare and forty-five in Galway East Riding. Therefore, Clifford Lloyd was associated with almost 18 per cent of the total arrests for the country under the PPP (Ireland) Act 1881. The league table (table 18, p. 120) for arrests in the country shows the dominant position of Loughrea, with Athenry in fourth place.

Five of the ten police districts with the most arrests (209) were under the supervision of Clifford Lloyd, indicating the disturbed nature of the districts and his vigorous response to the level of agitation.

Overall, the analysis of the arrests of suspects under the PPP (Ireland) Act has strong parallels with that of Samuel Clark. They include the preponderance of farmers and farmers' sons and the excess of persons in the commercial and industrial sector, indicating the close relationship between rural dwellers and townspeople that formed the 'challenging collectivity' proposed by Clark. The opportunity for communication provided by the number of publicans identified in the analysis is also significant. The majority of the arrests were for the relatively minor offences, but the number in the serious categories of murder and accessory to murder is exceptionally high. For this reason, the most controversial of the SRMs, Clifford Lloyd, was given the task of imposing the full rigour of the law on the community.

---

to Spencer. **13** Clifford Lloyd, *Ireland under the Land League*, p. 97. **14** *Freeman's Journal*, 21 May 1881. **15** Moody & Hawkins, *Florence-Arnold Forster's Irish journal*, p. 254. **16** Ibid., p. 382. **17** NAI CSO RP 1883/300, FCR, W Div 2/1/1883.

Table 18 Police districts with the most arrests under the PPP (Ireland) Act 1881 (source: NAI, PPP (Ireland) Act 1881, carton 1).

Police district	Number of arrests	Police district	Number of arrests
Loughrea, Co. Galway	95	Kilfinane, Co. Limerick	21
Dublin city	61	Ennistymon, Co. Clare	19
Tulla, Co. Clare	47	Roscommon	17
Athenry, Co. Galway	27	Killarney, Co. Kerry	15
Castleisland, Co. Kerry	22	New Pallas, Co. Limerick	15

CLIFFORD LLOYD AND HIS APPLICATION OF THE TWO COERCION ACTS[18]

At the end of June 1882, in addition to his duties in Limerick and Clare, Clifford Lloyd was appointed to Co. Galway. He took up his post immediately after the killing of Blake and Ruane and he reported to Assistant Under Secretary E.G. Jenkinson that Loughrea was 'a den of infamy and must be made to pay under the new act'[19] (the Prevention of Crime (Ireland) Act 1882). He obtained warrants for the arrest of twenty-three suspects of involvement in these killings. Among those arrested were the leading Land League activists still at liberty, as well as suspected IRB members, John McCarthy, John Farrell and Michael Dilleen. Clifford Lloyd reported that Andrew McEntee was overheard saying to another suspect, on the morning of the arrests, 'if they only had ... here there would be the pack of us'. Clifford Lloyd thought that the remark meant that those arrested were all members of an illegal secret society, whereas it is probable that many of them had no such affiliation and that McEntee was referring to their membership of the Land League.

Soon after his appointment, Clifford Lloyd arranged for the setting up of four police huts in Loughrea and another sixteen at crossroads within a radius of 6km (figs 3 & 4, p. 121). The huts were brought from the police depot in the Phoenix Park and erected on site. Permission to erect huts was often refused by landowners and tenants and in that case they were placed on the sides of roads and on the triangular areas where roads forked. As many as six soldiers and three policemen could be accommodated in them, and each hut was given an allowance of fourteen shillings per month for food.[20] There were constant day and night patrols and a total of two hundred police and military were stationed in the town.[21] On the road between Kilrickle and Dartfield, two policemen were on

18 The Protection of Person and Property (Ireland) Act 1881 and the Prevention of Crime (Ireland) Act 1882 (see below, ch. 11) 19 BL, Spencer papers, 77080, Lloyd to Jenkinson, 7 July 1882. 20 NAI CSO RP 1883/2214, report of Captain Lindsay, 2nd Battalion, Lothian Regiment, Tulla, Co. Clare, 1 Apr. 1882. 21 *Tuam News*, 11 Aug. 1882.

3 Exterior of a portable hut for police in Mayo (source: *Illustrated London News*, 28 May 1870).

4 The interior of a police hut (source: *Illustrated London News*, 28 May 1870).

constant patrol and two more at the Hardy estate at Dartfield. At the entrance to Loughrea, there were two policemen on guard, 'scrutinizing the features of every stranger and arresting suspicious characters'.[22]

As well as overseeing the large number of arrests in Loughrea in early July 1882, Clifford Lloyd was active elsewhere in the locality. In Dunsandle, he arrested seventeen men, who were bound over to keep the peace. On 17 July, as part of the continuing investigations of the killing of Peter Doherty, Clifford Lloyd brought a strong force of police to Craughwell and arrested six men, namely Thomas Connolly (Mannin), John Connaire (Caherdine), Thomas Pendergast (Carrigan), Michael Connolly (Ballywinna), Michael Fogarty (Shanbally) and Thomas Joyce (Grenage).[23] At the hearing before RM Byrne, Constable Judge claimed that they were all members of a secret society and they were charged with being accessories to the murder of Doherty. In total, fifteen suspects from the Craughwell area who had been imprisoned in Galway, Enniskillen and other jails were released on 17 and 23 August. Their return home was a joyous occasion. The windows were illuminated and bonfires blazed while a large crowd conveyed them to their homes.[24]

At this time, the *Western News* published a regular column entitled 'The State of Loughrea', which, in effect, was under siege. 'One thing is beyond doubt; if the present system of police terrorism is continued, the trade of the town will become paralysed. A gloom and a pall seem to have enveloped the district'. Clifford Lloyd remarked that he would 'make the grass grow through the streets of Loughrea, or else discover the murderer of Mr Blake'. The local interpretation was that the police and protection tax levied on the district would be so burdensome that people would have to emigrate.[25] The belief that the town was under siege was reinforced in early August by a search carried out by fifty soldiers of the 28th Regiment, accompanied by eighty policemen from all the surrounding stations. They were under the command of SI Dominick Barry (Loughrea), SI Alan Bell (Athenry) and RM Byrne. Three soldiers and three policemen guarded all points of entry and exit from Galway Road while the remainder searched the houses, backyards and piggeries. Nothing of a criminal nature was found during the search.[26]

In August 1882, Clifford Lloyd visited W.E. Forster and his family in London and expressed the hope that the Loughrea suspects, when they were released from Kilmainham, would find themselves 'less able to do harm than before'. In his opinion, brute force would not lead to permanent improvement, but he hoped that, 'as a result of the vigorous enforcement of the law, the side of order as against outrage may become the winning side, in which case the people will have a strong inducement to become well-disposed'.[27] Despite his experience at

22 *Western News*, 15 July 1882.   23 *Tuam News*, 21 July 1882.   24 *Tuam News*, 8 Sept. 1882.
25 *Western News*, 15 July 1882.   26 *Western News*, 5 Aug. 1882.   27 Moody & Hawkins (eds),

first hand of the turbulent state of the country during the Land War, he still did not appreciate the widespread disaffection and disillusionment with the law as administered in Ireland.

On 14 August 1882, Clifford Lloyd took up residence in Loughrea and on his arrival he was accompanied by 'an RM, several clerks, armed constables including four who were mounted and a few soldiers also armed'. The newspaper report described the mood in the town as despondent, with ratepayers fearing that they would not be able to pay the extra taxation related to the increased numbers of soldiers and police. It referred to Clifford Lloyd as 'a small man, [who] walks with his head stooped and though he is only about thirty-five or forty years of age [actually, thirty-eight] looks really as if the snows of sixty winters had fallen over his head. He appears very nervous and looks to the right and left when walking, like a hyena'.[28] In a speech delivered in Loughrea in September 1882, Clifford Lloyd claimed that 'it was not his intention or the intention of the government, whom he represented, to use any unnecessary harshness towards the people and that his mission was not one of oppression, but to restore law and order in Loughrea'.[29]

Despite his reputation for zealous attention to duty, Clifford Lloyd had already been looking elsewhere for a position. On 4 May 1882, he wrote to Spencer requesting employment in England or as a colonial governor. However, in the wake of the Phoenix Park murders, he withdrew the request.[30] He coveted the governorship of the Bahamas, but this post was awarded to his colleague SRM Blake, who was also awarded a knighthood. During 1883, Clifford Lloyd remained officially in post, although on prolonged sick leave. In September, the title of special resident magistrate was changed to divisional magistrate and Clifford Lloyd was not offered a post. It would appear, therefore, that his authoritarian attitude and public notoriety resulted in a reassessment of his suitability for postings requiring a more diplomatic approach. In a telegram dated 30 August 1883, Lord Granville at the war office sent Clifford Lloyd confirmation that he had been offered a post by the Egyptian government with a salary of £1,000 for six months' work. The post was that of inspector general for reform and it was attached to the ministry of the interior.[31] Following disagreements with the Egyptian authorities over his plans, he resigned the post at the end of May 1884 and returned to England. From March to November 1885, he returned for a brief period as RM for Co. Londonderry, before he achieved one of his ambitions, when he became lieutenant governor of Mauritius. Controversy arose with the governor, Sir John Pope Hennessy, and Clifford Lloyd resigned the post. His career ended as consul for Kurdistan. He died at Erzerum, Armenia, in June 1891.

Florence Arnold-Forster's Irish journal, p. 525. **28** *Western News*, 19 Aug. 1882. **29** *Western News*, 16 Sept. 1882. **30** BL, Spencer papers, 77080, Lloyd to Spencer, 4 May 1882. **31** BL, Spencer papers, 77080, telegram Lord Granville to Clifford Lloyd, 30 Aug. 1883.

After leaving Ireland, Clifford Lloyd had written a revealing letter to *The Times* in which his class and religious prejudices were evident. He expressed the opinion that 'the Northerners are essentially an orderly people (Belfast riots notwithstanding)' compared with 'the Southerners, [who are] the reverse'. He remarked that 'the Irish of the south and west are disloyal by tradition, impulsive, reckless, ignorant, emotional, priest-ridden and willing to be the slaves of the first who knows how to master them, and, as a consequence, are unstable, poor and forever in need'.[32] Throughout his tenure as resident magistrate and special resident magistrate, Clifford Lloyd made a determined effort to master the Irish nationalists but his tactics served to enrage rather than enslave.

---

32 *The Times*, 18 Mar. 1889 and quoted in Penny Bonsall, *The Irish RMs* (Dublin, n.d.), p. 39.

11 Political and social consequences of agrarian unrest in 1882

EVENTS LEADING TO THE RESIGNATION OF CHIEF SECRETARY FORSTER

Forster had come under sustained pressure in parliament regarding the failure of the PPP (Ireland) Act to stop outrages despite the arrest of so many Land League activists. In March 1882, Forster decided to undertake a tour of some of the 'disturbed areas' in Clare, Limerick and Galway. The first stop was Tulla in east Clare, which he described in a letter to Gladstone as 'the worst in Ireland – being possessed by a secret society, partly treasonable, partly murderous'.[1] During the tour, a number of extraordinary episodes occurred, not least when he gave an impromptu speech, in 'pithy and forcible terms', to a group of men sheltering in a shed from the rain, who listened to him in silence while he remonstrated with their 'silent acquiescence in the reign of terror organized by the agitators'.[2] He also visited Tulla Workhouse to speak to Michael Moroney, who had been shot by moonlighters near Feakle, and gave him a present of £10. Moroney died the following day. From Ennis, Forster travelled by train to Athenry, 'the worst bit of Galway', and held brief discussions with local people attending the weekly market.[3] His adopted son reported that people 'eyed him very curiously, but everyone has been civil enough'.[4] Civility clearly did not prevail in Gort, where a crowd gathered at the railway station 'headed by the priest of that district – a notorious Land Leaguer – groans and hoots, and cries of "Buckshot" rang out as the train went out of the station'.[5] The last stop was Tullamore, where he lectured a crowd from a hotel window regarding their duties to God and their lack of moral courage in failing to oppose those committing outrages.[6] His speech was in turn patronizing and blinkered in its perception of Irish concerns and demonstrated his own rigid concept of duty and the paramount importance of the law.

Forster continued to be perturbed by the number of agrarian homicides, seventy-five having been committed in the previous six months, which added to his alarm about the cessation of the PPP (Ireland) Act in September. In a letter to Gladstone, dated 7 April 1882, he proposed

> A vigorous and determined effort to secure convictions of men notoriously guilty. ... We cannot return to the old system of packing juries and tinkering; such a bitter system of challenging etc. may be an improve-

---

1 Wemyss Reid, *Life of Forster*, ii, p. 392.   2 Ibid., pp 393–4.   3 *Galway Express*, 4 Mar. 1882.
4 Wemyss Reid, *Life of Forster*, ii, p. 395.   5 Moody & Hawkins (eds), *Arnold-Forster's Irish journal*, p. 391.   6 Wemyss Reid, *Life of Forster*, ii, pp 398–403.

ment, but no cure for the present evil. I think we cannot stop short of taking temporary powers to try agrarian offences, without jury, by special legal commissioners. ... can we let this act expire? I dare not face the autumn and coming winter without it.[7]

He feared that secret societies were increasing their activities and thought further repressive legislation was needed.[8]

Political events progressed rapidly with the resignation of Lord Cowper as lord lieutenant and his replacement on 28 April 1882 by Earl Spencer. At the same time, an agreement was reached between Gladstone and Parnell. Known as the Kilmainham agreement, its main provisions were that:

a) the government would amend the Land Act 1881 to include tenants in arrears and
b) Parnell and his colleagues would endeavour to stop outrages.

Forster was dissatisfied with the agreement and when Parnell was released on 2 May, he submitted his resignation as chief secretary.

In May, the national incidence of outrages decreased to 401 and thereafter there was a progressive decline in the incidence of outrages throughout 1882 (table 8, p. 59).[9] The reduction in outrages accelerated from the introduction of the Prevention of Crime (Ireland) Act in mid-July 1882 with the statistics for Galway East Riding showing 131 outrages for the first half of 1882 and twenty-nine during the second half. The decline is attributable to several factors, including the imprisonment of many of the organizers of the Land League and their militant associates during the winter months. Although the release of suspects increased markedly from March 1882, it is likely that the activists' appetite for militant action was impaired by their sojourn in prison and the need to re-engage with their own occupations. The introduction in July 1882 of the repressive legislation that Forster had requested during the drafting of the Prevention of Crime Bill was also a factor in reducing the level of agitation. In addition, the failure of the 'No Rent' agitation and the decision of many tenant farmers to take their cases to the recently established land courts presaged the end of that phase of the Land War. The Kilmainham agreement also signalled a change in policy; it led to the establishment of the Irish National League in October 1882 and thereafter political efforts concentrated on parliamentary action and the achievement of home rule.

The decline of the agrarian agitation came too late to save Forster's position

---

7 Forster to Gladstone, 7 Apr. 1882, in Wemyss Reid, *Life of Forster*, ii, pp 417–18. 8 BL, Spencer papers, 77316A, memo to cabinet, 17 Apr. 1882. 9 BL, Spencer papers, 77314, memo by Courtney Boyle.

Political and social consequences of agrarian unrest in 1882 127

5 Loughrea prisoners released from Kilmainham Jail on 17 August 1882: back row (l–r): Patrick Morrissey, Peter Sweeny, Bernard Coyle, Patrick Sweeny, John McCarthy, unknown; second row: Martin Greene, Fardy O'Neill, William Delaney, William Manahan, Thomas Cunningham; front row: Patrick Kavanagh, Nicholas Barrett (original in possession of the family of the present author).

as chief secretary and within one month of taking office the new lord lieutenant, Earl Spencer, was able to write to Gladstone to inform him that:

> I can give a good report of crime, the daily returns show considerable improvement. I heard from Kerry and West Cork that there has not been a serious crime there for three weeks, much the same comes from Limerick, Clare, Galway and Mayo ... it seems a lull has generally set in and all think the word has gone forth that outrages are to cease.[10]

Spencer clearly believed that the Kilmainham agreement with Parnell was responsible for the improvement.

The number of arrests under the Coercion Act dwindled after March 1882, with the notable exception of July, when forty-seven were arrested, of which thirty-seven were taken into custody in the Loughrea police district, mainly in connection with the killings of Doherty, Blake and Ruane. During August and September, there were no further arrests and all the suspects had been released by the time the act lapsed at the end of September (fig. 5, above).

10 BL, Spencer papers, 76854, Spencer to Gladstone, 29 May 1882.

AGRARIAN DISTURBANCES, LIVING CONDITIONS AND EVICTIONS IN SOUTH GALWAY, FEBRUARY–OCTOBER 1882

In the early months of 1882, the Loughrea correspondent of the *Tuam News* regularly highlighted the disturbed state of the area. In February 1882, he reported that Lord Clanricarde and other owners of property in the Craughwell district had 'resorted to every form of terror in order to collect rent; processes and writs were served but none of the tenants was willing to pay and as a consequence several evictions took place'. One exception was John Donohue, who had paid rent and was then boycotted. He owned a corn mill and did a first-class business, but when the boycott started no one was willing to talk to him or enter his mill.[11] Threatening notices continued to be posted and one promised death to anyone taking a meadow from Walter Bourke. On 7 March, John Doherty was threatened with the same fate as his cousin Peter if he continued in the employment of Bourke.[12] In April, shots were fired into the house of a widow, Mary Burke, Caherfurrvaus, and potatoes were torn up and destroyed because she continued to herd for Michael Clasby.[13] This event provoked a great display of strength by the authorities, including the presence of the county inspector, a special resident magistrate, two sub inspectors and a large force of police who searched the surrounding country. Evictions continued, often accompanied by a great show of force by the police and military. The fact that the authorities acted with such vigour at the behest of landlords served only to strengthen the sense of victimhood in the local communities. In March, a man called Keary, from Craughwell, was evicted from his holding by a large force of military and police. This was quickly followed by the eviction of two families, the Sheridans and the Tullys, in Poulnabonny. Another eviction in Fiddane met with stern resistance and, in exchanges with the police, SI Alan Bell received head injuries.[14] During October 1881, a dispute over rent had occurred on land in Rathcosgrove, the property of a Mr Graham from Dublin. The estate was small and encumbered and the land poor.[15] Graham would allow only a small reduction in the rent, insisted on the full amount of arrears and threatened legal proceedings. In April 1882, the bailiff and sheriff, accompanied by a company of soldiers and police, commenced evictions. Following negotiations with Graham, he agreed to accept a 20 per cent reduction in the rent and also to cancel some of the arrears.[16] In Roveagh, at the end of that month, on land owned by Revd West, dean of Ardagh, ninety people from fourteen families were evicted and the doors and furniture were badly damaged to prevent repossession. It was later reported that

---

11 *Tuam News*, 17 Feb. 1882. 12 NLI, Parnell Special Commission, evidence of SI Alan Bell, i, p. 512. 13 Ibid. 14 *Tuam News*, 24 Mar. 1882. 15 Ibid. 16 *Tuam News*, 14 Apr. 1882

the families were sheltering in outhouses and sheds and were receiving support from the Craughwell Ladies' Land League.[17]

The Loughrea correspondent outlined the living conditions in the area. On a visit to Bookeen and Kiltulla, he observed a few scattered hovels, ruined homesteads and sheepwalks. Young people had emigrated in large numbers and the remainder were 'steeped in poverty' due to bad harvests and exorbitant rents. During the previous year, Lord Dunsandle had issued two hundred processes of ejectment but the majority of tenants avoided eviction by paying their rents. He described the parlous state of the parents of Patrick Keogh, who was in prison charged with the killing of James Connors in May 1881 (see above, p. 88). His father, born in 1798, was disabled and walked with the aid of crutches while his mother had been confined to bed for several years. The countryside between Loughrea and Craughwell was thinly populated and he described the homes in Caher, just outside Loughrea, as hovels.[18]

The disturbed state of Athenry during May is evident from a press report that enumerated the forces of the crown deployed there. There were thirty-six policemen, two mounted policemen, two sub inspectors and fifty soldiers under the command of Captain Snow.[19]

Also in May 1882, warnings were issued to Burton Persse's labourers, urging them to leave his employment unless he increased their wages. At Clostoken, five policemen were stationed in a police hut and the district around Craughwell 'was studded with police huts'. In Ballymana, notices were posted warning people not to rent farms from Mr Lynch JP. In June, immediately after Walter Bourke's killing, there were two death threats issued to John W. Lambert and another letter to John Doherty threatening him with his master's fate if he continued herding on the Bourke estate. Arms were stolen from a man called Denis Crowe by a moonlighting party and within a month of Walter Bourke's assassination in June, a wall on the estate was knocked down and warnings were issued regarding anyone attempting to rebuild it.[20]

On 30 October, a letter with a death threat was sent to Peter Doherty (Senior), if he sought compensation for his son's murder.[21] Also in October, on the estate of Peter Blake at Ganty near Craughwell, evictions were carried out under the protection of RM de Vere Pery, SI Bell and a large number of police. Local opinion considered that the appropriate rent should be eight shillings per acre rather than the actual rent being charged, which was between thirty and thirty-five shillings per acre. Observing the proceedings were three members of the Craughwell Land League, Patrick Cawley PLG, Nicholas Barrett and his brother Edward. The first person evicted was Michael Mack, who occupied

---

17 *Tuam News*, 5 May 1882.   18 *Tuam News*, 20 Apr. 1882.   19 *Tuam News*, 26 May 1882.
20 NLI, Parnell Special Commission, witness statement of DI Alan Bell, i, p. 512.   21 Ibid.

thirteen acres valued at £7 10s., on which he paid £18 rent per annum. Mack, who was married with a wife and nine children, lived in a small thatched house and owed two years' rent. Cawley appealed to the agent, John Blake, the magistrate de Vere Pery and SI Bell, but to no avail. The decision was that the law should take its course. However, after a further forceful appeal, Mack was allowed to re-enter his house as caretaker. James Fleming, a father of seven, lived on fourteen acres that were valued at £10 10s., and his annual rent was £21. At the time of the eviction, Fleming was working as a labourer some 10km away, trying to earn enough to maintain his family. Cawley offered one year's rent, on Fleming's behalf. This offer was accepted and Fleming was also allowed back as a caretaker. James Treacy occupied ten acres with his family and his parents. Following the eviction, his father, who was infirm, had to be taken to the workhouse in Loughrea, despite his wife's appeal to the agent, 'Ah John, ah John, ní ceart duit an éagcoir seo a tharraingt orainn'.[22] During the following months, the events at Ganty were used to castigate the members of the Galway Blazers when they assembled for their hunts.

22 *Tuam News*, 17 Oct. 1882. Translation: 'Ah John, ah John, it was not right to bring this injustice upon us'.

12 The Prevention of Crime (Ireland) Act 1882

In December 1881, John W. Byrne, RM in Loughrea, had reported that the numbers of police and patrols were unable to cope with the disturbed nature of the area. In a letter to the chief secretary's office, he outlined a number of provisions that he considered necessary to tackle the increased prevalence of crime. Many of his suggestions were subsequently incorporated in the Prevention of Crime (Ireland) Act 1882, commonly known as the Crimes Act.

The act, one of the most oppressive of all the coercion acts of the nineteenth century, was introduced to parliament by Sir William Harcourt, the home secretary in the immediate aftermath of the Phoenix Park assassinations of Thomas Burke and Lord Cavendish on 6 May 1882. Irish MPs vigorously opposed the provisions of the act in debates that featured bitter exchanges. It came into effect on 13 July 1882 in sixteen counties, including all the Connacht counties, and three days later three more counties and the city of Galway were added.

PRINCIPAL PROVISIONS OF THE CRIMES ACT

The principal provisions of the act were as follows

Sections 1–4	approved the establishment of a special commission of judges to try agrarian and political cases without a jury. They also gave authority to the attorney general to direct that certain criminal cases be tried before special juries.
Section 6	gave the attorney general the power to change the venues of trials. It allowed for payment of defence counsel and the expenses of defence witnesses.
Section 7	made provision for summary prosecution of intimidation and incitement to intimidation. It also applied to editors and proprietors of newspapers accused of incitement. This section was applied to the whole country, not just to the disturbed areas.
Section 8	allowed summary jurisdiction over public order offences such as riot and unlawful assembly, taking and holding forcible possession, aggravated assault and assault on police and bailiffs.
Section 10	gave power to the lord lieutenant to prohibit by proclamation any meeting which he had 'reason to believe to be dangerous to the public peace or public safety'.

Sections 11–12   gave the power to impose curfews and to arrest on suspicion.
Section 13   provided for the seizure of publications containing 'matter inciting to the commission of treason or of any act of violence or intimidation'.
Section 14   allowed searches at night.
Section 16   provided for detailed preliminary investigation of serious crimes.

ADMINISTRATION OF THE CRIMES ACT

Even before the Crimes Act became law, troops were deployed to aid the police, particularly in the disturbed areas. Additional troops were sent to Ireland and by 1 May 1882 the number had increased to 28,653 from 25,763 in the previous year.[1] The companies usually comprised fifty soldiers commanded by two officers. They participated in protection duties, thus freeing police to conduct their normal duties, and they also had a duty in aid of the police that was first requested by Clifford Lloyd. The war office gave its authorization, 'on the understanding that the men shall remain under the general command of their officers, and that a commissioned officer and a certain number of non-commissioned officers should accompany the soldiers'.[2] Mounted patrols had an intimidatory effect on the local population because of their high visibility but their value in preventing outrages was questionable. The fact that a detachment of fifty soldiers could only provide four patrols per week also limited their effectiveness. The Army Act of 1881 was employed for the acquisition of vehicles in places where the troops were boycotted and, in addition, long cars and brakes were purchased in order to improve the mobility of patrols and the transport of prisoners.[3]

NOTES ON CERTAIN SECTIONS OF THE CRIMES ACT

Sections 1–4   approved the establishment of a special commission of judges to try agrarian and political cases without a jury and gave authority to the attorney general to direct that certain criminal cases be tried before special juries.

The special commission of judges to hear cases without a jury was strongly opposed by the lord chancellor, Hugh Law, and the judges, and it was never

---

[1] NAI CSO RP 1883/2214, memo of Ross of Bladenburg. [2] NAI CSO RP 1883/2214.
[3] Ibid.

implemented. However, a Dublin commission was established in which special juries tried cases transferred by the attorney general from other parts of the country. Anticipating the passage of the act, George Otto Trevelyan, the new chief secretary, wrote to the lord lieutenant requesting a list of people awaiting trial for agrarian offences: 'The thing I am now far the most anxious about is to have all the arrears of murder and outrage tried under the new tribunals'.[4] On the previous day, the assistant under secretary for crime, Henry Brackenbury, had written to Trevelyan, enclosing a report from SI Horne, who was in charge of the Letterfrack murder case.[5] The report stated that a man called Patrick Walsh was due to be tried for the killing of John Lyden and his son Martin. SI Horne advised that the juries of Galway are

> so demoralised by fear owing to the recent outrages and the general state of intimidation which prevails, that not only no jury dare find Pat Walsh guilty, but that no one man on such a jury dare propose to find him guilty, and that there is a certainty of acquittal.

Brackenbury supported Horne's advice and argued strongly for a change of venue and stated that the law adviser, John Naish, and the under secretary, Sir Robert Hamilton, approved. The Walsh case was transferred to the Dublin Commission in August 1882 and, although the jury disagreed in the first trial, he was retried, found guilty and hanged in Galway Jail on 22 September 1882.

The composition of the juries in this case is of interest. At the first trial, there were eleven Protestants and one Roman Catholic and the second jury was composed entirely of Protestants.[6] Brackenbury expressed the opinion that if Pat Walsh was convicted, further evidence might be forthcoming in the trial of his brother, Michael, charged with the same crime.[7] During the selection of the jury for Michael's trial two individuals asked to be excused on the grounds that they had served on the jury in the trial that found Patrick guilty. Judge Lawson ruled that this was not a sufficient cause for exemption and directed that they should serve on the jury. However, the prisoner's counsel successfully challenged their participation.[8] Michael Walsh was found guilty and sentenced to death. The jury made a strong recommendation for mercy on the grounds of the prisoner's youth and because he did not fire the fatal shot.[9] The death sentence was commuted and he was given a sentence of penal servitude for life.

A number of other Galway cases were transferred to the Dublin Commission. Michael Flynn and Patrick and Thomas Higgins were convicted of the killing of Joseph Huddy and his grandson on the Ardilaun estate. They were hanged in Galway Jail in January 1883. The most notorious case heard at the Dublin

4 BL, Spencer papers, 76946, Trevelyan to Spencer, 9 July 1882. 5 NAI CSO RP 1882/28047.
6 NAI CSO RP 1882/44750. 7 NAI CSO RP 1891/28047, Brackenbury to Trevelyan (copy), 8 July 1882. 8 *Freeman's Journal*, 28 Sept. 1882. 9 *Freeman's Journal*, 30 Sept. 1882.

Commission in November 1882 was that of the prisoners charged with the Maamtrasna killings. Myles and Patrick Joyce and Patrick Casey were convicted and hanged in Galway Jail in December 1882. Two approvers[10] were set free and five other prisoners were sentenced to life imprisonment.[11] The leading crown prosecutor was James Murphy QC, who was paid the princely sum of £486 for his achievements[12] and promoted shortly afterwards to the bench. Another trial to arouse considerable controversy was that of Francis Hynes, who was charged with the killing of John Doloughty near Ennis, Co. Clare. At the selection of the jury, the crown solicitor for Co. Clare, Alexander Murphy, asked all Roman Catholics and those of liberal principles to stand aside and a further twenty-six were challenged by the crown counsel. Additional concerns arose following allegations of rowdy and drunken behaviour by jury members at their hotel on the night before Hynes was convicted. This aspect received wide publicity in a letter from William O'Brien to the *Freeman's Journal*.[13] A judicial enquiry was held but it did not alter the conviction and hanging of Hynes.

In his analysis of the effect of the Crimes Act on agrarian crime, the then attorney general, John Naish, stated that it was impossible to obtain convictions in nine counties, namely Clare, Kerry, Limerick, Galway, Roscommon, Westmeath, King's County (Offaly), Tipperary and Meath. Naish singled out Clare, Limerick and Kerry, where he considered there was 'a glaring failure of justice' because the panels were mainly composed of farmers. Trial venues were most commonly changed to Dublin in sixty-nine cases, Cork in forty cases and Sligo in nineteen. The venue was changed in eleven of the twelve Galway cases. There were 350 cases in which either the venue was changed or special juries were obtained. In a further 177 cases there was no order for a change of venue but special juries served and several of these cases were heard at the winter assizes which effectively resulted in a change of venue. For instance, the Connacht cases were tried at the winter assizes in Sligo and Carrick-on-Shannon and for Munster the winter assizes were held in Cork. Between 1 January 1880 and July 1882, forty-seven murders were deemed to be agrarian or political in nature. Convictions were obtained in twenty cases, with special juries acting in all of them and in a further thirteen cases the venue was changed.[14]

Whereas the detection rate for agrarian crime remained low, the success of the change of venue and provision of special juries can be gauged from the fact that during the winter assizes of 1882, 52 per cent of cases resulted in conviction. When change of venue cases were analysed separately, there was a 79 per cent conviction rate. In relation to the Galway cases tried at the Dublin Commission between July and December 1882, fifteen individuals were charged

10 An approver was someone who participated in a crime and afterward became an informer. 11 Waldron, *Maamtrasna: the murders and the mystery*. 12 NAI CSO LB 403, crown solicitor's letter book. 13 *Freeman's Journal*, 14 Aug. 1882. 14 NAI CSO RP 1891/28047, memo by Rt Hon. John Naish on sections 4–6 of the Prevention of Crime (Ireland) Act 1882.

with agrarian murders. Two of them became approvers and thirteen were convicted and sentenced to death. Of these, six had the death sentences commuted to life imprisonment and the remaining seven were hanged.[15] In the case of the Craughwell prisoners, the change of venue from Galway to Sligo and the trials before special juries resulted in guilty verdicts for both men.[16]

When the renewal of the Crimes Act was under consideration in 1885, Earl Spencer commented in a memo for cabinet that both provisions in relation to trial venues and special juries should be retained, because 'without them it would not be possible to secure convictions in any political or agrarian case'.[17]

Section 7   made provision for the summary prosecution of intimidation and incitement to intimidation. It also applied to editors and proprietors of newspapers accused of incitement. This section was applied to the whole country, not just to the disturbed areas.

During 1880 and 1881, boycotting became widespread and was strongly approved of by the national leaders of the Land League. The successful use of this tactic depended on unified community support for Land League objectives and an abhorrence of land grabbing. This unity was not always achieved because of the disparate interests of large farmers, small farmers, labourers, shopkeepers and other town dwellers, but when unity was achieved it constituted a formidable social weapon. An early success was the boycotting of Murty Hynes followed by his rapid capitulation to the power of social ostracism in September 1880 (see above, pp 35–6). This episode had a peaceful outcome but on many other occasions there were not only threats of violence but also their implementation. The legal difficulties associated with the successful prosecution of those involved in boycotting had been evident for some years. In December 1880, Edward Fowler, JP of Cleaghmore, Ballinasloe, asked for the law adviser's opinion regarding the legality of the practice. In the course of his reply, John Naish stated that

> The mere passive refusal of a shopkeeper or other person to deal with the person boycotted is not an offence criminally punishable. [However,] if threats or intimidation are addressed to third parties for the purpose of preventing them dealing with the person boycotted, the instigators could be proceeded against under various existing laws.[18]

One of the aims of the PPP (Ireland) Act 1881 had been to prevent boycotting and 462 (47 per cent) of the arrests under the act cited intimidation and boycotting. In the Loughrea and Athenry police districts, 63 (52 per cent) of the

---

[15] NAI CSO RP 1883/2142, verdicts in Crimes Act trials.   [16] Finnegan, *The case of the Craughwell prisoners*, pp 95–102.   [17] BL, Spencer papers, 77314.   [18] NAI CSO RP 1880/32524, Fowler to U.S. Burke, 18 Dec. 1880 and reply of J. Naish, 24 Dec. 1880.

arrests were in this category. Nevertheless, boycotting and intimidation continued throughout the winter of 1881 and the spring of 1882, and very few convictions were obtained because of lack of evidence and the unwillingness of victims to appear in court. It is no surprise, therefore, that Spencer was very keen that intimidation should be included in the Crimes Act and that incitement to intimidation should be regarded as an offence.[19]

An early prosecution for intimidation under the Crimes Act was that of Michael Fallon (Loughrea) for an assault on Thomas Carty and also for intimidating him in order to prevent him from erecting police huts. The injuries sustained appear to have been trivial, but Fallon's attitude was described as very menacing and threatening, although one witness claimed that Carty was the aggressor. In finding Fallon guilty, RM Byrne stated 'happily the Prevention of Crime Act was passed and was in force in this county, and the state of society, the condition of the town and district called forth for the strictest enforcement of that act'. Fallon was sentenced to three months' imprisonment.[20] A sentence of six months was possible under the Crimes Act, but more commonly the sentences were for shorter periods.

By the end of 1882, 346 persons had been prosecuted for intimidation and two hundred were convicted and at the end of 1884 there had been 985 prosecutions and 572 convictions.[21] The effectiveness of this section of the act is evident in the police and resident magistrates' reports for December 1882 and January 1883 in which they recorded a marked decline in boycotting. HC McAlumney (Gort) reported no fresh cases of boycotting and cited only the cases of a shopkeeper called John Forrest and a farm belonging to Mrs Lahiff at Caherbroder.[22] In January 1883, Clifford Lloyd reported that 'boycotting is dying out and intimidation is not practised on any organized scale', although there were isolated instances. However, he went on to comment on the number of boycotted farms that were lying idle, an example of the 'terror the Land League has left behind'.[23]

When renewal of the Prevention of Crime Act was under consideration in 1885, DM Andrew Reed claimed that section 7 suppressed intimidation of persons who came forward as witnesses for the crown. To support his claim, he cited the statistics for crime in the western division. Between 1 June 1880 and 12 July 1882, there had been eight hundred serious agrarian offences, an annual average of 320. From the introduction of the Crimes Act on 14 July 1882 to 1 May 1885, 252 serious crimes occurred at an annual average of ninety-two. Although this demonstrated a marked reduction in the prevalence of agrarian crimes, there was only a modest improvement in the conviction rate from 13 per cent to 20 per cent for the same periods.[24] This outcome would suggest that

19 BL, Spencer papers, 76854, Spencer to Gladstone (copy), 29 May 1882. 20 *Western News*, 5 Aug. 1882. 21 Ball, *Policing the Land War*, p. 379. 22 NAI CSO RP 1883/300, FCR, W Div., 31 Dec. 1882. 23 NAI CSO RP 1883/2886, FCR, W Div., 31 Jan. 1883. 24 NAI CSO

intimidation of witnesses was a continuing problem for the authorities. The lord lieutenant, Earl Spencer, was also convinced of the importance of section 7.

> This is the only check on boycotting and intimidation. The dropping of the clause would give an impetus to the operations of the League and it would be represented to the members that boycotting was no longer a crime.[25]

Section 7 as applied to editors and proprietors of newspapers accused of incitement.[26]

In the latter part of the nineteenth century, local nationalist papers played a vital role in the politicization of the public through the dissemination of national and local news. During the Land War, they published long and detailed reports of speeches at Land League meetings and the proceedings of court cases. Trenchant criticism of Dublin Castle, the police, magistracy, landlords and their agents was a regular feature. Government antipathy to the nationalist press had been evident for some time on the grounds that it was dangerous to peace and order in the country. During Clifford Lloyd's tenure as special resident magistrate in Galway, he became well acquainted with the local press, which regularly criticized and taunted him. The *Tuam News* frequently commented on his physical deformities that were probably attributable to chronic gout. In early 1883, Clifford Lloyd stated

> A treasonable press seriously impedes the work in which we are engaged. Indeed, it is difficult to conceive the amount of harm done and even crime committed from the writings in such papers as the *Tuam News*.[27]

It is not surprising, therefore, that the government tried to control the press through legislation and the Crimes Act was employed to suppress newspapers and prosecute editors and proprietors. The most outspoken nationalist papers in Co. Galway were the *Tuam News* and the *Western News*, which was published in Ballinasloe, and the editors of both papers were prosecuted under section 7 of the Crimes Act in 1882–3.

As early as 1879, the RIC had been instructed by Dublin Castle to examine articles published on the land agitation and to report any papers that encouraged crime, the non-payment of rent or sedition.[28] After the proclamation of the

---

RP 1885/5600. 25 BL, Spencer papers, 77314, memo to cabinet, 25 Dec. 1885. 26 For a detailed discussion on Dublin Castle and the nationalist press, see Stephen Ball, *Policing the Land War*, pp 93–112; Marie-Louise Legg, *The Irish provincial press, 1850–92* (Dublin, 1999). 27 NAI CSO RP 1883/7913, Lloyd to Jenkinson, 27 Mar. 1883. 28 NAI CSO RP 1879/9495

Land League in October 1881, the authorities had utilized existing powers to ban *United Ireland*. In the following August, Richard Kelly, proprietor and editor of the *Tuam Herald*, was charged under one of the earlier statutes that allowed imprisonment for not less than three years and not exceeding ten years. Kelly was a member of the Land League executive and a man of conservative opinions. He was charged with printing a letter by James Redpath, an American reporter and frequent visitor to Ireland during the Land War. Mr William French Henderson, sessional crown solicitor, prosecuted and said that the crown had ordered the prosecution in order to show other papers that 'the red flag of slaughter could not be flaunted abroad with impunity'.[29] The letter was originally published in the *Toledo Blade* and appeared in the *Tuam Herald* on 15 July 1882. The charge stated that the article encouraged individuals to murder landlords. The letter recalled the killing of Walter Bourke and Corporal Robert Wallace and Bourke's highhanded behaviour as a landlord. It referred to the article in the *Illustrated London News*[30] that contained 'a picture of this dead ruffian in the act of serving processes on his tenants' while holding a gun. It went on to state that this person was a magistrate and that 'if any peasant had presented a loaded pistol at the head of any landlord he would have been sent to jail with hard labour for five to seven years. But magistrates and landlords can commit these and kindred outrages with absolute impunity in Ireland'.[31] Kelly defended the publication of the letter and stated that he would continue to publish such correspondence.[32] However, at the special petty sessions in Tuam on 5 August 1882, Kelly blamed his foreman for the publication, stating that it had been done without his knowledge and he repudiated its contents. Nevertheless, he was sent for trial and allowed bail of £25.[33] Soon afterwards, the crown, without stating a reason, decided not to pursue the case.[34]

John McPhilpin, editor and proprietor of the *Tuam News*, was prosecuted under the Crimes Act for three articles 'of an intimidatory character' that had been published during 1882. The main focus was on articles published under the heading 'Loughrea Jottings' contributed by the Loughrea correspondent, James McDermot, who had been arrested as a suspect after the killing of Blake and Ruane. At the time of the trial, he was again in prison following the events at a proclaimed meeting at Ballymana (see below, p. 148). McDermot's articles were frequently hostile towards Clanricarde and his agent Blake and toward other local landlords such as the Dalys and Persses. The language employed was often very abusive; for example,

> In this very town [Craughwell], the fearful spectacle of eviction has been witnessed on the property of that execrable tyrant 'Clanrackrent' by the

in 1879/10454. **29** *Freeman's Journal*, 7 Aug. 1882. **30** *Illustrated London News*, 14 May 1881. **31** *Tuam Herald*, 15 July 1882. **32** *Tuam Herald*, 22 July 1882. **33** *Tuam News*, 11 Aug. 1882. **34** *Tuam News*, 18 Aug. 1882.

edict of that cruel, shaking, shivering old exterminator, Shawn Beagh (John Henry Blake), and under the immediate superintendence of the crooked, cadaverous, sneaking bailiff'.[35]

The first article cited in the prosecution was published on 8 December and described the eviction of Mrs Corless and her nine children, including a baby a few months old, by a landowner called Denis Deely at New Inn. The article referred to the 'horrid record of landlordism' and reported comments from the crowd such as 'Your stock will rot before you get anyone to herd for you in this district. You and the like of you are Ireland's ruin – beggars who aspire to be gentlemen at the expense of humanity and decency'. During the eviction, a sum of £10 was collected for the family, 'a fitting answer to those who say that our people are indifferent as to the clear sweeping away of landlordism'.[36] This was language that could be considered mild in the context of the eviction of a woman and her helpless family.

The second article reported the visit of Algernon Persse, agent for his father Dudley, to the holding of Michael Fallon (Moneen), who had been evicted in 1880 (see above, p. 56). Persse, accompanied by a number of policemen, demanded the departure of the family. On 4 December, the case was brought to court at Ardrahan and when Mrs Fallon offered to pay the full rent, Persse replied 'No, I will not take the rent. I will not admit them as tenants under any consideration – out they must go. I press for the full penalty'. The court chairman fined Fallon forty shillings.[37] The third article led to a charge of 'using and inciting others to use intimidation' towards Walter Lambert of Castle Ellen because he had enforced payment of rent due to him.

The papers relating to all three articles were referred to John Naish, the law adviser, and his opinion was that a charge could be maintained under section 7 in respect of using and inciting others to use intimidation against Denis Deely for an act he had a legal right to do, namely to take possession of a farm to which he was entitled. Naish went on to say that his opinion was very much influenced by the fact that

> the country around Loughrea is in a disturbed and dangerous state – and the writing of such denunciatory statements in reference to individuals has a direct tendency to expose them to danger and consequently to intimidate them by putting them in a state of apprehension. Under ordinary circumstances, mere denunciation could not or at least ought not be dealt with under the Crimes Act, but in a place like Loughrea, I think this is different.[38]

35 *Tuam News*, 14 Apr., 8 and 15 Dec. 1882, copies in NAI CSO RP 1891/28047. 36 *Tuam News*, 8 Dec. 1882. 37 *Tuam News*, 15 Dec. 1882. 38 NAI CSO RP 1891/28047.

On 1 January 1883, McPhilpin was tried before a special court in Tuam, found guilty and sentenced to two months' imprisonment. He was paraded through the streets of Galway en route to jail in Mullingar, dressed in prison garb and handcuffed like a common criminal. The reporters jailed for their part in the Clostoken and Ballymana meetings (see below, p. 148), including James McDermot, who had written the offending articles, accompanied him on the train journey.

The third prosecution was that of John Callanan, proprietor and editor of the *Western News*, on 1 December 1883. Earl Spencer expressed his displeasure that the case was taken without the approval of Dublin Castle.[39] The offending article had been published in the issue of 27 October and was deemed to have intimidated John Crehan from herding for Philip Smith of Colemanstown, Ballinasloe. Crehan had taken the position in Colemanstown previously held by Pat Byrne, a prominent organizer of the Shepherds' Association,[40] who had been dismissed by Philip Smith. As a result, a number of other herds and labourers employed by Smith had refused to work for him anymore. A police hut and extra police were sent to Colemanstown because Crehan said he was 'in mortal terror of the local people'. Callanan was convicted and sentenced to two weeks in jail.[41]

Like many of the provisions of the Crimes Act, the attempt to muzzle the press served only to foster antipathy to perceived tyrannical government policies. It is probable that the prosecutions of editors and proprietors enhanced the popularity and influence of publications that continued to promote the activities of the Irish National League during the second phase of the Land War. The papers, therefore, played a very important part in the development of a national consciousness. There is little doubt that they also had a definite subversive role because of their support for radical nationalist opinion and actions.

Section 8   allowed summary jurisdiction over public order offences such as riot and unlawful assembly, taking and holding forcible possession, aggravated assault and assault on police and bailiffs.

Before the Crimes Act, these offences rarely led to guilty verdicts because of the sympathetic attitude of juries. From July 1882, however, resident magistrates delivered summary judgments often after perfunctory court proceedings and inadequate legal representation for defendants. The first of several examples in Loughrea occurred in early September when HC Payne arrested Nicholas Barrett. He was charged with 'assembly with bad and notorious characters' even though SI Barry refused to identify who they were. In the eyes of the police,

---

39 NAI, Prevention of Crime (Ireland) Act 1882, carton 6.   40 The South and East Galway Shepherds' Association was founded in 1882 and it was based in Loughrea. It functioned as a trade union representing the interests of herds: see Cunningham, 'A spirit of self-preservation'. 41 NAI CSO RP 1891/28047.

merely living in Loughrea at that time meant inevitable contact with 'bad and notorious characters'. Barrett, an ex-suspect, was brought before RM de Vere Pery and RM Sir Harry Goodricke at the Loughrea Petty Sessions and de Vere Pery suggested that he should leave Loughrea but Barrett refused, saying that he would like to take up his previous job in the post office or start a business. He was released on bail of £20 and two sureties of £10 each, to be of good behaviour for six months.[42]

Another example of harassment of ex-suspects occurred in Loughrea when John Sweeny and Thomas Cunningham were charged at Loughrea Petty Sessions with having unlawfully assaulted and obstructed Sub Constable McDonagh on 2 November. McDonagh said he observed a crowd of people on Dunkellin Street obstructing the footpath. He told them to go away and he was then approached by Sweeny, who jostled him. Sweeny asked why he was interfering with people coming out of his public house and accused him of being drunk. The constable promptly arrested Sweeny for assault. On the way to the police barracks, Thomas Cunningham caught McDonagh by the arm and told him to release the prisoner. An eyewitness, William Ryan, gave evidence that McDonagh was drunk and staggering on the footpath. The bench retired to the magistrate's room and after a few minutes they returned verdicts of guilty, stating that 'on no account were the police to be interfered with in [the] discharge of their duty'. Sweeny was fined forty shillings and when he gave notice of appeal it was disallowed because the fine was not in excess of £2.[43]

The successful application of this part of section 8 is evident from the reduction in cases during 1883 and the achievement of an increased number of convictions. During the first year of its operation, 280 persons were prosecuted and two thirds were convicted and imprisoned, usually for a period of one month, in order to prevent the appeal of the sentence. The reduction in the level of disturbance leading to the pacification of the country can be inferred from the annual figure of 147 for 1883 compared with 246 prosecutions in the second half of 1882.[44]

Section 8   in relation to taking and holding of forcible possession.

The defence of property rights was the reason for the inclusion of this clause and it addressed the repossession of properties by evicted persons. These occasions often resulted in violent confrontations with the police. The case of Michael Fallon was dealt with in chapter 5 (see above, pp 56–8) and a similar case of serial evictions, repossessions and imprisonments occurred in relation to Patrick Healy of Boherduff, who was evicted by Lord Clanricarde on 15 November 1883.[45]

42 *Tuam News*, 8 Sept. 1882.   43 *Tuam News*, 11 Nov. 1882.   44 Quoted in Ball, *Policing the Land War*, Appendix 7, p. 379.   45 NAI CSO RP 1885/4374, report of DM Andrew Reed.

Between July 1882 and June 1885, 813 persons were prosecuted under this heading, resulting in 448 convictions.[46] The marked increase in evictions during the Land War and individual cases such as those discussed here had a dramatic effect on public opinion and raised the spectre of eviction for the whole community. The public perception was that the letter of the law was applied with vigour and the rights of property were upheld through the persecution of unfortunate families. The authorities seemed to be blind to the effect on public opinion of such callous behaviour and did not appreciate the contempt for the law that was inevitably engendered.

Section 10   gave power to the lord lieutenant to prohibit by proclamation any meeting that he had 'reason to believe to be dangerous to the public peace or public safety'.

In December 1882, this section was used to prohibit meetings in Clostoken and Ballymana. Magistrates and police dispersed the meeting at Clostoken (see below, p. 148). Edward and Nicholas Barrett, Thomas Cunningham and James McDermot were arrested. At their trial in Loughrea, they informed the court that they were present at the meeting in order to report the proceedings for local and national papers. However, they were convicted and given sentences for periods of three to four weeks in jail.[47] Following the meeting in Ballymana (see below, pp 148–50), thirty participants were jailed for three weeks on charges of riotous behaviour.[48]

Section 11   gave power to impose curfews.

An example of the draconian powers available to the police was the arrest of two tailors, Patrick Burke from Ballinasloe and James Mackey from Loughrea. They were charged at Loughrea Petty Sessions with being abroad after curfew time at 10.30pm without an adequate explanation. Sub Constable Christian testified that, when he asked them why they were out, they replied 'they were going out on patrol'. RM Byrne declared that section 11 met their case 'most rigorously' and clearly did not appreciate their levity and their claim that they were ignorant of the provisions of the Crimes Act. A three-month prison sentence could be imposed but as it was the first case tried in Loughrea, Byrne magnanimously imposed a sentence of one month with hard labour.[49]

Another incident occurred in Athenry on 15 August, when Owen Doherty and two others were arrested at 10.30pm. The accused gave contradictory accounts of their movements and only one sentence of one month in jail was

---

46 Ball, *Policing the Land War*, Appendix 7.   **47** *Western News*, 30 Dec. 1882.   **48** *Western News*, 7 Jan. 1883.   **49** *Western News*, 5 Aug. 1882.

handed down. Two weeks later, Nicholas Barrett was arrested in Kilrickle under section 11. He had helped some friends with the harvest of crops and later that night he was enjoying a celebration. The charge was absence from his dwelling at an hour after sunset. He was brought before Mr Hardy, JP of Dartfield, and remanded to Galway Jail for eight days on unspecified charges. Clifford Lloyd intervened and ordered his release from jail.[50]

In November, Barrett wrote to the *Tuam News*, complaining about the harassment of ex-suspects by means of frequent nocturnal raids that had occurred in Kiltulla, Derryhoyle, Killeenadeema and elsewhere. Tim Healy MP raised the matter in parliament when he asked about similar occurrences in Millstreet, Co. Cork. In reply, Chief Secretary Trevelyan merely said that it occurred occasionally that the police visited houses of people who were suspected of being out at night.[51]

Section 11 was not used very frequently in Co. Galway and conviction rates were low. In Galway East Riding, between July 1882 and 31 December 1884, twenty-five people were arrested and only four were imprisoned. However, the clause almost certainly had a preventative effect on agrarian incidents, with individuals fearing arrest if they were found abroad at night.

Section 12   gave the power to arrest on suspicion.

The facile manner in which this section was employed is illustrated by the case of Coleman Naughton, a native of the Aran Islands, who had been arrested under the Coercion Act on 25 January 1882 and imprisoned in Omagh and Kilmainham jails. Patrick Sweeny befriended him in Kilmainham and they conversed in Irish throughout their stay. On their release Sweeny invited him to Loughrea for a holiday and on the morning after his arrival Naughton decided to take a walk beside the lake. While returning from his walk, he met a constable of the RIC and was questioned about his business. He was attired in traditional Aran clothes and he replied to the questioning in Irish, a language the policeman did not understand. The constable decided that he was probably French and brought him to the police barracks. Fortunately, an Irish speaker was available to interpret Naughton's explanations and Naughton was released but told to leave Loughrea immediately.[52]

The arrest of strangers also occurred in the celebrated case of Henry George, an American newspaper reporter, and James Lee Joynes, an assistant master at Eton College.[53] On the evening of 8 August 1882, having travelled from Ballinasloe, where they had an interview with Matthew Harris, they arrived in Loughrea and RM Byrne ordered their arrest. Their papers were examined and,

50 *Western News*, 16 Sept. 1882.   51 *Tuam News*, 10 Nov. 1882.   52 *Western News*, 2 Sept. 1882.   53 An extended account of the affair was published by J.L. Joynes, 'Adventures of a tourist in Ireland' in Davitt, *The fall of feudalism* (1904), pp 421–6.

as nothing to suggest a criminal intent was found, they were discharged. They travelled to Athenry and Mr George met Thomas Madden, who was under boycott because he took part of an evicted farm, and John Broderick, an ex-suspect released in April. DI Alan Bell regarded these meetings as highly suspicious and he arrested Henry George on the station platform. A search of George's papers revealed the names and addresses of the 'most prominent agitators in Ireland and notes on persons under police protection in the Athenry area, which were considered prejudicial to their safety'. The magistrate took a more sensible view of the evidence than Bell and ordered the release of George.[54]

THE CONSEQUENCES OF THE ADMINISTRATION OF THE CRIMES ACT

The powers available under the Crimes Act hastened the decline in outrages and by the end of August 1882, Clifford Lloyd, in the Fortnightly Crime Report, noted a most marked improvement in Loughrea and surrounding districts. He stated that no outrage had occurred for two months and that this was attributable to the intensive police and military presence. He also commented on the importance of 'the firm administration of the law lately in Dublin,[55] the fearless tone of the judges' remarks and the failure to intimidate juries'.[56] In the FCR for December, he advocated the banning of all public meetings in proclaimed districts in order to 'restore public order and the government's authority'.[57] RM de Vere Pery stated that the Loughrea area was 'very peaceable and quiet' and there were no outrages to report. Boycotting was decreasing and although threatening letters continued to be written they were sent less frequently. He advised that the Land and Labour Leagues had merged into the Irish National League and a secret society still existed with its headquarters in Loughrea. In Clifford Lloyd's opinion, however, 'superficially during the past fortnight there has been peace in the west – but I am bound to add that it is what must be called an armed peace'. He concluded with the comment that 'no crime has been committed in the district since June'. Spencer's response reflected his trust in Clifford Lloyd and his unwavering support:

> It is well to see the views of one who had the experience of the National Land League during the last few years in the worst parts of Ireland. At present the elements of power which made the Land League so formidable are absent. The farmers are tired of agitation, they fear the labourers and money not coming from America. The National League

54 NAI CSO RP 1885/4374, report of DM Andrew Reed.   55 A reference to the use of the Dublin Commission to achieve convictions.   56 NAI CSO RP 1882/44222, FCR, W Div., Lloyd, 31 Aug. 1882.   57 NAI CSO RP 1882/46921, FCR, W Div., 15 Dec. 1882.

will need very careful watching and in districts like Loughrea and Tulla meetings must not be permitted.⁵⁸

In 1885, DM Andrew Reed echoed the hopes of the government when the Crimes Act was introduced that the restoration of peace and order had enabled farmers to avail of the benefits of the 1881 Land Act.⁵⁹

58 Ibid. 59 NAI CSO RP 1885/5600, Reed to under secretary, 11 May 1885.

13 The foundation of the Irish National League

On 17 October 1882, the Irish National League was founded in Dublin at a meeting attended by Parnell, Davitt, Dillon and other veterans of the Irish National Land League. Four days before that, a county land convention had been held in Athenry. The attendance included many of the local activists of the early phase of the Land War who had been imprisoned as suspects under the PPP (Ireland) Act of 1881. Among those present were Matthew Harris and James Kilmartin (Ballinasloe), Peter Broderick, Patrick C. Kelly, Michael Connolly and Anthony McGann (Athenry), John McCarthy, Thomas Cunningham, John Sweeny, Patrick Kennedy, William Delaney and Andrew Keary (Loughrea), Michael Glennon (Kilchreest), Patrick Cawley, William O'Loughlin, Edward and Nicholas Barrett (Craughwell), Thomas Cunniffe (Carrigan), Thomas and Patrick Monaghan, William Farrell and John Fahy (Ballywinna), Martin O'Halloran and Martin Huban (Kiltulla), Peter Kelly and Henry Pilkington (Killeenadeema), John Hazel (Gort) and Anthony and Thomas G. Griffin (Gurteen). There were delegates also from Ahascragh, Bullaun, Castleblakeny, Duniry, Leitrim, Letterfrack, Killimor, Kilrickle and Tynagh. Patrick Cawley was nominated as chairman. A letter of apology was received from Bishop Duggan, who urged prompt action on land reform 'so as to secure to the tenants immediately the amount of benefit deducible from the principles of the Land Act'. This indicates a change in attitude compared with a year previously. He now evidently accepted that the time for a trial of the act was over in favour of a vigorous pursuit of the potential benefits.

The first resolution was proposed by James Kilmartin and

> placed the national issue in pride of place in asserting the right of our country to national independence and declare our steadfast determination to strive for its attainment by every legitimate and honourable means.

The second resolution addressed the land question and stated 'that we accept the great principle – that the land of every country belongs to the people of that country' but it did not advocate any particular system of land reform. Matthew Harris, in supporting the resolution, said that 'the essence of the principle was a more just and equitable distribution of wealth'. In proposing the third resolution, Thomas Griffin referred to the 1881 act as a failure 'that had pauperised the poor tenant farmer' and he believed each man should have 'as much land as he and his family could till'. The fourth resolution advocated a peasant proprietary and that 'all bona fide farmers of thirty acres and under be empowered to

The foundation of the Irish National League 147

purchase their holdings – the sale of all such to be compulsory on landlords'. After a spirited debate, an amendment to include tenants with holdings greater than thirty acres was passed. Other resolutions related to compensation for improvements to holdings, the transfer of taxes on land to grazing farms, the improvement of living conditions and the provision of access to commonage land for labourers, the purchase and reclamation of waste land and the encouragement of industry. The controversy known as 'Stopping the hunt' was raised by Michael Glennon when he proposed that 'the convention pledge itself to prevent the county hounds from hunting over our lands'. In seconding the resolution, Matthew Harris indulged in a sweeping condemnation of landlords' behaviour and their failure to support the building of a branch railway line from Attymon to Loughrea. The resolution was passed with acclamation.[1]

To promote the new organization, a series of public meetings was planned and Michael Davitt and T.D. Sullivan addressed a very large and enthusiastic crowd in Navan, Co. Meath, on 26 November. The bishop of Meath, Dr Nulty, sent his carriage to convey Davitt and the other MPs from the railway station. Davitt advised that no rent should be paid from November to May and that a portion of this sum be paid into a national relief fund for those requiring help to survive. Timothy Harrington spoke on the operation of the Irish National League, which combined more interests than the previous league, and he advised that the interests of the farmers and labourers lay in harmonious action.[2]

Earl Spencer expressed his concerns about the renewed land agitation and referred to the seditious speeches of Davitt, Delany, Quinn and Healy. He stated that 'up to this, meetings have fallen flat but there is evidence that they are becoming much more lively and important'.[3]

On 15 December, a meeting of the organizing committee of the Irish National League was told that seventy-six branches, including the Gurteen branch in Co. Galway, had paid subscriptions and a further forty-three branches had held meetings, including the branches in Ballymana, Craughwell, Loughrea and Ballinasloe.[4]

Meeting at Kilconierin, 26 November 1882
On 26 November, a meeting was held in Kilconierin to establish a branch of the Irish National League. Contingents from Kiltulla and Craughwell marched to the meeting in military order and the Craughwell group, numbering 400–500 men, wore green scarves and laurel leaves in their hats. Revd Furlong PP was in the chair and the platform party included Patrick Cawley, Edward and Nicholas Barrett and John Cunniffe from Craughwell, John Sweeny and William Delany from Loughrea and Edward Keane PLG (Clostoken). The atmosphere was

1 *Western News*, 20 Oct. 1882. 2 *Freeman's Journal*, 27 Nov. 1882. 3 BL, Spencer papers, 76951, Spencer to Trevelyan, 29 Nov. 1882. 4 *Freeman's Journal*, 16 Dec. 1882.

enlivened by speeches of great passion and commitment, reminiscent of the early Land League meetings. Mr Humphrey McInerney BL, in his address, referred to 'the state of Loughrea with its silent streets, levelled homesteads and starving people, living in hovels without food or clothing or any prospect of employment'. His references to the large number of deaths in Loughrea during the famine were greeted with cries of 'Clanrackrent' and 'Dunsandle'. The clearances in Knockatoher in 1847 were recalled when Lord Dunsandle evicted eight hundred people. There were also derogatory remarks about Mrs Blake, the chief manager of the Hollypark estate, and the evictions that had taken place during October at Ganty. McInerney outlined the programme of the Irish National League that 'would be the redemption of the nation'. Patrick Cawley referred to the 1881 Land Act as a mockery when it did not prevent the evictions he had recently witnessed in Ganty. John Sweeny spoke about the great importance of organization – 'that the people should rely on themselves and on themselves alone'.[5]

Meeting at Clostoken, 10 December 1882
The momentum for the promotion of the Irish National League was set to continue at Clostoken on 10 December and placards announcing the meeting had been displayed for the previous two weeks. On the day prior to the meeting, notices prohibiting the meeting under the terms of the Crimes Act were distributed all over the locality. By 2pm, five hundred people had assembled at the crossroads near the church, watched over by a number of police under the command of SI Chambers. RM de Vere Pery read out the proclamation and advised the crowd to disperse within ten minutes or they would be dispersed by force. The crowd was gradually leaving when a number of press reporters were approached by de Vere Pery and Chambers and told to leave immediately. The reporters – Thomas Cunningham, Edward and Nicholas Barrett and James McDermot – protested that they were reporting for local, national and London papers and representing the public interest. The police noted their names and they were arrested later in the month. In addition, ten young men were arrested and sentenced to seven days' imprisonment.[6]

Meeting at Ballymana, 17 December 1882
On the following Sunday, 17 December, posters advertising a meeting of the Irish National League at Ballymana were put up throughout the locality. A crowd of about two hundred marched from Ardrahan and a like number from Craughwell who were followed by contingents from Kilconierin, Clostoken, Kilchreest and Killeenadeema. A force of fifty police arrived under SI Alan Bell, RM de Vere Pery and RM Goodricke, who read the proclamation and ordered

5 *Tuam News*, 1 Dec. 1883. 6 *Galway Observer*, 23 Dec. 1882.

the crowd to disperse within ten minutes. The crowd began to move away and occupied various vantage points while others played football. There was much cheering, groaning and hooting at the police and a number of young women jeered and made fun of Bell and de Vere Pery. The meeting commenced some distance from the announced place and, although there are no reports of speeches, a number of resolutions were passed. The resolutions professed support for the Irish National League and Parnell, advocated complete national independence and condemned the practice of state sponsored emigration. A confrontation between members of the press and the authorities was not mentioned in the newspaper article reporting on the meeting.[7]

An account of the meeting was immediately sent to Clifford Lloyd by SI Bell,[8] stating that at 12 noon he attended at Ballymana with twelve police. The lord lieutenant's proclamation was posted in Athenry, Craughwell, Ballymana, Riverville, Kilchreest and Loughrea. Clifford Lloyd instructed that warrants for arrest be issued on a charge of riot and thirty-three individuals (see below, appendix 3) were arrested on 20 December and taken to Galway Jail. The prisoners appeared the following day at a court of summary jurisdiction in Loughrea and were remanded for eight days.[9] At the petty sessions court held in Loughrea on 28 December, the handcuffed prisoners were brought before RM Paul and RM Crotty.

The cases of a number of men arrested in relation to the Clostoken meeting had been postponed from an earlier court and were heard first. Mr French Henderson argued that the meeting was intended to be of 'an inflammatory character, provocative of sedition and calculated to create discontent in several persons of Her Majesty's subjects, and possibly promote treason against Her Majesty'. Edward Barrett (Craughwell) was charged with failing to disperse within the appointed time and RM de Vere Pery gave evidence that Barrett did not leave for five minutes after the time allotted had elapsed. The defence counsel argued that Barrett had attended the meeting in his role as reporter for the *Western News* and John Callanan, proprietor of the paper, confirmed that he had instructed Barrett to provide a report for the paper. The justices decided that they would not consider that his occupation was a defence and sentenced Barrett to seven days in jail without hard labour. The other reporters – Nicholas Barrett, Thomas Cunningham and James McDermot – pleaded guilty and were sentenced to two days' confinement in Loughrea Bridewell.

On the following day, the prisoners arrested in connection with the Ballymana meeting were charged with being guilty of riot. During cross examination by Mr McInerney, Constable Murtagh agreed that, apart from shouting, booing and calling names, there was 'no act calculated to put an ordinary subject of Her Majesty in fear and terror and that he himself was not in fear and terror'. SI Bell

7 *Western News*, 23 Dec. 1882. 8 NAI CSO RP 1883/153. 9 *Galway Observer*, 23 Dec. 1882.

agreed that there was no violence of any kind, except the gross abuse of the police, 'but there might have been'. RM de Vere Pery described the crowd as riotous but he heard no expressions made by the prisoners. After thirty minutes deliberation, the magistrates returned verdicts of illegal assemblage and failing to disperse after the reading of the proclamation. Thomas Stratford, James Coy and John Duane, who were alleged to have led a military style parade, were sentenced to two months' imprisonment with hard labour. Thomas Cunningham and the Barrett brothers were given one month with hard labour. The eight-day sentence given to Edward Barrett the previous day was allowed to run concurrently. James McDermot and the others, including Michael Connolly, Michael Fogarty and Patrick Finnegan, were given three weeks imprisonment with hard labour.[10] The outcome of the trial of Edward Barrett was condemned by the editor of the *Western News*, who criticized the arbitrary actions of the police.[11] The editorial in the *Freeman's Journal* asked 'was it now established that a representative of the press can be sent to prison merely for attending a meeting and reporting the facts?'[12]

The founding of the Irish National League and the revival of meetings and public protest was clearly perceived by the Dublin Castle authorities as an important renewed threat to the rule of law. A return to the days of the Land League and the widespread agitation and violence could not be tolerated. It was evident that the full rigour of the extensive powers provided by the Prevention of Crime Act 1882 would be employed to suppress public dissent.

10 *Western News*, 7 Jan. 1883. 11 *Western News*, 30 Dec. 1882. 12 *Freeman's Journal*, 1 Jan. 1883.

14 Conclusion

The foundation of the Land League and the initiation of the Land War of 1879–82 have been the subject of intensive study by historians such as T.W. Moody, James S. Donnelly, Samuel Clark, Paul Bew and Donald Jordan. In Donnelly's view, 'material progress can help to undermine the established order of things, especially if it is threatened with temporary check or reversal as it was in the late 1870s'.[1] An improvement had occurred in the agricultural economy in the period 1862–76, resulting in a marked increase in the prices for livestock and agricultural produce. The succession of poor harvests that followed caused a dramatic reduction in farmers' incomes, particularly after the disastrous harvest of 1879. Solow comments that 'the years of worst crop failure thus coincided with the years of relatively low prices, and income declines for tillage farmers were drastic indeed'.[2]

Another important social factor was the state of indebtedness of tenant farmers, not only to landlords but also to shopkeepers who themselves had become active in the purchase of land in competition with the farmers. The assistant commissioners to the Richmond Commission, Prof. Thomas Baldwin and Major Robertson, reported that 'in many places they [farmers] owe on an average from three to five years' rent to shopkeepers alone'. Baldwin explained that the state of indebtedness had come about because

> people have been from a variety of remote causes deficient in thrift. Then came the great bound of modern prosperity. The growth of wealth led to the establishment of a great many banks; the banks gave money on easy terms to shopkeepers, and then ... all of a sudden that has collapsed.[3]

A similar view was expressed by William O'Brien, stating that the farmers in Co. Mayo owed £200,000 to shopkeepers.[4] Although relationships between farmers and shopkeepers were good during years of plenty, there is evidence that excessive levels of interest were charged by shopkeepers. For the farmers, the combination of discharging debts to shopkeepers and the payment of rent to landlords often resulted in an intolerable burden. The prospect of famine now faced communities, particularly among the families of impoverished small farmers in the west of Ireland. It is not surprising that the radical policies of the

---

1 Donnelly, *The land and the people of nineteenth-century Cork*, pp 249–50. 2 Solow, *The land question and the Irish economy*, pp 121–5. 3 Cited in Jordan, *Land and popular politics in Ireland*, p. 192. 4 *Freeman's Journal*, 25 Aug. 1879.

nascent Land League generated such enthusiastic support at the early land meetings in Mayo and Galway.

Clark focuses on a 'challenging collectivity' comprising farmers, townspeople and the Catholic clergy that united the community in opposition to British rule.[5] The close links between farmers and townspeople and the important support of the clergy is also evident in the present study, and the over-representation of townspeople is confirmed by the number arrested as suspects in 1881–2. Bew disagrees regarding the degree of unity achieved, and draws attention to the significant conflicts of interest:

> The Land League was above all a class alliance of the rural bourgeoisie, the middle and poor peasantry, and the agricultural proletariat: one of the most remarkable things about the League is the way in which its different sections pushed in different directions. The large and middle farmers were looking for rent reductions, the smallholders of the west were looking for land redistribution, while the labourers of the south were contemplating at least a general strike for better wages.[6]

THE FOUNDATION OF THE LAND LEAGUE

The foundation of the Land League set in train a chain of events that achieved major changes in land tenure and ultimately resulted in the end of landlordism. That the land agitation started in the west of Ireland owes much to the familiarity of Michael Davitt with the area and the preparatory efforts of the Ballinasloe Tenants' Defence Association. The association flourished due to the organizational skills of the veteran Fenian, Matthew Harris, James Kilmartin and M.M. O'Sullivan. Their activities came to the attention of James Daly, who, together with John O'Connor Power and J.J. Louden, had supported the establishment of similar bodies in Co. Mayo. Daly had an important influence on the movement by promoting land tenure reform at numerous meetings and through publicity in his paper the *Connaught Telegraph*. During Davitt's visit to the west of Ireland in 1878, he met Harris and it is believed that he was given the names of IRB members in Mayo by the Fenian County Centres. He formed the opinion that agitation for land tenure reform could be organized on a wide scale. The assistance of some of the well-known Fenians in Mayo – John and P.W. Nally, John Walshe and John O'Keane – led to the organization of the initial mass meetings.

The momentum generated by the meetings held in Irishtown, Westport,

---

5 Clark, *Social origins of the Irish Land War*, ch. 8.   6 Bew, *Land and the national question in Ireland, 1858–82*, p. 223.

Claremorris and elsewhere in Mayo resulted in the establishment of the National Land League of Mayo in August 1879. Parnell had already attended meetings in Ballinasloe and Castlebar and he also realized the potential of the new organization to further the twin causes of land tenure reform and home rule. As McCartney observes, 'it was the explosive combination of Davitt's organizational and inspirational skills and Parnell's power of command and genius for leadership that turned the Land League into a highly effective weapon of agitation'.[7]

Davitt's contacts with John Devoy and Clan na Gael during his visit to America in 1878 were of great importance in the forging of links between the Fenians and the land agitation. They mobilized support among the Irish American community that resulted in the generation of funding for the Land League and prompted the 'new departure' that envisaged cooperation between constitutional nationalism, land agitation and the Fenians. The availability of funding for the Land League helped to relieve distress during the crisis of 1879–80 and it facilitated the widespread formation of Land League branches.

Although the leaders of the Fenians – Kickham and O'Leary – were opposed to involvement in the Land League, there was widespread participation of Fenians at all levels of the League organization. Several members of the central executive were Fenians, including Davitt, Patrick Egan, Thomas Brennan and M.M. O'Sullivan. The overlap of membership is also clearly evident in the prominent role of the Fenians in the organization of the Land League in Galway. The Fenians Matthew Harris, John Sweeny, Thomas Cunningham and many others were prominent Land League organizers until their arrest as suspects and again after their release, and the widespread importation of arms by the Fenians undoubtedly facilitated the level of violence in south Galway.

The relationship between the agrarian secret societies and the Fenians during the Land War is unclear. The term Ribbon-Fenianism has been coined because of the great difficulty in clarifying the precise nature of both groups due to the paucity of documentation relating to their activities. Furthermore, there are problems of credibility regarding police reports and communications from informers. There is no doubt that in the disturbed districts there were large numbers of young and disaffected men who were available for violent intervention in local disputes and who also enjoyed easy access to arms.[8] In addition, the Fenian connection provided the discipline and a degree of military organization for the serious violent incidents. The political purpose of the Fenians was expressed by their challenge to the governing authorities and while an open, armed rebellion was never likely, there was ample evidence that the government believed that Ireland was degenerating into a state of anarchy.

7 Donal McCartney, 'Parnell, Davitt and the land question' in King (ed.), *Famine, land and culture in Ireland* (2000), p. 80. 8 NAI, Fenian B files, B2, Lloyd to Brackenbury, 29 June 1882.

Bew expresses the opinion that

> It would be misleading to describe the attitude of the western peasantry in this period as revolutionary; it was rather a species of desperate pragmatism. They were keen to follow any course that might improve their social conditions and alleviate their poverty.⁹

There is truth in this claim, but it does not do justice to the more sophisticated political aims of the town-based leadership of the Land League in south Galway. This organization was dominated by committed Fenians who never lost sight of national aims and at the land meetings in the area affirmed the desire for national independence. Their involvement in the initial efforts to found the Gaelic Athletic Association was also connected with their overall interest in the promotion of national aims.

Townshend claims that the 'effect of the land war in 1880 was obtained through the intensification of old methods of struggle rather than the development of new ones'.¹⁰ This view underestimates the degree of politicization, the capacity for organization and the new confidence to challenge the entrenched principles of the rights of property that had evolved.

COUNTY COMPARISONS

Other county studies of the Land League and Land War have been carried out in relation to Cos Cork, Mayo and Kerry and Queen's County (Laois). In Donnelly's study of Cork in the nineteenth century, there are many similarities to the present study.¹¹ There was a rapid spread of Land League branches joined by all segments of the farming community as well as townsmen, especially shopkeepers and publicans, who also provided local leadership. In the period August to December 1880, there were as many as ninety-one meetings each month, compared with fourteen per month earlier that year. A meeting addressed by Parnell in Cork city in October was attended by an estimated thirty thousand people. Evictions were common, but the repossession rate was very high; for instance, of two hundred evicted tenants in Mitchelstown, 180 were reinstated. Although there was a high level of agrarian crime in both counties, the number of suspects arrested under the PPP (Ireland) Act 1881 differed greatly, with 166 in Co. Galway and 72 in Co. Cork. During 1879–82, two murders were committed in Co. Cork, whereas seventeen occurred in Galway

---

9 Bew, 'The Land League ideal: achievements and contradictions' in Drudy (ed.), *Irish studies 2, Ireland: land, politics and people* (1982), pp 77–92. 10 Charles Townshend, *Political violence in Ireland: government and resistance since 1848* (Oxford, 1983), p. 115. 11 Donnelly, *The land and the people of Cork in the nineteenth century*, pp 251–307.

Conclusion

and many of the arrests of the Galway suspects were related to those killings. The activities of the Millstreet agrarian secret society in Co. Cork led to fifty-six individuals being charged with treason felony in 1882. Two were found guilty of Whiteboy offences and the others were discharged. As elsewhere, the issuing of threatening letters and notices were the most frequent offences and the frequency of outrages decreased rapidly during 1882.

In relation to Queen's County, the main common feature with the Galway experience was the clerical support from Bishop Moran. The militant attitude of many of the clergy was voiced at the meetings that were allowed to take place. It is interesting that the administration started to use the proclamation of meetings at an early stage and enforced them with large numbers of military and police. The proximity of the Curragh camp undoubtedly facilitated the availability of military forces. For instance, a force of 360 soldiers and one hundred RIC prevented a meeting at Cullahill.[12] The press was not supportive of the Land League and the *Leinster Express* carried on a sustained campaign of outright hostility. The local MP, Bernard Fitzpatrick, son of Lord Castletown, also showed his antipathy, on one occasion proposing that accommodation be provided for two hundred soldiers and fifty horses in the workhouse of Donoughmore Union. The proposal was not approved.

There was a very low level of agrarian crime in Queen's County, with only ninety-nine instances reported for the county and twenty-two suspects arrested under the 1881 Coercion Act. The benevolence of some of the large landowners, such as Sir Charles Coote and the earl of Portarlington, may have tempered militancy when they accepted rents at Griffith's valuation. Predictably, the *Leinster Express* disapproved of this action on the grounds that it would encourage the demands of tenants on other estates.

In relation to Co. Mayo, Jordan gives a detailed account of the decline in Land League action that occurred as early as the summer of 1880. At the conclusion of the book, he states that 'without additional local studies of the land agitation, it is difficult to determine how unique the Mayo experience was'.[13] A comparative account of events in the neighbouring counties of Mayo and Galway is, therefore, of particular interest. The tenant farmers of Mayo had been the original enthusiastic supporters of the agitation on the land question when they flocked in their thousands to the meetings at Irishtown and elsewhere in Mayo during 1879. However, by the following year there was widespread disillusionment because the small farmers thought they had been neglected by the central executive of the Land League who appeared more concerned with the interests of the large farmers in the south and east of the country. In addition, the Fenians, led by P.W. and John Nally, John Walshe and John O'Keane, were

---

12 J.W.H. Carter, *The Land War and its leaders in Queen's County, 1872–82* (Portlaoise, 1994), p. 93.   13 Jordan, *Land and popular politics in Ireland*, p. 312.

disaffected because they thought the Land League was not radical enough. Initially, the antipathy displayed by Archbishop John McHale had discouraged the clergy from taking leadership roles and participating in public meetings and meetings of Land League branches. This changed in early 1880, when they began to take a more active role helping to form new branches and were often elected as officers.[14] This had a restraining effect on members, leading to a moderation of attitudes.

By contrast, support for the Land League remained strong in Co. Galway and mass public meetings recommenced when concerns over the agricultural crisis abated in August 1880. Enthusiastic support continued into 1881 and declined only following the arrests of prominent organizers of branches after the introduction of the PPP (Ireland) Act and particularly after the proclamation of the Land League in October 1881.

In Co. Galway, clerical support for the Land League was evident from the beginning, particularly that of Bishop Duggan, who had long been a forthright supporter of radical land tenure reform. His enthusiasm was evident in the numerous letters of encouragement read out at mass Land League meetings. The clergy were also eager participants, often taking leadership positions and displaying a militant attitude in their public speeches.

The contrast between the two counties is evident in the application of the 1881 Coercion Act. In Mayo, fourteen suspects were arrested, whereas in Galway the total was 166. The majority of the Galway suspects (92) were arrested between October 1881 and February 1882 at the time when agrarian outrages were most numerous, indicating the persistent level of agitation. In Mayo, the number of outrages peaked much earlier, between December 1880 and January 1881. Another obvious difference was the very large number of arrests in Galway for the more serious categories of offences against the person and property.

A major factor in the decline of Land League activities in Mayo was the disaffection of some of its early organizers. The Fenians had been committed supporters and organizers, but they soon became disillusioned with the failure of the Land League to pursue a radical campaign of agrarian reform. The Fenians were wary of involvement in constitutional politics and the support given by the Land League to the Irish Parliamentary Party.

In Co. Mayo, James Daly was a very influential figure because of his early involvement, with O'Connor Power and Louden, in tenants' support and his advocacy of the agrarian cause. Initially, he was a supporter of boycotting but he became more moderate in his views and opposed this tactic. Daly also began to question the centralization of power within the central executive of the Land League and he was concerned about the alleged misappropriation of funds by

14 Ibid., p. 253.

Land League members. There was dissension between Daly and James Louden because Daly considered that Louden, who was a substantial landowner, had begun to act like a landlord.[15] Furthermore, Daly criticized the Fenians, whom he blamed for the increase in violence in late 1880 and early 1881. All of these factors played a part in the decline of the Land League in Co. Mayo, and Jordan concludes that 'the Land War had moved away from Mayo, leaving the small farmers to find their own solution to the land agitation – emigration'.[16]

The study of the Land War in Kerry is of particular interest and there are many similarities with events in Galway.[17] In Kerry, there was little clerical involvement in Land League activities in the early stages and there was evidence of direct opposition when the parish priest of Tralee, Revd O'Leary, urged the government to suppress a meeting 'on the grounds that it would lead to abusive speeches and boycotting'.[18] However, following the passage of the PPP (Ireland) Act in March 1881, clerical influence increased and at the national convention of the Land League in April, five of the eight delegates from Kerry were priests. Thereafter, they had a moderating influence and their views often coincided with those of the conservative large tenant farmers. Timothy Harrington, as editor of the *Kerry Sentinel*, provided extensive coverage of the branch meetings of the Land League. He also had a national role in the central branch of the Land League and promoted their policies. These included the 'Rent at the point of a bayonet' that was also approved of by wealthy tenant farmers. As in Galway, there was a marked increase in agrarian violence after the proclamation of the Land League. Between October 1880 and October 1881, twelve agrarian outrages occurred but in the succeeding fourteen months four murders, twelve instances of firing into dwellings and twenty-one of firing at the person were recorded. Much of the violence was political and was attributed to the continuing influence of the Fenians.

In Galway, the same individuals who were involved in the early stages were present at the Land Convention in October 1882, many of them suspects recently released from prison. The leadership of the Land League was still dominated by Fenians, including Matthew Harris, John McCarthy, John Sweeny and others, who remained committed to continued agitation for radical solutions to the land tenure question. The immediate adoption of the Irish National League and the organization of mass meetings showed their determination not to let the core aims of the original Land League organization wither away. Their capacity for organization was destined to continue into the second phase of the Land War (1886–91) when the Plan of Campaign commenced on the Clanricarde and Dunsandle estates and the area was again thrown into turmoil.

15 Moran, 'James Daly and the rise and fall of the Land League', 201.   16 Jordan, *Land and popular politics in Ireland*, p. 312.   17 Donnacha Seán Lucey, *Land, popular politics and agrarian violence in Ireland: the case of County Kerry, 1872–86* (Dublin, 2011).   18 Lucey, *Land, popular politics and agrarian violence in Ireland*, p. 80.

The national campaign of agitation caused a social and political revolution that resulted in the reforming Land Act of 1881 and it is significant that Gladstone acknowledged the importance of the Land League in achieving this reform.[19] In addition, the Arrears Act of 1882 provided a remedy for one of the defects of that legislation. The foundation was laid for a succession of reforming land acts over the ensuing half century that ultimately achieved the ambitious aim of the founders of the movement.

---

19 Hansard's parliamentary debates, third series, vol. 341, 1686, 3 Mar. 1890.

Appendix 1

Transcript of the diary of John Sweeny (fig. 6)[1]

– 1881 –
– Coercion Act –
Date of arrest
of Messrs
J. Sweeny,
T. Cunningham
& J.M. Huban
Wednesday June 15th
– Charge –
Reasonably suspected
of being accessory
to the Crime of
'Murder'[2]

Sub Inspector Barry accompanied by Head Constable Leonard knocked loudly at my door about 3 O'C, hearing the noise I awoke pulled on my trousers, lit a candle and opened the door when the warrant was handed to me by the sub inspector who remarked that it was a disagreeable business and said quite calmly 'I suppose you were expecting it John'. I replied calmly that while I was quite prepared I did not expect it, particularly on such a hideous charge. Having asked when they required me I was answered immediately and had scarce time to dress. My poor Mrs [wife], seeing me put on my clothes, got frightened, jumped out of bed and asked me what was the matter. I tried to keep the matter quiet but she became impatient whereupon I informed her the police were downstairs and required me. At the same time entreating her to bear with the awful ordeal, particularly as the children upstairs, Mary Agnes and Alice Bridget, or as we more familiarly call her Siss, both crying loudly at hearing the mother. By permission of the sub inspector, I was allowed to go see my father, mother and brother Peter, being accompanied by the head constable. Having knocked at the window, my father asked who was there. When I answered and told him, whereupon he at once opened the door and saw the police accompanying me. I said the worst had come and bade my loving mother good bye. I really thought she was frantic at hearing the sad news and could not pacify her. The police being

---

1 In possession of the present author. 2 Suspected of the murders of James Connors and Peter Dempsey (see above, ch. 8).

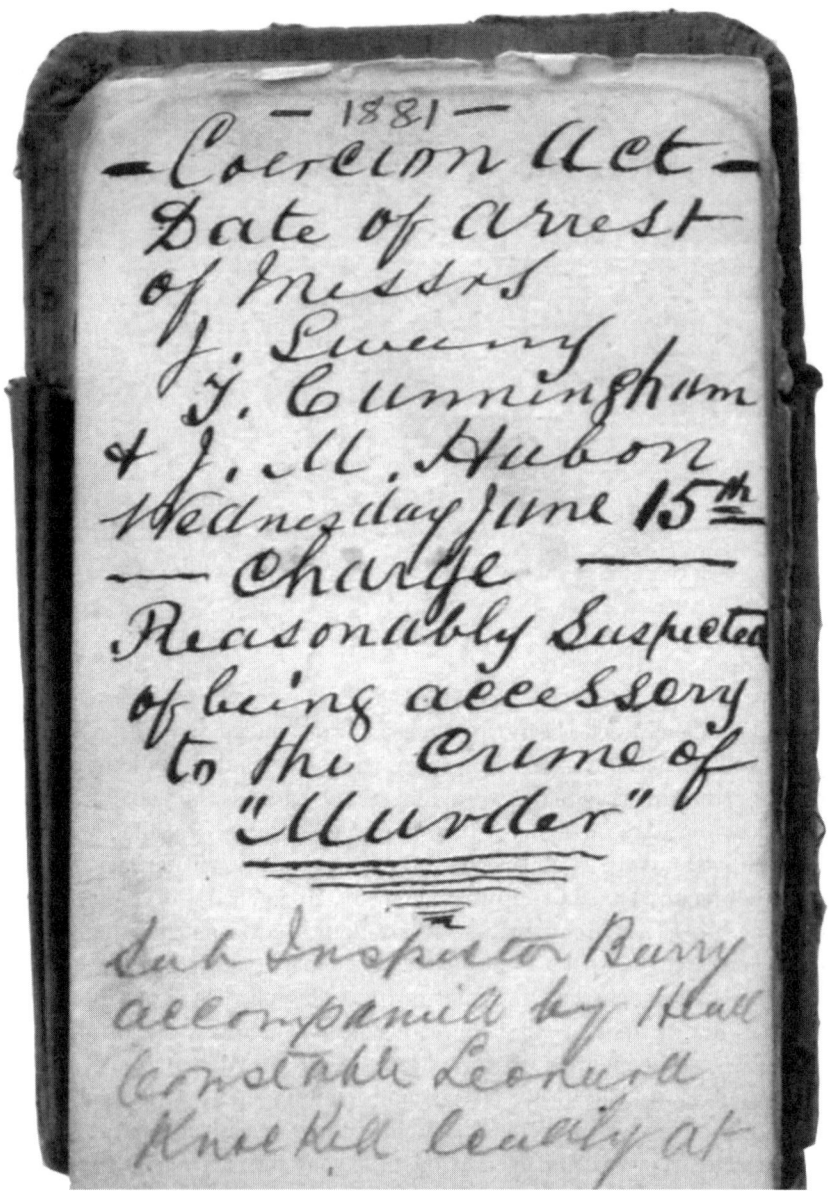

6 Page from the diary of John Sweeny (source: private possession of the present author).

impatient, I then retired. I should have stated that on going down to my father's house I saw police posted outside the house of John Farrell wherein resided my brother suspect, Thomas Cunningham, and I at once guessed that it was for him they were waiting. On arriving at my own house, I hurriedly packed my clothes

Appendices 161

into my portmanteau and amid an indescribable scene bade goodbye to my dear wife and little children. On arriving at the police barracks, my friend T. Cunningham was inside and we greeted each other as usual. Police were there in great numbers among them being several from Ballinasloe who arrived during the night on cars belonging to a fellow called Fleming and Colohan and on which we were to be conveyed. Immediately after entering the barrack the Revd Patk Egan, president of St Brendan's College and also president of the local branch of the Land League, entered and in his usual sympathetic yet patriotic manner spoke words of consolation. On presenting him with my warrant, he felt somewhat amazed and at once characterized the accusation as a libel stating emphatically that I would be the last man living in his estimation to encourage crime or outrage of any kind and further added that henceforth the work of the League should be pushed forward with renewed energy. By this time, a number of friends had assembled, among whom I noticed the following: My Mrs, father and mother and brothers Peter and Martin, Mr & Mrs John Farrell, my sister Lizzie & her husband John McGann, Mr Thomas Mulkern, Pat Donohue, Mrs Luke Quirke, Micky Loftus and others. By this time, all was in readiness and the cars laden with police all armed with loaded rifles got in motion. There were four cars in all, together with a dozen police and SI Barry. Conveyed by road to Ballinasloe and when outside Aughrim turned down by Kilcloney and on to the police station at Ballinasloe where we arrived about 7 O'C or a little later. I sent a messenger to Mr Michael McGiverin, auctioneer and valuer, an old and valued friend of mine who shortly turned up and heartily sympathized with me. While thus conversing, the sub inspector and Head Constable Barniville brought in Mr Joseph M. Huban, having arrested him at Corbetts Hotel, where he had been staying with the intention of delivering a Lecture on the following evening. Subject: The Bards and Music of Ireland. Just as the latter suspect was entering the barrack, it was my intention to dispatch a messenger but was spared the trouble. At 8 O'C the cars and police were again in readiness and conveyed us to the railway station, from whence after a few minutes the train arrived and we were handed into a second-class carriage accompanied by the Sub Inspector A.C. Clements, Constables Hodgens, Roe, Murtagh, McGuiness and one other whose name I don't know. At none of the stations along the way were we permitted to have any refreshment. Arrived at the Broadstone there were a number of detectives in plain clothes together with a large force of the RIC decked with the new helmet awaiting our arrival and subsequently escorted us thro the city in cabs. The police save those with us riding on outside cars to the Amiens St. Station. By this time, being completely exhausted, I complained to the officer in charge of the treatment we were being subjected to. Whereupon he gave permission to have some tea given to us. Sub Constable McGuinness endeavoured to obtain a drop of whiskey but there was none sold at the bar of the Amiens St. Station so that we had to content ourselves with a cup of most miserable tea, despatched a messenger to Mr J.P. Quinn of the Central League, who did not arrive. Started at 2 O'C for Dundalk [Jail], where we arrived about 4.30 and were at once handed over to the governor's care. The escort in the meantime retiring, we were then ushered into a room, our height taken and entered in a book, weighed next, stated occupation or calling in life, whether married or single, religion and asked whether or not we had any money on us, which was taken up and amount entered, any pipes or tobacco. The regulations were then read or as we subsequently called it the Riot Act. Then we were brought into a room in which were four other suspects who each in turn shook hands with us and congratulated us on our new quarters. Their names were James and Henry Flood of Westmeath, Dannie McSweeney of Carrowcannon House, Falcarragh, Donegal, Francis B. O'Gallagher, Glassagh, Bunbeg, Donegal. Having arrived during the hours set apart for exercise, all hands repaired to the garden wherein we were permitted to walk and converse as best we choose, two wardens being at a convenient distance. Immediately after going out, we were informed by our brother suspects that they had already established within their own circle a society of which Mr McSweeney was president and unto which they had given the name of the Red Branch Knights. Previous to admission there are certain indispensable qualifications, so that we were then individually asked by the president the following questions. ?Have you paid any rent this year. Answer ########## [The answer and subsequent questions and answers are blanked out.] The answers given to the various questions put were then submitted to the remaining suspects when we were unanimously admitted as members. So that henceforth all were united so as to make light of the punishment imposed. At six o'clock, a bell was rung summoning all to return to their cells. On entering which, I realized for the first time my imprisonment. The cell consists in a neatly white washed room 13 feet x 6'10½ and having a brick arched ceiling 8'4 from the floor to cove or wall line, also a semi Gothic or elliptical metal sash with fourteen squares of glass the whole being 3'8 long by 15" high at either end and having a swill of 3" in the centre. Beside the window is a ventilator 10" x 9" and under the same is another 19 x 4½" both having a sliding door in ploughed wood frame and inside which are iron bars of 3¾" iron. The furniture consists of a neat iron bedstead and all requisites which have been supplied by the Ladies' Land League together with a chair and small table 2' x 1–5. The right angle next door contains 2 shelves on which to lay our cup and saucer, knife, spoons, small plate, tumbler & egg stand together with some books. The left angle next window contains an iron bracket for a copper basin with which to wash, while underneath stands a galvanized relieving officer. The inside of door painted black & casings are of iron and having 38 bolts with riveted heads on the inside. There is a trap on the centre of the door 8" x 6½" for the purpose of warders looking in each night and morning. In addition to a Spy glass through which the inmates can be seen on the outside by lifting aside a large iron escutcheon. In addition to other cell furniture, each has a towel and soap, looking glass, comb and hairbrush, the latter also supplied by the ladies.

N.B. I should have mentioned that immediately after arriving we were visited by Mr Roe of the Democrat and Mr P. Sellars uncle to Revd J. Sellars to whom as he informed us Revd Father Egan had telegraphed.

Shortly after entering cells, a hearty meal of tea, bread and chops was supplied of which I partook of but very little. Later on I wrote to my dear wife describing the journey and also arrived safe. I slept very little that first night and tears rolled down my cheeks while writing, thinking of home and children. Thursday morning was composed of the ringing of bells and banging of trap doors at 6 O'C. Got up, washed, and paced up and down or wrote until breakfast came at 8 O'C, eat very little, the warder remarking that 'you will not do at this rate'. 10 O'C at length came and again self and friends enjoyed each others society until one.

N.B. I forgot to mention that all attended Mass at 8 O'C it being the Corpus Christi holiday. Wrote home and also to some friends until 3 when exercise again came on. 6 at length found the cell door again locked. Friday 17th while at exercise three more suspects, viz John Ryan, John Darcy and Martin Bermingham, arrived and were admitted immediately to our ranks, the charge in the warrant was similar to mine and others [conspiracy to murder].[3]

---

[3] John Ryan was suspected of the murder of James Connors, while John Darcy and Martin Bermingham were suspected of the murder of Peter Dempsey (see above, ch. 8).

Appendix 2

Persons from the Loughrea and Athenry police districts arrested under the Protection of Person and Property (Ireland) Act 1881.[1]

Name	District	Arrested	Released	Suspected crime
Martin O'Halloran	Loughrea	08.03.1881	19.04.1882	Preventing rent payment
Timothy Dolan	Loughrea	04.06.1881	17.08.1882	Murder
Patrick Keogh	Loughrea	04.06.1881	17.08.1882	Murder
Edward Fahey	Loughrea	04.06.1881	17.08.1882	Murder
John Sweeny	Loughrea	15.06.1881	17.08.1882	Accessory to murder
Thomas Cunningham	Loughrea	15.06.1881	17.08.1882	Accessory to murder
Joseph Huban	Loughrea	15.06.1881	16.04.1882	Accessory to murder
John Ryan (1st)	Loughrea	17.06.1881	21.05.1882	Accessory to murder
John Darcy	Loughrea	17.06.1881	17.08.1882	Accessory to murder
Martin Bermingham	Loughrea	17.06.1881	17.08.1882	Accessory to murder
Edward Barrett	Athenry	18.06.1881	23.08.1882	Posting threatening notices
Michael Connolly	Loughrea	09.07.1881	14.03.1882	Treasonable practices
Michael Glennon	Loughrea	09.07.1881	17.08.1882	Posting threatening notices
Martin Spellman	Loughrea	09.07.1881	01.04.1882	Boycotting
Martin Hooban	Loughrea	05.11.1881	30.04.1882	Intimidation against rent
John Burke	Loughrea	05.11.1881	29.06.1882	Intimidation against rent
Patrick C. Kelly	Athenry	09.11.1881	23.08.1882	Boycotting
Peter Broderick	Athenry	09.11.1881	23.08.1882	Boycotting
James Noakley	Loughrea	10.11.1881	17.08.1882	Firing into a dwelling
Patrick Tuohill	Loughrea	10.11.1881	17.08.1882	Firing into a dwelling
Andrew Keary	Loughrea	10.11.1881	17.08.1882	Boycotting
Thomas G. Griffin	Athenry	11.11.1881	19.05.1882	Intimidation against rent
Patrick Morrissey	Athenry	25.11.1881	23.08.1882	Accessory to murder
Thomas Morrissey	Athenry	14.11.1881	23.08.1882	Accessory to murder
Thomas Coyne	Athenry	17.11.1881	23.08.1882	Intimidation against rent
Thomas Cunniffe	Athenry	25.11.1881	23.08.1882	Murder
John Connors	Loughrea	24.11.1881	19.05.1882	Intimidation against rent
Peter Coughlan	Loughrea	24.11.1881	08.04.1882	Intimidation against rent
Peter Plower	Loughrea	28.11.1881	11.04.1882	Intimidation against rent
Michael Leahy	Loughrea	24.11.1881	17.05.1882	Accessory to murder
Anthony Griffin	Athenry	03.12.1881	12.04.1882	Intimidation against rent
Henry L. Pilkington	Loughrea	16.12.1881	10.04.1882	Intimidation against rent
John Connaughton	Loughrea	16.12.1881	18.05.1882	Intimidation against rent
John Glennon	Loughrea	16.12.1881	08.04.1882	Intimidation against rent
Patrick Corbett	Athenry	29.12.1881	21.05.1882	Intimidation against rent
John Keane	Athenry	29.12.1881	23.08.1882	Intimidation against rent
Denis Cunningham	Loughrea	29.12.1881	12.03.1882	Intimidation against rent
Thomas Duggan	Loughrea	29.12.1881	26.05.1882	Intimidation against rent
Martin Mullavel	Loughrea	29.12.1881	20.04.1882	Intimidation against rent
Michael Calligy	Loughrea	29.12.1881	16.03.1882	Intimidation against rent

1 NAI Protection of Person and Property (Ireland) Act. List of persons arrested, carton 1.

Name	Place	Date	Date	Offence
Thomas Cunningham	Loughrea	29.12.1881	22.06.1882	Intimidation against rent
Michael Furlong	Loughrea	29.12.1881	25.03.1882	Intimidation against rent
Peter Kelly (1st)	Loughrea	29.12.1881	03.05.1882	Intimidation against rent
Thomas Finnigan	Loughrea	27.01.1882	06.06.1882	Intimidation against rent and boycotting
Michael Cooney	Loughrea	27.01.1882	11.04.1882	Intimidation against rent
Lewis Quinn	Loughrea	27.01.1882	11.04.1882	Intimidation against rent
James Kennedy	Loughrea	27.01.1882	02.05.1882	Intimidation against rent
Thomas Keighrey	Loughrea	27.01.1882	10.04.1882	Intimidation against rent
John McCarthy (1st)	Loughrea	27.01.1882	08.06.1882	Intimidation against rent
John Farrell (1st)	Loughrea	27.01.1882	25.02.1882	Intimidation against rent
Nicholas Barrett	Loughrea	27.01.1882	17.08.1882	Intimidation against rent
Martin Huban (1st)	Loughrea	27.01.1882	17.08.1882	Intimidation against rent
Bernard Coyle	Loughrea	27.01.1882	17.08.1882	Intimidation against rent
Michael Dilleen (1st)	Loughrea	27.01.1882	04.06.1882	Intimidation against rent
Peter Sweeny (1st)	Loughrea	27.01.1882	11.04.1882	Intimidation against rent
Martin Greene (1st)	Loughrea	27.01.1882	31.03.1882	Intimidation against rent
Hugh Kennedy	Athenry	02.02.1882	22.08.1882	Intimidation against rent
Patrick Ruane	Athenry	27.01.1882	07.06.1882	Intimidation against rent
John Carley	Athenry	27.01.1882	23.08.1882	Intimidation against rent
Martin Hynes	Athenry	27.01.1882	23.08.1882	Intimidation against rent
John Moran	Athenry	27.01.1882	23.08.1882	Intimidation against rent
John Melia	Athenry	27.01.1882	15.04.1882	Intimidation against rent
Martin Kennedy	Athenry	02.02.1882	09.06.1882	Intimidation against rent
Michael Ward	Athenry	02.02.1882	23.06.1882	Intimidation against rent
John Broderick	Athenry	27.01.1882	10.04.1882	Intimidation against rent
John Connelly	Athenry	02.02.1882	08.06.1882	Intimidation against rent
Patrick Carley	Athenry	27.01.1882	23.08.1882	Intimidation against rent
Patrick Raftery	Loughrea	10.02.1882	19.05.1882	Intimidation against rent
Martin Minihan	Loughrea	10.02.1882	21.05.1882	Intimidation against rent
Patrick Haverty	Loughrea	16.02.1882	11.04.1882	Intimidation against rent
James Buckley	Loughrea	10.02.1882	08.04.1882	Intimidation against rent
Bernard Stratford	Loughrea	10.02.1882	17.05.1882	Intimidation against rent
Michael Stratford	Loughrea	10.02.1882	17.05.1882	Intimidation against rent
James Coy	Loughrea	10.02.1882	17.08.1882	Intimidation against rent
James Finnigan (1st)	Loughrea	10.02.1882	31.03.1882	Intimidation against rent
Thomas Halloran	Loughrea	10.02.1882	07.06.1882	Intimidation against rent
John Buckley	Loughrea	10.02.1882	09.04.1882	Intimidation against rent
Michael Cunningham	Loughrea	10.02.1882	09.04.1882	Intimidation against rent
Thomas Haire (1st)	Loughrea	10.02.1882	21.05.1882	Inciting to murder
James Coane	Athenry	28.02.1882	23.08.1882	Shooting at person
Thomas Coane	Athenry	28.02.1882	23.08.1882	Shooting at person
John McGann	Athenry	28.02.1882	23.08.1882	Shooting at person
Patrick Gilligan	Athenry	28.02.1882	11.04.1882	Shooting at person
Patrick Finnegan	Athenry	17.04.1882	23.08.1882	Murder
John McCarthy (2nd)	Loughrea	04.07.1882	17.08.1882	Accessory to murder
Peter Sweeny (2nd)	Loughrea	04.07.1882	17.08.1882	Accessory to murder
Martin Kennedy	Loughrea	04.07.1882	17.08.1882	Accessory to murder
William Manahan	Loughrea	04.07.1882	17.08.1882	Accessory to murder
Patrick Burke	Loughrea	04.07.1882	17.08.1882	Accessory to murder
Patrick Morrissey	Loughrea	04.07.1882	17.08.1882	Accessory to murder
John Ryan (2nd)	Loughrea	04.07.1882	17.08.1882	Accessory to murder

Michael Dilleen (2nd)	Loughrea	04.07.1882	17.08.1882	Accessory to murder
Michael Butler	Loughrea	04.07.1882	17.08.1882	Accessory to murder
James Finnigan (2nd)	Loughrea	04.07.1882	17.08.1882	Accessory to murder
Martin Huban (2nd)	Loughrea	04.07.1882	17.08.1882	Accessory to murder
James McDermot	Loughrea	04.07.1882	17.08.1882	Accessory to murder
Andrew McEntee	Loughrea	04.07.1882	17.08.1882	Accessory to murder
Patrick Sweeny	Loughrea	04.07.1882	17.08.1882	Accessory to murder
Michael Clarke	Loughrea	04.07.1882	17.08.1882	Accessory to murder
Martin Greene (2nd)	Loughrea	04.07.1882	17.08.1882	Accessory to murder
Patrick Corry	Loughrea	04.07.1882	17.08.1882	Accessory to murder
Thomas O'Brien	Loughrea	04.07.1882	17.08.1882	Accessory to murder
Fardy O'Neill	Loughrea	04.07.1882	17.08.1882	Accessory to murder
Patrick Kavanagh	Loughrea	04.07.1882	17.08.1882	Accessory to murder
William O'Flynn	Loughrea	04.07.1882	17.08.1882	Accessory to murder
John Farrell (2nd)	Loughrea	04.07.1882	17.08.1882	Accessory to murder
Michael Leahy	Loughrea	07.07.1882	17.08.1882	Accessory to murder
Thomas Connolly	Loughrea	17.07.1882	17.08.1882	Accessory to murder
John Connaire	Loughrea	17.07.1882	17.08.1882	Accessory to murder
Peter Kelly (2nd)	Loughrea	18.07.1882	17.08.1882	Inciting to murder
Edward Costello	Loughrea	18.07.1882	17.08.1882	Inciting to murder
Thomas Haire (2nd)	Loughrea	18.07.1882	17.08.1882	Inciting to murder
John Sheill	Loughrea	18.07.1882	17.08.1882	Accessory to murder
Michael Fogarty	Loughrea	18.07.1882	17.08.1882	Accessory to murder
Thomas Pendergast	Loughrea	18.07.1882	17.08.1882	Accessory to murder
Thomas Joyce	Loughrea	18.07.1882	17.08.1882	Accessory to murder
Patrick Connelly	Loughrea	19.07.1882	17.08.1882	Accessory to murder
Michael Cusack	Loughrea	21.07.1882	17.08.1882	Accessory to murder
Michael Connolly	Loughrea	19.07.1882	17.08.1882	Accessory to murder
Michael Connolly	Loughrea	21.07.1882	17.08.1882	Accessory to murder

Appendix 3

Persons arrested after the Irish National League meetings in Clostoken and Ballymana in December 1882.[1]

Thomas Cunningham	Loughrea
Edward J. Barrett	Craughwell
Nicholas J. Barrett	Loughrea
James McDermott	Loughrea
Michael Connelly	Ballymana
John Joyce	
Peter Joyce	Grenage
Martin Kelly	Roo
Tom Kelly	Roo
Thomas Holland	
Thomas Cunniffe	Cahergal
Michael Cloonan	Caherfurvaus
Peter Skehill	Craughwell
Pat Kinneen	Craughwell
Thoman Carr	Killora
John Connean	
Patrick Finnegan	Aggard
Michael Fogarty	Shanbally
John Kennedy	Ballylin E.
Michael [Martin?] Roland	
John Glynn	Craughwell
John Newell	Carrigans
John Ryan	Mannin
Thomas Stratford	
James Coy	
Pat Connelly	Lisnagrieve
Thomas Finnigan	Kilconieran
Patrick Raftery	
Michael Connolly	Ballywinna
Martin Kennedy	
Martin Whelan	
John Duane	Rathruddy
Martin Mannion	

Thomas Stratford, James Coy and John Duane were released on bail pending their appeal. The appeal was upheld by Judge T. Rice Henn Esq., QC.[2]

1 *Western News*, 30 Dec. 1882. 2 *Galway Vindicator*, 27 Jan. 1883.

Bibliography

MANUSCRIPT SOURCES

British Library, London
Spencer papers

Dublin City Library
Mansion House Relief Committee Correspondence and Irish Bishops files

Dublin Diocesan Archive
McCabe Relief of Distress Papers and Irish Bishop files

James Hardiman Library, NUIG
PRO, CO 904
Special Collections

Military Archives, Bureau of Military History, Cathal Brugha Barracks, Rathmines, Dublin

National Archives of Ireland, Dublin
Chief Secretary's Office, Crown Solicitor's Letter Book
Chief Secretary's Office, Registered Papers
Crime Branch Special
Fenian A files
Fenian B files
Irish Crimes Records
Irish Land League and Irish National League documents
IRB index of names 1866–71
Protection of Person and Property (Ireland) Act 1881
Prevention of Crime (Ireland) Act 1882

National Library of Ireland, Dublin
Clonbrock papers, MS 19,678
Parnell Special Commission (London, 1890)

Private possessions
Diary and photograph of John Sweeny in possession of the present author
Letter of John (Soldier) Morrissey in possession of Maura Lyons
Photographs of William Duffy and John McCarthy in possession of Norman Morgan

Parliamentary papers
HC 1845 (657), xxi, 1–1004. Evidence taken before Her Majesty's commissioners of inquiry into the state of the law and practice in respect to the occupation of land in Ireland (Devon Commission).

Bibliography

HC 1878 (249), xv, 1–466. Report from the select committee on Irish land act, 1870 together with the proceedings of the committee, minutes of evidence, and appendix.

HC 1878 [C.1938], lxxvii, 511. Agricultural statistics of Ireland for the year 1877.

HC 1878–79 [C.2221], lxxv, 703. Emigration statistics of Ireland for the year 1878.

HC 1880 [C.2501], lxxvi, 985. Emigration statistics of Ireland for the year 1879.

HC 1880 [C.2534], lxxvi, 815. The agricultural statistics of Ireland for the year 1879.

HC 1880 [C.2567], lxxvi, 1003. General abstract of the numbers of marriages, births, and deaths registered in Ireland during the year 1879.

HC 1880 (131), lx, 199. Return of agrarian outrages reported by Royal Irish Constabulary, 1879–January 1880.

HC 1880 (254), lx, 361. Evictions (Ireland). Copy of return prepared from reports made to the inspector general of the Royal Irish Constabulary of cases of eviction which have come under the knowledge of the constabulary, showing the number of families evicted in each county in Ireland in each of the four quarters of the years 1877, 1878, 1879, first quarter of the year 1880, and up to 20 June 1880.

HC 1881 [C.2779–I], xviii, 597, 600, 604 and 626. Report of her majesty's commissioners of inquiry into the working of the Landlord and Tenant (Ireland) Act 1870, and the acts amending the same (Bessborough commission report, 4 Jan. 1881).

HC 1881 [C.2828], xciv, 703. Emigration statistics of Ireland for the year 1880.

HC 1881 [C.2894], xciv, 721. General abstract of the numbers of marriages, births, and deaths registered in Ireland during the year 1880.

HC 1881 [C.2926], xlvii, Annual report of the Local Government Board for Ireland.

HC 1881 [C.2932], xciii, 685. The agricultural statistics of Ireland for the year 1880.

HC 1881 (13), lxxvii, 607. Agrarian offences (provinces) (Ireland). Return, by provinces, of agrarian offences throughout Ireland reported to the Inspector General of the Royal Irish Constabulary between 1 January 1880 and 31 December 1880.

HC 1881 (2), lxxvii, 713. Evictions (Ireland). Return (compiled from returns made to the Inspector General of the Royal Irish Constabulary) of cases of eviction which have come to the knowledge of the constabulary in each quarter of the year ended 31 December 1880.

HC 1881 (5), lxxvii, 793. Land League meetings and agrarian crime (Ireland). Return showing for each month of the years 1879 and 1880, the number of Land League meetings held and agrarian crimes reported to the Inspector General of the Royal Irish Constabulary in each county throughout Ireland.

HC 1881 (185), lxxvii, 725. Evictions (Ireland). Return by provinces and counties (compiled from returns made to the Inspector General, Royal Irish Constabulary), of cases of evictions which have come to the knowledge of the constabulary in each of the years from 1849 to 1880, inclusive.

HC 1882 [C.3125], lv, 275. Proclamation by the lord lieutenant of Ireland, dated 20 October 1881, relative to association styling itself Irish National Land League.

HC 1882 [C.3268], lxxix, 1. Census of Ireland 1881, Part 1, Vol. IV Province of Connaught.

HC 1882 (7), lv, 615. Outrages (Ireland). Return of outrages reported to the Royal Irish Constabulary office in each month of the year 1880, 1881 and in the month of January 1882.

HC 1882 (8), lv, 1. Agrarian offences (counties) (Ireland). Return of the number of agrarian offences in each county in Ireland reported to the constabulary office in each month of the year 1881, distinguishing offences against the person, offences against property, and offences against the public peace, with summary for each county, for the year.

HC 1882 (9), lv, 229. Evictions (Ireland). Return (compiled from returns made to the Inspector General of the Royal Irish Constabulary), of cases of eviction which have come to the knowledge of the constabulary in each quarter of the year ended 31 December 1881.

HC 1882 (72), lv, 17. Return, by provinces, of agrarian offences throughout Ireland reported to Inspector General of Royal Irish Constabulary.

HC 1882 (156), lv, 635. Return of all Persons who have been or are in Custody under 'The Protection of Person and Property (Ireland) Act 1881', up to the 31st of March 1882.

HC 1882 (276), lv, 661. Return of numbers of suspects in gaols in Ireland, whose meals are supplied from without.

HC 1882 (403), lv, 609. Nocturnal attacks (Ireland). Return giving the names and occupations of all persons arrested for or convicted of having taken part in nocturnal attacks between the months of June 1880 and June 1882.

HC 1883 [C.3465], lvi, 99. Evictions (Ireland). Return (compiled from returns made to the Inspector-General of the Royal Irish Constabulary) of cases of eviction which have come to the knowledge of the constabulary in each quarter of the year ended 31st day of December 1881.

HC 1883 (6), lvii, 1047. Outrages (Ireland). Return of outrages reported to the Royal Irish Constabulary Office in each month of the years 1881 and 1882, and in the month of January 1883.

HC 1883 (6), [C.3511], lv, 13. Agrarian outrages (Ireland). Return of the number of agrarian outrages which were reported to the Inspector-General of the Royal Irish Constabulary during the month of February, 1883.

HC 1883 [C.3566], lvi, 17. Agrarian outrages (Ireland) – during March 1883.

HC 1883 [C.3608], lvi, 21. Agrarian outrages (Ireland) – during April 1883.

HC 1883 [C.3664], lvi, 25. Agrarian outrages (Ireland) – during May 1883.

HC 1883 [C.3681], lvi, 29. Agrarian outrages (Ireland) – during June 1883.

HC 1883 [C.3743], lvi, 33. Agrarian outrages (Ireland) – during July 1883.

HC 1883 (12), lvi, 1. Agrarian offences (provinces) (Ireland). Return by provinces, of agrarian offences throughout Ireland reported to the Inspector-General of the Royal Irish Constabulary between 1 January 1882 and 31 December 1882.

HC 1883 (204) Third report from the Select Committee of the House of Lords on Land Law (Ireland).

HC 1884 [C.3894], lxiv, 13. Agrarian outrages (Ireland). Return of the number of agrarian outrages which were reported to the Inspector-General of the Royal Irish Constabulary during the months of August, September, October, November, December, 1883.

HC 1884 [C.3950], lxiv, 1. Agrarian offences (provinces) (Ireland). Return by provinces, of agrarian offences throughout Ireland reported to the Inspector-

General of the Royal Irish Constabulary, between 1st January, 1883, and 31st December, 1883.

HC 1884 (80), lxiii, 529. Return of awards by lord lieutenant of Ireland under Crimes Act, and by grand juries in Ireland under Peace Preservation (Ireland) Act, 1875.

Hansard's parliamentary debates, third series, vol. 271.
Hansard's parliamentary debates, third series, vol. 341.

Acts
Encumbered Estates (Ireland) Act, 12 & 13 Vict., c. 77, 1849.
Landlord and Tenant (Ireland) Act, 33 & 34 Vict., c. 46, 1870.
Peace Preservation (Ireland) Act, 38 Vict., c. 4, 1875.
Seed Supply (Ireland) Act, 43 Vict., c. 1, 1880.
Relief of Distress (Ireland) Act, 43 Vict., c. 4, 1880.
Protection of Person and Property (Ireland) Act, 44 & 45 Vict., c. 14, 1881.
Peace Preservation (Ireland) Act, 44 & 45 Vict., c. 5, 1881.
Land Law (Ireland) Act, 44 & 45 Vict., c. 49, 1881.
Prevention of Crime (Ireland) Act, 45 & 46 Vict., c. 25, 1882.
Arrears of Rent (Ireland) Act, 45 & 46 Vict., c. 47, 1882.
15 & 16 George III, c. 21, section 2. Criminal Law Amendment (Ireland) Bill – The Whiteboy Act 1831 and later statutes.

Newspapers

Connaught Telegraph
Connaught Tribune
Dublin Gazette
Freeman's Journal
Galway Express
Galway Observer
Galway Vindicator
Illustrated London News
Irish Times
Irish World
Kerry Sentinel
The Times
Tuam Herald
Tuam News
Western News

UNPUBLISHED SOURCES

Ball, Stephen Andrew, 'Policing the Land War': official responses to political protest and agrarian crime in Ireland, 1879–91' (PhD, U London, 2000).

Finnegan, Anne B., 'The Land War in south-east Galway, 1879–1890' (MA, UCG, 1974).

Griffin, Brian, 'The IRB in Connacht and Leinster, 1858–78 (MA, Maynooth, 1983).

Lane, P.G., 'The social impact of the encumbered estates court on counties Galway and Mayo, 1849–58' (MA, UCD, 1969).

PUBLISHED SOURCES

Ball, F.E., *The judges in Ireland, ii: 1221–1921* (London, 1926).
Bane, Liam, 'John McEvilly and the Catholic Church in Galway, 1857–1902' in Moran and Gillespie (eds), *Galway* (1996).
Beames, Michael, *Peasants and power: the Whiteboy movements and their control in pre-famine Ireland* (Brighton, 1983).
Bew, Paul, 'The Land League ideal: achievements and contradictions' in P.J. Drudy (ed.), *Irish studies 2, Ireland: land, politics and people* (Cambridge, 1982).
Bew, Paul, *Land and the national question in Ireland, 1858–82* (Dublin, 1978).
Bonsall, Penny, *The Irish RMs* (Dublin, n.d.).
Boucicault, Dion, *Selected plays of Dion Boucicault* (Gerrards Cross, 1987).
Boyle, John W., 'A marginal figure: the Irish rural laborer' in Clark & Donnelly Junior (eds), *Irish peasants* (1983).
Buckley, K., 'The fixing of rents by agreement in County Galway, 1881–85', *Irish Historical Studies*, 7:27 (1951).
Bull, Philip, *Land, politics and nationalism* (Dublin, 1996).
Campbell, Fergus, *Land and revolution* (Oxford, 2005).
Carter, J.W.H., *The Land War and its leaders in Queen's County, 1872–82* (Portlaoise, 1994).
Cashman, D.B., *The life of Michael Davitt, founder of the National Land League* (London, n.d.).
Clark, Samuel, *Social origins of the Irish Land War* (Princeton, NJ, 1979).
Clark, Samuel, & James S. Donnelly Junior (eds), *Irish peasants: violence and political unrest, 1780–1914* (Manchester, 1983).
Clifford Lloyd, Charles Dalton, *Ireland under the Land League* (London, 1892).
Comerford, R.V., *The Fenians in context* (Dublin, 1985).
Connolly, S.J., 'The Houghers' in Philpin (ed.), *Nationalism and popular protest* (1987).
Cornewell Lewis, G., *On local disturbances in Ireland* (London, 1836).
Cunningham, John, 'A spirit of self-preservation: herdsmen around Loughrea in the late 19th century' in Joseph Forde, Christina Cassidy, Paul Manzor and David Ryan (eds), *The district of Loughrea, i: history, 1791–1918* (Loughrea, 2003).
Curtis, L.P., 'Stopping the hunt' in Philpin (ed.), *Nationalism and popular protest* (1987).
Davitt, Michael, *The fall of feudalism in Ireland* (London & New York, 1904).
De Búrca, Marcus, *History of the GAA* (Dublin, 1980).
Donnelly, James S. Junior, *The land and the people of nineteenth-century Cork: the rural economy and the land question* (London, 1975).
Donnelly, James S. Junior, 'Pastorini and Captain Rock' in Clark & Donnelly Junior (eds), *Irish peasants* (1983).
Donnelly, James S. Junior, 'The land question in nationalist politics' in Thomas E. Hachey & Lawrence J. McCaffrey, *Perspectives on Irish nationalism* (Lexington, 1989).
Donnelly, James S. Junior, *The great Irish potato famine* (Stroud, 2001).
Dooley, Terence A.M., 'Landlords and the land question, 1879–1909' in King (ed.), *Famine* (2000).

Drudy, P.J. (ed.), *Irish Studies 2, Ireland: land, politics and people* (Cambridge, 1982).
Finnegan, Pat, *The case of the Craughwell prisoners during the Land War in Co. Galway, 1879–85* (Dublin, 2012).
Gordon, Peter, *The Red Earl* (Northampton, 1981).
Grey, Marguerite (ed.), *Gort Inse Guaire* (Gort, 2000).
Hawkins, Richard, 'Liberals, land and coercion in the summer of 1880: the influence of the Carraroe ejectments', *Journal of Galway Archaeological and Historical Society*, 34 (1974–5).
Hawkins, Richard, 'An army on police work, 1881–2', *Irish Sword*, 11 (1973).
Jordan, Donald E., *Land and popular politics in Ireland: County Mayo from the Plantation to the Land War* (Cambridge, 1994).
Joynes, J.L., 'Adventures of a tourist in Ireland' in Michael Davitt, *The fall of feudalism in Ireland* (London & New York, 1904).
Kelly Desmond, Catherine, 'John Henry Blake: villain or victim?' in Kieran Jordan (ed.), *Kiltullagh Killimordaly* (Midleton, 2000).
Kinealy, Christine, 'The response of the Poor Law to the Great Famine in County Galway' in Moran and Gillespie (eds), *Galway* (1996).
King, Carla (ed.), *Famine, land and culture in Ireland* (Dublin, 2000).
King, Carla, and Conor McNamara (eds), *The West of Ireland: new perspectives on the nineteenth century* (Dublin, 2011).
Laird, Heather, *Subversive law in Ireland, 1879–1920* (Dublin, 2005).
Lane, Padraig G., 'The general impact of the Encumbered Estates Act of 1849 on Counties Galway and Mayo', *Journal of Galway Archaeological and Historical Society*, 33 (1972–3).
Lane, Padraig G., 'Agricultural labourers and rural violence, 1850–1914', *Studia Hibernica*, 27 (1993).
Lane, Padraig G., 'The Encumbered Estates Court and Galway land ownership, 1849–58' in Moran and Gillespie (eds), *Galway* (1996).
Lane, Padraig G., 'The tedious business of unwanted tenants: Galway and Mayo in the 1850s', *Journal of Galway Archaeological and Historical Society*, 60 (2008).
Legg, Marie-Louise, *The Irish provincial press, 1850–92* (Dublin, 1999).
Lourdes Fahy, Sr Mary de, *Kiltartan: many leaves, one root* (Kiltartan, 2004).
Lucey, Donnacha Seán, *Land, popular politics and agrarian violence in Ireland: the case of County Kerry, 1872–86* (Dublin, 2011).
Mandle, W.F., *The Gaelic Athletic Association and Irish nationalist politics, 1884–1924* (London & Dublin, 1987).
McCartney, Donal, 'Parnell, Davitt and the land question' in King (ed.), *Famine* (2000).
McGee, Owen, *The IRB* (Dublin, 2005).
Moody, T.W., *Davitt and Irish revolution, 1846–82* (Oxford, 1981).
Moody, T.W., & R.A.J. Hawkins (eds), *Florence Arnold-Forster's Irish journal* (Oxford, 1988).
Moran, Gerard, 'Near famine: the Roman Catholic Church and the subsistence crisis of 1879–82', *Studia Hibernica*, 32 (2002–3).
Moran, Gerard, 'Laying the seeds for agrarian agitation: the Ballinasloe Tenants' Defence Association, 1876–80' in Carla King and Conor McNamara (eds), *The west of Ireland: new perspectives on the nineteenth century* (Dublin, 2011).

Moran, Gerard, 'James Daly and the rise and fall of the Land League in the west of Ireland, 1879–1882', *Journal of the Irish Historical Society* 39:114 (1994).
Moran, Gerard, & Raymond Gillespie (eds), *Galway: history and society* (Dublin, 1996).
O'Brien, William, & Desmond Ryan (eds), *Devoy's post bag, i & ii* (Dublin, 1948).
O'Callaghan, Margaret, *British high politics and a nationalist Ireland* (Cork, 1994).
O'Neill, Tim P., 'Famine evictions' in King (ed.), *Famine* (2000).
Orridge, Andrew W., 'Who supported the Land War?: an aggregate data analysis of Irish discontent, 1879–82', *Economic and Social Review*, 12:3 (1981).
Palmer, Norman Dunbar, *The Irish Land League crisis* (New Haven, CT, 1940).
Palmer, S.H., *Police and protest in England and Ireland, 1780–1850* (Cambridge, 1988).
Philpin, C.H.E. (ed.), *Nationalism and popular protest in Ireland* (Cambridge, 1987).
Ryan, David, 'Disaffection and rebellious conspiracy in the Loughrea area, 1791–1804' in Joseph Forde, Christina Cassidy, Paul Manzor and David Ryan (eds), *The district of Loughrea, i: history, 1791–1918* (Loughrea, 2003).
Ryan, David, 'The trial and execution of Anthony Daly' in Joseph Forde, Christina Cassidy, Paul Manzor and David Ryan (eds), *The district of Loughrea, i: history, 1791–1918* (Loughrea, 2003).
Ryan, Mark, *Fenian memories* (Dublin, 1946).
Shaw Lefevre, G., *Incidents of coercion in Ireland* (London, 1889).
Solow, Barbara L., *The land question and the Irish economy, 1870–1903* (Cambridge, MA, 1971).
Thom's Directory.
Townshend, Charles, *Political violence in Ireland, government and resistance since 1848* (Oxford, 1983).
Tynan, P.J.P., *The Irish National Invincibles and their times* (London, 1894).
Vaughan, W.E., *Landlords and tenants in mid-Victorian Ireland* (Oxford, 1994).
Waldron, Jarlath, *Maamtrasna: the murders and the mystery* (Dublin, 1992).
Wemyss Reid, Thomas, *Life of the Rt Hon. W.E. Forster*, i & ii (New York, 1970).

Index

Abbeygormican, 40
Aggard House, 40, 86, 91
agrarian crimes, outrages, 11, 40, 58, 61, 68, 76–7, 81, 136, 156–7
agrarian (and political) murders (killings), 9, 11, 37, 60–2, 65, 69–71, 73, 76, 84, 88–102, 114, 117–23, 129, 133–5, 138, 154–8, 163–6
agrarian reform, land tenure reform, 13–15, 19, 32, 50, 64, 103, 146, 152–3, 156, 158, 163–6
agrarian secret societies, 14, 18, 62–7, 69–73, 91, 96n, 99, 110–12, 117, 120, 122, 125–6, 144, 153, 155
agrarian statistics, 21–3, 109
agricultural crisis, 13, 21–3, 27–8, 35, 52, 59, 64, 153, 156
agricultural labourers, 12, 25–6, 49, 63–5, 67, 103, 115–16, 129, 135, 140, 144, 147, 152
agricultural produce, 12, 21, 30, 51, 63; crops (hay, potatoes, oats), 21–3, 29; livestock, 21–3, 115, 151
agricultural sector, 115–16, 119
Ahascragh, 40, 146
Amiens St. station, 161
Anderson, Samuel Lee, 69, 71n, 111
Antoine Ó Dálaigh, 63
approver, 134–5
Aran Islands, 114, 143
Arbor Hill, 96
Ardilaun estate, 133
Ardrahan, 13, 36, 39, 45, 49, 56–7, 77, 87–9, 91, 102, 139, 148; dispensary, 45; Petty Sessions, 45, 57
arms, 11, 41, 61, 63, 65–8, 70–1, 73, 76, 80, 90–2, 95, 110, 129, 153, 161
Army Act 1881, 132
Arnold-Forster, Florence, 35, 45
Arrears of Rent (Ireland) Act 1882, 104
arrest on suspicion, 77, 132, 143
Ashtown, Lord, 12
assassination, 71, 93, 98, 131; landlord, 60, 129; political, 60; Society, 99
assizes, Carrick-on-Shannon, winter, 134; Cork, winter, 134; Galway, spring, 47, 57, 93; winter, 47; Sligo, summer, 90; winter, 57, 94, 134; Wicklow, 73
Athenry, 11, 25, 28, 35–6, 39, 41, 44, 70, 77, 84–5, 88–90, 92, 101–2, 104, 110, 113, 116, 122, 125, 129, 144, 149; baronies of Athenry and Loughrea, 100; Fenian membership, 65, 72; Ladies' Land League branch, 84, 113; land conference (convention), 38, 146; Land Court, 38; Land League branch, 25, 31, 34, 38, 79, 84; Loughrea and Athenry police districts, 11, 60, 96, 99, 112, 114, 117, 135, 164; meetings, 30, 62, 65, 83; station, 87; suspects (arrests), 87, 110–12, 114, 116–17, 119–20, 142, 164–5
Attymon, 37, 147
Aughamore, 14
Aughrim, 62, 161

Baldwin, Thomas, 51, 151
Ball, Stephen A., 60, 117
Ball Greene, 51
Balla, 17–18
Ballinagar, 40, 79
Ballinasloe, 16–17, 27, 38, 79, 91, 98, 104, 111, 135, 137, 140, 143, 146, 161; arrests, 114, 142, 147, 153; fair, 23; Fenians, 65; Land League branch, 31; land meetings, 30, 83, 107, police station, 161
Ballinasloe Tenants' Defence Association (BTDA), 15, 17, 152
Ballybane, 35
Ballycrissane, 43, 48
Ballydugan, 42, 48
Ballyglass, 91
Ballymacward, 40
Ballymana, 39, 57, 96, 105, 129; arrests, 167; Craughwell and Ballymana Land League branch, 108; INL branch, 147; INL meeting, 138, 140, 142, 148–9; Land League meeting, 38
Ballymore House, 39, 113
Ballywinna, 122, 146, 167
Barnacarroll, 96
Barniville, Head Constable, 161

175

Barrett, Edward J., 41, 83, 129, 142, 146–50, 164, 167
Barrett, Mary, 56, 108
Barrett, Mr, 66
Barrett, Nicholas J., 110, 127–9, 140–3, 146–50, 165, 167
Barry, Dominick, 35, 88–92, 101, 105, 111, 122, 140, 159, 161
Beaconsfield, Lord (Benjamin Disraeli), 32, 65
Bell, Alan, 70, 77, 83, 87, 90, 92, 110–11, 122, 128–30, 144, 148–9
Belleek, 55
Bellew, Henry Gratten, 44
Benn, J., 39, 105, 113
Benn, Mrs, 108
Benn-Walsh, John, 51
Bennett, James Gordon, 24
Beresford, RM, 111
Bermingham, Martin, 35–6, 90–1, 103, 163–4
Berridge estate, 55
Bessborough Commission, 16, 103, 113
Bessborough, earl of, 103
Bew, Paul, 151–2, 154
Biggar, Joseph, 19
Bladenburg, Ross of, 110n, 132n
Blake estate, 45, 148
Blake, Henrietta Frances, 97, 102
Blake, Henry Arthur, 66n, 109–12, 123
Blake, John Henry (Shawn Beagh), 9, 79, 94, 97–9, 102–3, 110, 114, 120, 122, 127, 130, 138–9
Blake, Mr, Towerhill, 55
Blake, Mrs, Hollypark, 148
Blake, Peter, Hollypark, 34, 41, 90, 111, 129
Blake Lewis, Charles, 96
Blindwell, 55
Board of Public Works, 26
Boherduff, 141
Boland, Constable, 46
Bookeen, 88, 129
Bourke, Isidore, 47, 102
Bourke, Ulick, 18
Bourke, Walter, 11, 33, 47, 79, 95–8, 100, 102, 128, 129, 138
boycotting, 70, 79–80, 82, 117, 135–7, 144, 156–7; as suspected crime, 164–5; for paying rent, 128; of job and land grabbers, 39, 88, 90, 95, 101, 144; of landlords, 40–1, 60, 92; of police, 39, 132; 'the boycott', 102

Boyton, Michael, 68, 83
Brackenbury, Henry, 69, 133
Brennan, Thomas, 19, 33, 68, 71, 82, 107, 153
Bright, John, 19n, 80; Bright clauses, 19
Broadstone, 161
Broderick, John, 70, 72, 144, 165
Broderick, Peter, 9, 35, 39, 70, 72, 83–7, 104, 113, 146, 164
Browne, Edward, 62
Bruce, G., 66n
Bruce, Robert, 66
Brusk, 85
Buckley, James, 165
Buckley, John, 165
Buckley, K., 106
Bull, Philip, 50
Bullaun, 146
Burke, John, 92, 164
Burke, Dr John, 24, 92, 97
Burke, Mary, 128
Burke, Patrick, 142, 165
Burke, Thomas H., 66–7, 69, 76, 109, 111, 131
Butler, A.S., 67
Butler, Michael, 166
Butterfield, Mr, 71
Byrne, CI, 94, 98, 105
Byrne, J. Alexander, 100
Byrne, John W., 92–3, 105, 109–12, 122, 131, 136, 142–3
Byrne, Pat, 140

Caher, 129
Caherbroder, 136
Cahill, Michael, 45, 48
Cahill, Thomas, 97
Cairns Commission, 51
Callanan, John, 140, 149
Callanan, Patrick, 79
Callanan, P.A., 39
Calligy, Michael, 38, 110, 164
Cappanoole, 37
Cappataggle, 40, 48, 77
Carberry, Mrs, 84
Carley, John, 165
Carley, Patrick, 165
Carr, Thomas, 167
Carra, 48
Carrabane, 11
Carraroe, 31, 32n, 55
Carrick-on-Shannon, winter assizes, 134

Index

Carrigan, 33, 39, 46, 84, 86, 92, 95, 101, 122, 146
Carroll, James, 24, 30, 50
Carty, Thomas, 136
Casey, Patrick, 134
Castle Ellen, 34, 41, 106, 139
Castleblakeny, 146
Castleisland, 120
Castletaylor, 95, 102
Castletown, Lord, 155
categories of offence, 116–17, 119, 136, 156
Cavan, Co., 62
Cave, Thomas L., 51
Cavendish, Lord, 69, 131
Cawley, Patrick, 57, 105, 129–30, 146–8
Chamberlain, Joseph, 80
Chambers, SI, 94, 148
Christian, Sub Constable, 142
civil bills court, 106
Clancarty, Lord, 12
Clanmorris, Lord, 44
Clanricarde, Lord, 11–12, 30–1, 39n, 78, 97, 106, 113, 128, 138, 141; his agent, 79, 97, 138; estate, 37n, 79, 157; Clanrackrent, 78, 97, 138
Clan na Gael, 20, 66–7, 153
Clare, Co., 20n, 63–4, 73, 81, 119, 125, 127, 134
Claregalway, 18
Claremorris, 17, 95, 102; land meeting, 18, 153
Clarinbridge, 38, 43
Clark, Samuel, 114–16, 119, 151–2
Clarke, Mary Anne, 93–4
Clarke, Michael, 93–4, 166
Clasby, Michael, 33, 39, 128
Cleaghmore, 135
Clements, A.C., 161
Clifden, arrests, 11; Castle, 55; land meeting, 18
Clifford Lloyd, C.D., 9, 11, 57, 71–2, 81, 83, 98–9, 109, 118–20, 122–4, 132, 136–7, 143–4, 149
Clonbern, 66
Clonbrock, Lord, 44; papers, 110n
Clonbur, 115
Cloonan, Michael, 167
Cloonan, Miss, 108
Clostoken, 26, 39, 113, 129, 147; Fife and Drum Band, 113; meetings, 37, 140, 142, 148–9, 167
Clough, 113

Coane [Coen], James, 113, 165
Coane [Coen], Thomas, 113, 165
Coen, William, 45, 48
coercion, 80, 107; acts, 9, 58, 62, 78, 120, 131; bill, 78; Crimes Act, 11, 131–145, 148; Protection of Person and Property (PPP) (Ireland) Act 1881 (Coercion Act), 11, 43, 49, 81–4, 90, 117–20, 156; arrests (suspects) under PPP (Ireland) Act, 43n, 59, 73, 81–4, 87, 89–91, 94, 97–100, 109–22, 125, 127, 135–6, 138, 143, 154–6, 159, 164–6 (also see suspects)
Colemanstown, 140
Comerford, R.V., 15
compensation, 19; Compensation for Disturbance Bill, 32, 35, 40; for eviction, 33; for improvements to holdings, 147; hearing, 100–2; payment, 101–2; to victims of crimes, 90, 100, 129
Comyn, Andrew, 44
Connacht, 66; Crimes Act in, 131, 134; crop production, 23; evictions, 53–5; Fenians, 65n; Invincibles, 71; IRB, 15, 65n, 70; police district, 63
Connaire, John, 122, 166
Connaire, Michael, 45–6
Connaught, province, 116; Rangers, 95–6
Connaught Telegraph, 15, 152
Connaughton, John, 113, 164
Connean, John, 167
Connell, James, 72
Connell, John, 45, 48
Connelly, John, 165
Connelly, Michael, 167
Connelly, Pat(rick), 166–7
Connolly, Michael, Ballywinna, 122, 150, 166–7
Connolly, Thomas, 122, 166
Connolly, Michael, Brusk, 85, 146
Connolly, Michael, Loughrea, 97
Connolly, Michael, Brucken, 166
Connors, James, 88, 91, 98, 100, 129, 159n, 163n
Connors, John, 164
Connors, Julia, 90, 100
Considine, T.B., 39, 56, 77–8
constitutional, agitation, 71; nationalism, 16, 153; politics, 68, 156; reform, 13; rights, 107
Convent of Mercy, 24
Coole Park, 106
Cooney, Michael, 165

Coote, Charles, 155
Corbett, Patrick, 86, 164
Corbett, Thomas, 91
Corbetts Hotel, 161
Cork, city, 32, 154; Co., 127, 154; agrarian secret society, 155; estate rentals, 51; murders, 154; suspects, 106, 143, 154; trial venue, 134; winter assizes, 134
Corless, Mrs, 139
Cornewell Lewis, G., 63
Corofin, 64
Corry, Patrick, 166
Costello, Edward, 166
cottiers, 53
Coughlan, Peter, 164
county council, 47
County Galway Hunt, 43, 45
Cowper, Lord, 76–7, 99, 126
Cox, J.R., 86
Coy, James, 150, 165, 167
Coyle, Bernard, 110, 127, 165
Coyne, Thomas, 113, 164
Craughwell, 11, 26, 33–4, 36, 39, 57, 63, 77, 95–6, 101–2, 111, 128, 129, 146, 149; and Ballymana branch of the Land League, 31, 105, 108, 129; arms raid, 41; arrests, 83, 85, 97, 122, 149, 167; eviction, 128, 138; INL branch, 147–8; Ladies' Land League, 39n, 56–7, 111, 113, 129; meetings, 39, 147; prisoners, 33n, 71, 135; railway station, 41; secret society, 91; tenants, 30, 34
Cregclare, 45–6
Creggs, 31
Crehan, John, 140
Crimes Act, 11, 131–45, 148
Croke, Thomas, 32, 73, 107
Crotty, RM, 149
Crowe, Denis, 129
crown, the, 138; counsel, 47, 94, 134; estates, 14; forces, 62, 129; law officers, 106; prosecutor, 90, 134; protection, 96; solicitor, 69, 94, 134, 138; witness, 136
Cullahill, 155
Cunniffe, John, 147
Cunniffe, Thomas, 33, 84, 146, 164, 167
Cunningham, Denis, 164
Cunningham, J., 78, 105
Cunningham, John, 9
Cunningham, Michael, 50, 165
Cunningham, Thomas, 57, 72–3, 87, 91, 110, 127, 141–2, 146, 148–50, 153, 159–61, 164–5, 167
curfew, 132, 142
Curragh camp, 155
Curraghmore Hunt, 45
Curraleigh estate, 102
Currandula, 18
Cusack, Michael, 73, 166

Dalton, P.R., 95–6
Daly, Anthony, 62–3
Daly, James, 15, 17–18, 33, 39n, 152, 156–7
Daly, John Archer, 44, 103
Daly, William, 50, 82, 101, 103, 138
Dalystown, 48
Darcy, John, 91, 163–4
Dartfield, 120, 122, 143
Davin, Maurice, 75
Davis, Thomas, 14
Davitt, Michael, 16–20, 24, 30–1, 35, 40, 52, 57, 66, 68, 78, 81, 93, 107, 146–7, 152–3
Deane, Colonel, 25
Deely, Denis, 139
Defenders, 62
Delaney, William, 127, 146
Dempsey, Mary, 101
Dempsey, Peter, 67, 90–1, 95, 98, 101, 112, 159n, 163n
Dempsey, widow, 38
Derrygimley, 55
Derryhoyle, 143
Derryoober, 49
detective, 161; department, 69n, 89; director of constabulary, 69
de Vere Pery, RM, 45–6, 129–30, 141, 144, 148–50
Devon Commission, 11
Devoy, John, 16, 21, 24, 66–7, 153
Dilleen, Michael, 93–4, 98, 120, 165–6
Dillon, John, 9, 20, 24, 32–3, 80, 82–3, 85–6, 107, 146
disturbed, areas, 11, 62, 77, 110, 114, 119, 125, 128, 131–2, 135, 139, 153; nature of the country, 52, 59; relations between landlords and tenants, 91; town, 9, 129
divisional magistrate, 123
Doherty, John, 33, 128, 129
Doherty, Kate, 101
Doherty, Mary Anne, 101
Doherty, Owen, 142
Doherty, Peter (Junior), 67, 70, 84, 95, 100–1, 112, 122, 127

Index

Doherty, Peter (Senior), 33, 101, 129
Dolan, Timothy, 88–9, 164
Doloughty, John, 134
Dolphin, Peter H., 90
Donegal Rifles, 39
Donnelly, James S. (Junior), 9, 21, 51, 151
Donohue, John, 128
Donohue, Pat, 161
Donoughmore Union, 155
Dooley, Terence A.M., 52
Down, Co., 55, 92, 101
Duane, John, 150, 167
Dublin, 24, 69, 73, 98, 106–7, 128, 144, 146; Arbor Hill, 96; Castle, 23, 38, 40, 62, 69, 70, 72, 76, 81, 109, 111, 137, 140, 150; city police district, 120; Commission, 133–4; convention, 105; Fenians, 71; lord mayor, 24; Metropolitan Police (DMP), 69; papers, 73, 110; Rotunda, 32, 82; state trials, 80; tradesmen, 96; Trinity College, 118; weather data, 22
Dublin Gazette, 96
Duff, Harvey, 93n
Duffy, William J. (Willy), 73–4
Duggan, Patrick, 19, 25–7, 29, 31, 73, 78, 105, 146, 156
Duggan, Thomas, 110, 164
Dundalk Jail, 86, 91, 162
Duniry, 146
Dunkellin, barony of, Fenian Head Centre, 96; Street, Loughrea, 9, 141
Dunmore, 66
Dunsandle, estate, 26, 50, 88, 103, 122; Lord, 12, 26, 30, 35–7, 50, 52, 80, 82, 100, 129, 148, 157
Duro, Joe, 72

East Galway Hunt, 49
Easter Rising, 97
Eastwell, 45
Egan, P., 24, 77, 82, 93, 161, 163
Egan, Patrick, 19, 35, 68, 71, 80, 107, 153
'Emergency Men', 41, 57, 79–80
emigration, 11–12, 16, 21, 28, 52, 63, 96, 122, 129, 157; assisted, 55, 69, 103, 149; national statistics, 28
Encumbered Estates (Ireland) Act, 12
encumbered properties, 12, 102, 128
Enfield rifles, 65
Ennis, 31, 76, 125, 134
Enniskillen, 70; Jail, 122
Ennistymon, 122

Errislannon, 55
evictions, ejectments, 11–12, 16, 19, 30–8, 40–5, 52–61, 64, 76, 80, 82, 87–8, 90–1, 95, 97, 102–4, 107–8, 128–30, 138–9, 141–2, 148, 154
execution, hanging, 63, 114, 133–5
Eyre, Mr, 55
Eyrecourt, 44, 48, 73

Fahey, Edward, 88–9, 164
Fahey, Jerome, 25
Fahey, John, 45, 48
Fahy, John, 146
Fahy, Mary, 108
fair rent, 14, 17, 19, 37, 42, 50, 82, 103–4
Fallon, John, 57
Fallon, Michael (Mike), 36, 42, 56–7, 87, 136, 139, 141; family, 56–7, 108
Fallon, Mrs, 56–8, 139
farm(er)s, farming, 12, 33, 63–4, 79, 144–5, 154; boycotted, 79, 101, 129, 136; class, 63–7, 73, 115–16, 120; clubs, 12; commercial, gentlemen, graziers, large, 11–12, 15, 21, 25, 32–3, 42, 48–9, 52, 62, 82, 104, 134–5, 155; consolidation of, 11–12; evicted, vacant, 33, 37, 73, 77, 79–80, 90, 136, 144; harvest and produce, see agricultural produce; sales, 79–80; small, tenant, 15, 17, 19, 22, 26, 30, 32, 34–5, 37, 40, 42, 45, 47–50, 56, 65–6, 78–9, 87–8, 105, 107, 112–13, 126, 146–7, 151, 155, 157
farm labourers, see agricultural labourers
Farrell, John, 72–3, 110, 121, 160–1, 165–6
Farrell, William, 146
Feakle, 125
Fenian, 9, 15–17, 37, 39, 64, 66–8, 70–3, 82, 84, 152–3; agitation, 66, 153, 157; Centre, Barony of Dunkellin, 96; IRB, 69–71; Loughrea, 65, 72; Galway, 65, 70, 153; leaders, 20, 33, 68, 153, 155, 157; Mayo, 68, 152, 155–7; membership, 72; movement 15–16, 41, 65, 71; organization, 62, 65, 67–8, 90, 153–4; Ribbonism, 67, 69–71, 153; rising, 65
Fenton, John, 31
Fiddane, 128
Finnegan, Patrick, 150, 165, 167
Finnegan, P.J., 9
Finnigan, James, 165–6
Finnigan, Thomas, 111, 165, 167

Fitzgerald, Mr, 50
Fitzgerald, P.N., 66
Fitzpatrick, Bernard, 155
fixity (security) of tenure (see also '3 Fs'), 14, 103
Flatley, Thomas, 104
Fleming, James, 130
Fleming & Colohan, 161
Flood, Henry, 162
Flood, James, 162
Flynn, Michael, 114, 133
Fogarty, Michael, 122, 150, 166–7
Forde, Miss, 108
Forge Hill, 88
Forrest, John, 136
Forster, William Edward, 11, 27, 32, 34–5, 45, 59, 76–7, 80, 105, 107, 109, 111, 117–19, 122, 125–6
Fortnightly Crime Report (FCR), 144
Fowler, Edward, 135
Franks, David B., 67, 95
Freeman's Journal, 17–18, 134, 150
free sale (right to sell; see also '3 Fs'), 14–15, 30
French, James Ellis, 69
French Henderson, William, 45, 93, 138, 149
Furlong, Revd, 147
Furlong, Michael, 110, 165

Gaelic Athletic Association (GAA), 73, 75, 154
Galway, Blazers, 42–5, 130; changes of trial venues, 80, 90, 94, 131, 133–5; City, 37, 65, 84, 94, 116, 131, 140; clearances, evictions, 11–12, 16, 31, 34–8, 40–2, 45, 48, 52–7, 59–61, 80, 82, 87, 90–1, 95, 97, 103, 108, 127–30, 138–9, 141, 148; clerics, 17–19, 23–7, 29–31, 38–9, 50, 56, 64, 77–9, 82, 84–5, 90, 93, 104–5, 112–13, 146, 156, 161, 163; Co., 11–13, 15–19, 30–1, 37n, 42–4, 47, 49, 60, 62, 65, 69, 79, 81, 127, 134, 143, 155–7; County Club, 43; County Hunt, 43, 45; Courthouse, 46; crop production and livestock numbers, 21–3; East Galway Hunt, 49; East Riding, 12, 52–5, 59–60, 67, 70, 72, 120, 126, 143; election 1872, 103; emigration, 11–12, 16, 28, 55, 96, 122, 129; executions (hangings), 115, 133–4; Fenians, 65–6, 70, 82, 84, 96, 152–5, 157; hunts, 37, 42–9, 86, 130, 147; INL, 147; intelligence activities, 72; Jail, 9, 56–7, 84–7, 91, 93, 115, 133–4, 143, 149; juries, 47, 94, 133; labour force, 115–16; Ladies' Land League, 84, 86, 108, 111, 113, 129, 162; landlords, 12, 17–18, 25, 30, 36–7, 43–4, 47, 50, 55–6, 64, 97, 103, 105–6, 110, 128–9; Land Convention, 43, 146, 157; Land League, 30–2, 34–43, 47–53, 56–7, 64, 70–3, 76, 79–80, 82–4, 88, 91–3, 98, 103–5, 107, 110–12, 116, 120, 125–6, 129, 138, 152–4, 156–7, 161; land meeting, 15, 17–18, 26, 30–1, 33, 35–42, 45, 52–3, 56–7, 61–2, 77–8, 81–3, 88, 92–3, 95, 105, 107, 112, 137–8, 140, 142, 147–50, 152–4, 156–7, 167; MPs, 26–7, 30, 35, 37, 48, 73, 112–13; murders (killings), 88–102; nationalist papers, 137; occupations of suspects, 114–15, 149, 162; outrage statistics, 59–61, 126, 136; Plan of Campaign, 73, 157; police and military, 31, 48–9, 55, 77, 88, 96, 99–100, 105, 110, 120, 128, 144; population change, 11–13; Record Court, 100; rents, 106, 114; RMs, 38, 44–6, 48, 67, 72, 87, 92–3, 95, 105, 109–12, 122–3, 129, 131, 136, 141–4, 148–50; Ribbonism, 70; secret societies, 66; Shepherd's Association, 140n; south, 33, 40, 63–4, 127, 153–4; SRM, 11, 109, 137; spring assizes, 93; suspects, 112, 115–20, 122, 154–7; West Riding, 12, 52–5, 59, 60; Whiteboyism, 62; winter assizes, 47

Galway Vindicator, 43, 86
Ganty, 45, 129–30, 148
general election, 1880, 32, 34, 103
gentry, 12, 42–3, 47, 49, 62–3
Geoghegan, T.D., 28, 39, 77, 105
George, Henry, 143–4
Gibbons, Michael, 88
Gildea, Governor, 85
Gilligan, Patrick, 112, 165
Gladstone, W.E., 15, 32, 34, 52, 69, 76–7, 81, 99, 106–7, 110, 125–7, 158
Glenarde, 90
Glennon, John, 113, 164
Glennon, Michael, 73–4, 83, 146–7, 164
Gloves, 78
Glynn, John, 167
Glynn, Patrick, 90
Goodricke, Harry, 141, 148
Gordon, Patrick J., 83

Index

Gort, 39, 46, 79, 95, 102, 104; band, 39; distress, 25; Fenians, 65; INL, 146; Ladies' Land League, 108; land meeting, 18, 78; petty sessions, 95; police, 96, 136; poor law union, 11–12, 21–2; produce of crops and livestock, 21–3; railway station, 125; RM, 67; Right Boys, 62; suspects, 83, 114; Terry Alt, 63
Graham, Mr, 128
grand jury system, 47
Grangepark, 73
Granville, Lord, 123
Greally, Dr, 28
Greaney, Miss, 108
Great Famine, 11, 21–2, 27–8, 48, 58, 63, 82; evictions, 52–3, 63
Greene, Martin, 110, 127, 165–6
Gregory, W.H., 106
Grenage, 91, 122, 167
Griffin, Anthony, 113, 146, 164
Griffin, Brian, 65
Griffin, J.J., 37
Griffin, Thomas G., 111, 113, 146, 164
Griffith's valuation, 32, 32n, 37–8, 40, 50–2, 103, 106, 155
Gunning estate, 49
Gurteen, Co. Galway, 37, 50; INL branch, 146–7; land court, 38; Land League branch, 31, 36, 38, 111
Gurteen, Co. Sligo, 39n

habeas corpus, suspension of, 58, 76–7
Haire, Thomas, 165–6
Halloran, John, 97
Halloran, Thomas, 165
Hamilton, Robert G.C., 69, 133
Harcourt, William, 118, 131
Hardiman Burke, James, 11
Hardy estate, 122
Hardy, JP of Dartfield, 143
Harrington, Timothy, 9, 83, 85–6, 147, 157
Harris, Matthew, 15–19, 30–2, 36–7, 42, 47, 56–7, 65, 68, 70, 72, 80, 82, 85, 87, 98, 143, 146–7, 152–3, 157
Harrison, John, 26
Hartington, Lord, 118n
Haverty, Patrick, 165
Hayden, Robert, 57
Hazel, John, 83, 146
Headford, 49
Healy, Patrick, 141
Healy, Tim, 71, 104n, 143, 147; clause, 104

Hennessy, John Pope, 123
herd, herdsmen, 39, 41, 64, 111, 115–16, 127, 129, 139–40
Higgins, Patrick, 114, 133
Higgins, Thomas, 114, 133
Hill, Benjamin, 38
Hillier, George, 69
Hoarty, Michael, 72
Hodgens, Constable, 161
Holland, Thomas, 45–8, 167
Hollypark, 34, 41, 90, 111, 148
Holmes, Hugh, 66
home rule, 30, 126, 153
homicide (killing, murder), 9, 11, 37, 59–63, 65, 69–70, 73, 76, 84, 88–102, 114, 117, 119–20, 122–3, 125, 127, 129, 133–5, 138, 154–5, 157, 159, 163n, 164–5
Hooban, Martin, 164
Horne, SI, 133
'Houghers', 62
House of Commons, 27, 32–3, 35, 52, 80, 105, 119
House of Lords, 35
Howley, James, 45
Huban, Joseph M., 36, 40, 67, 73, 78, 80, 85, 91, 159, 161, 164
Huban, Martin, 110, 146, 165–6
Huddy, Joseph, 114, 133
Hughes, R., 89
hunt (hunting), 37, 42–9; stopping the, 42, 48, 147; County Galway Hunt, 43, 45; Curraghmore Hunt, 45; East Galway Hunt, 49; Kilcornan hunt, 43–4, 86; Kildare Hunt, 45; People's Hunts, 48–9
Huntington, Lord, 50
Hussey, Samuel, 98
Hynes, Francis, 134
Hynes, Martin, 165
Hynes, Murty, 35–6, 90, 135
Hynes, Patrick, 93

Ichem, Bere, 46
Illustrated London News, 121, 138
incitement, 83; by newspapers, 137; to intimidation, 131, 135–6; to murder, 117; to violence, 81
informer, 60, 69, 71–2, 100, 134n, 153
Insurrection Act, 62
intelligence, 25; activities, 69, 72; service, 69
internment (detention) without trial, 11, 58, 81

intimidation, 64, 79, 81, 107, 132, 135–6; against payment of rent, 11, 94, 111–12, 114, 117, 164–5; and incitement to intimidation, 131, 135; by publications, 132, 138–40; of juries, 133, 144; of land grabbers, 31, 60, 95; of witnesses, 136–7
Invincibles, 67, 70–1, 96
Irish Free State, 104n
Irish National Land League, see Land League
Irish National League, 45, 72–3, 140, 144, 147, 149–50, 157; foundation, 126, 146; Ballymana, 148–50, 167; Clostoken, 148, 167; Kilconierin, 147; programme, 148
Irish office, London, 112
Irish Parliamentary Party, 33, 104, 156
Irish Republican Brotherhood (IRB), 67–70, 96, 100; County Head Centre, 73; groups, 61, 64–5; members, 16, 68, 71–3, 75, 99, 111, 120, 152; supreme council, 15–17, 66, 68
Irish Times, 76
Irish World, 104
Irishtown, 17, 33, 68, 152, 155

jail (prison), Dartmoor, 16; Dundalk, 86, 91, 162; Enniskillen, 70, 122; Galway, 9, 56–7, 84–7, 91, 93, 114, 133–4, 143, 149; Kilmainham, 70, 86, 106–7, 122, 128, 143; Monaghan, 110, 112; Mullingar, 140; Naas, 110; Omagh, 110, 113, 143; Portland, 81, 107
Jenkinson, E.G., 99, 120
Jordan, Donald E., 18, 33, 114, 151, 155, 157
Joyce, DI, 71n
Joyce, Dominick, 91
Joyce, John, 167
Joyce, Myles, 134
Joyce, Patrick, 134
Joyce, Peter, 167
Joyce, Thomas, 91, 122, 166
Joynes, James Lee, 143
Judge, Constable, 108, 122
jury, composition, 133; Dublin Commission, 133–4, 144n; Galway, spring assizes 1882, 94; winter assizes 1881, 47, 134; intimidation of, 133, 144; packing, 125; panel, 134; religion of, 133–4, Catholics, 133–4, Protestants, 133; selection, 133–4; special juries, 131–5; state trial of Parnell and others, 80; trial without, 126
justice of the peace (JP), 24, 90, 129, 135, 143

Kavanagh, Patrick, 127, 166
Keane, Edward, 147
Keane, James, 45–8
Keane, John, 86, 109, 164
Keary, Andrew, 113, 146, 164
Keary, of Craughwell, 128
Keighrey, Thomas, 165
Kelly, Charles, 76
Kelly, Columbus, 24
Kelly, John J., 72
Kelly, Martin, 167
Kelly, Mary, 88
Kelly, M.E., 24
Kelly, Patrick C. (Pat), 84–6, 146, 164
Kelly, Peter, 73–5, 109, 113, 146, 165–6
Kelly, Richard, 19, 138
Kelly, Tom, 167
Kenmare, earl of, 76
Kennedy, Edward, 93–4
Kennedy, Hugh, 165
Kennedy, James, 165
Kennedy, John, 167
Kennedy, Martin (Athenry), 165, 167
Kennedy, Martin (Loughrea), 166
Kennedy, of Gort, 79
Kennedy, Patrick, 146
Kenny, Joseph E., 28
Keogh, James, 88
Keogh, Patrick, 88–90, 129, 164
Kerry, Co., 55, 59, 98, 120, 127, 134, 154, 157
Kerry Sentinel, 157
Kettle, Andrew, 19, 82, 107
Kickham, Charles, 16, 68, 85, 153
Kilchreest, 13, 65, 73, 83, 146, 148–9
Kilcloney, 161
Kilcolgan, 48
Kilconierin, 34, 111, 147–8; church, 90
Kilconnell, 40
Kilcornan, 43–4, 106; hunt, 86
Kildare, convention, 44; Hunt, 45
Kilfinane, 120
Kilkenny, 69
Killariff, 88, 100
Killarney, 120
Killeenadeema, 28, 35–6, 39, 50, 104–5, 109, 111, 143, 146, 148; Fife and Drum Band, 113
Killeeneen, 13, 63n, 86, 112
Killimor, 40, 146; court, 38
Killora, 13, 167
Kilmainham, agreement, 104, 126–7; Jail, 70, 86, 106–7, 122, 127, 143

Index 183

Kilmallock, 83
Kilmartin, James, 15, 104, 146, 152
Kilogilleen, 13
Kilrickle, 45, 79, 83, 120, 143, 146
Kiltulla, 36, 50, 81, 90, 97, 105, 111, 129, 143, 146–7; Land League branch, 35, 37, 88; meeting, 78
King's County (Offaly), 58, 134
Kinkead, Dr, 84
Kinneen, Pat, 167
Kirwan, Mrs, 55
Knockatogher, 52
Kylebeg, 38

Labane, 57
labour force, Co. Galway, 115–16; national, 63, 115–16
Labour League, 144
Ladies' Land League, 86, 108, 162; allowances, 56, 83–4, 108, 113, 129; branches, 83; Athenry, 84, 113; Craughwell, 39n, 56–7, 108, 111, 113, 129; Gort, 108; Killeenadeema, 111; Loughrea, 108, 111; Shanaglish, 108
Lahiff, Mrs, 136
Lalor, James Fintan, 14–15
Lambert, Frank, 44
Lambert, Giles, 44
Lambert, John W., 40–1, 86, 91–2, 129
Lambert, Walter P., 34, 41, 106, 139
land, acts, 158; administration, 32; (tenure) reform, 13–15, 19, 32, 50, 64, 103, 146, 152–3, 156, 158
Land Act 1870, 15, 35, 103; Bright clauses, 19; Compensation for Disturbance Bill, 32, 35, 40
Land Act 1881, 51–2, 61, 104–5, 126, 145–6, 148, 158
Land Act 1887, 104
Land Bill 1881, 82
land commission, 104; Land Commission, 51–2, 106
land conference (convention), Athenry, 38, 146–7; Galway, 43, 157; Rotunda, Dublin 1880, 32–3, 82; 1881, 104–5
land court, 104, 108; Athenry, 38; Gurteen, 38; Loughrea, 112; O'Halloran's, 82; Sweeny's, 91
land grabber(s), 31, 34–5, 39, 88; land grabbing, 33, 58, 60, 82, 135
Land Law (Ireland) Act 1881, 103

Land League, Irish National, 13–14, 19, 30, 34, 146; branches, Athenry, 25, 31, 34, 38, 79, 84; Ballinasloe, 31; Craughwell, 31, 105, 108, 129; Creggs, 31; Gort, 18; Gurteen, 31, 38, 111, 147; Kiltulla, 35, 37, 88; Loughrea, 9, 73, 91, 93; Mountbellew, 31; central executive, 32, 35, 42, 70, 108, 153, 155–6; clerical support, 17–19, 23–7, 29–31, 38–9, 50, 56, 64, 77–9, 82, 84–5, 90, 93, 104–5, 112–13, 146, 155–7, 161, 163; Co. Cork, 106, 154–5; Galway, 30–2, 34–43, 47–53, 56–7, 64, 70–3, 76, 79–80, 82–4, 88, 91–3, 98, 103–5, 107, 110–12, 116, 120, 125–6, 129, 138, 152–4, 156–7, 161; Mayo, 18, 33, 152–7; Queen's Co., 154–5; court, 38, 82, 91, 104, 108, 112; foundation, 13, 18, 37; hunts, 48–9; Ladies', see above; meetings, see land meetings below; opposition to, 79, 157; policy, programme, 31, 33, 37n, 78, 80, 104, 107–8, 126; proclamation of (inc. meetings), 48, 70, 81, 105, 107–8, 113, 118, 137–8, 144, 148–50, 155–7; relief funds, 31; rules, 34, 36, 50; suppression, 32, 103; and Clan na Gael, 20, 67, 153; and Fenians, 16, 33, 39, 67–72, 153–7; and the IRB and other secret societies, 16, 18, 61, 64–8, 70–3, 100
Landlord and Tenant (Ireland) Act 1870, 15
landlordism, 35–6, 49–50, 78, 139, 152; abolition, 30, 35, 82
land meetings, 18, 23, 30, 35, 37–8, 41, 45, 48, 53, 61, 77, 81–3, 95, 105, 116, 137, 144–5, 150, 152, 154, 156–7; Abbeygormican, 40; Ahascragh, 40; Athenry, 30, 38, 62, 65, 83, 146; Attymon, 37; Balla, 18; Ballinasloe, 15, 17, 30, 83, 107, 147, 153; Ballydugan, 48; Ballymacward, 40; Ballymana, 38–9, 138, 140, 142, 147–9, 167; Cappanoole, 37; Cappatagle, 40; Castlebar, 153; Claregalway, 18; Claremorris, 18, 153; Clifden, 18; Clostoken, 26, 37, 140, 142, 148–9, 167; Cork, 154; Craughwell, 39, 105, 147; Currandula, 18; Dublin, 107; east Galway, 15, 40, 107; Ennis, 31; Galway, 37; Gloves, 78; Gort, 18, 77; Irishtown, 17, 33, 68, 152, 155; Kilconierin, 147; Kilconnell, 40; Killeenadeema, 36, 105; Killimor, 40; Kilrickle, 83; Kiltulla, 35, 78, 88; Labane,

57; Leitrim, 40; Loughrea, 9, 30–1, 33, 40, 62, 77, 83, 95, 147; Maryborough, 82; Mayo, 16; Milltown, 18; Mountbellew, 40; Mullagh, 50; Navan, 147; New Inn, 40; Portumna, 40; Queen's County, 155; Riverville, 35–7, 42, 92; Strokestown, 82; south Galway, 31, 40; south Roscommon, 15; Tuam, 18; Tynagh, 40; Westport, 17, 152; Woodford, 82

land question, 14, 16–17, 19, 29, 40, 50, 146, 155

land reform, 13–15, 19, 32, 50, 64, 103, 146, 152–3, 156, 158

Land War 1879–82, 11, 50, 52, 55, 58, 60, 64, 76, 118, 123, 126, 137–8, 142, 146, 151, 153–4, 157; second phase 1886–91, 140, 157

Lane, Padraig G., 52, 64

Lardner, Johnny, 87

Lardner, Michael, 87

Law, Hugh, 80, 132

Lawson, James, 47–8, 133

Leahy, Michael, 164, 166

Leamy, Edmund, 71

Lee, Sub Constable, 70

Leeds, 106

Leighton, CI, 84, 111

Leinster Express, 155

Leitrim, 40, 146

Leitrim, Co., 55

Leitrim, Lord, 53

Leonard, Dr, 67, 88, 90, 97

Leonard, Head Constable, 159

Letterfrack, 72, 146; murder case, 133

Lewis, Hannah, 40, 79

Limerick, 41; Co., 59, 83, 119–20, 125, 127, 134

Lindsay, Captain, 120n

Linton, James, 40, 73, 78, 92–4, 98, 100–1

Lismany, 44, 49

Local Government Board (LGB), 23, 25–6, 28

Loftus, Micky, 161

Lomasney, William Mackey, 66

Longford, Co., 55

Louden, John James, 16, 152, 156–7

Loughrea, 11, 30, 35–6, 38–9, 57, 62–3, 85, 94, 98, 102, 106, 136, 139, 143–4, 146–8; agitation, 33, 41, 62; arms, 41, 65, 67, 73, 92–3, 110; arrests, 82, 87, 89–91, 93–4, 98–9, 110, 112, 114, 117, 119–20, 122, 128, 135, 140–4, 164–7; 'Assassination Society', 99; Athenry Road, 77; (board of) Poor Law Guardians, 24–5, 27, 29, 38, 57, 83, 85, 109; Brass Band, 93–4; Bridewell, 49, 149; Church Street, 92–3; clergy, 77, 82, 105; Convent of Mercy, 24; courthouse, 88–9, 142, 149; crops and livestock, 21–3, 25, 29; 'den of infamy', 9, 11, 99, 120; destitution, distress, 25–7, 148; Dunkellin Street, 9, 141; emigration, 28; evictions, 97; fair, 25; Fenians, 9, 65, 72; GAA, 73–4; INL, 144, 147, 167; IRB, 71–2; Ladies' Land League branch, 108, 111; land court, 112; Land League, branch, 31, 38, 72–3; members, 9, 71–4, 91, 110; land meeting, 31, 40, 57, 73–4, 77, 82–3, 93, 145, 148; living conditions, 129, 148; Main Street, 92–4; Mount Carmel convent, 94; murder, 40, 88, 92, 97–8; Nevin's Hotel, 50; Petty Sessions, 34, 141–2, 149; Piggot's Lane, 97; police, 40, 78–9, 90, 92, 94, 96, 98, 100, 105, 110–13, 120, 122–3, 140–1; police district, 11, 60, 99, 110, 112, 114, 117, 128, 135, 164; poor law union, 11–12, 21–3, 29, 38, 83; population, 11–12, 27, 116; property auctions, sales, 79; Protestant church, 92; relief committee, 24–7; RMs, 109–10, 131, 141, 143–4, 149–50; St Brendan's College, 24, 161; Scanlon's Hotel, 98; SRM, 98, 123; suspects, prisoners, 87, 89–91, 94, 98–9, 110, 113–14, 116, 122, 127, 141, 149, 164–7; Town Commissioners, 78, 99, 114; typhus fever, 28; 'Walks', 33; West Bridge, 99, 105; Workhouse, 25, 56, 130; 'Loughrea Jottings', 138; 'The State of Loughrea', 122

Loughrea and Athenry, baronies of, 100

Louth, Co., 62; Baron, 109n

Lyden, John, 133

Lyden, Martin, 133

Lynam, James, 73

Lynch, Francis, 97

Lynch, JP, 129

Lynskey, John, 72

Maamtrasna killings, 134

McAlumney, HC, 136

McCabe, Archbishop, 24–5, 29

McCarthy, John, 72–4, 93–4, 98, 110, 120, 127, 146, 157, 165

McCartney, Donal, 153

Index

McDermot, James, 138, 140, 142, 148–50, 166–7
McDermot, The, 47, 100–1
McDonagh, Sub Constable, 141
McDonnell Bodkin, Mathias, 47
McDonogh, James, 66
McEntee, Andrew, 99, 120, 166
McEvilly, John, 18, 25
McGann, Anthony, 146
McGann, John, 112, 162, 165
McGiverin, Michael, 161
McGuiness, Constable, 161
McHale, John, 17–18, 156
McInerney, Humphrey, 45–6, 148–9
Mack, Michael, 129–30
Mackey, James, 142
Macklin, John, 11
McPhilpin, John, 138, 140
McPhilpin, Peter J., 25, 38, 79, 104, 112–13
McSweeney, Dannie, 162
Madden, Thomas, 34, 144
Mahon, John Ross, 79
Malahide, Lord, 12
Mallon, John, 69–71, 96
Manahan, William, 127, 165
Mannin, 122, 167
Mannion, James, 72
Mannion, Martin, 167
Mansion House, Relief Committee, 24–8; Relief Fund, 24, 28
Marlborough, Duchess of, 24; Fund, 24–5, 28
martial law, 109
Martin estate, 55
Martyn, Edward, 106
Maryborough, 82
Mason, George, 86
Mason, Mrs, 84
Masonbrook, 30, 41
mauvais sujets, 58
May, Lord Chief Justice, 80
Mayo, Co., 15–18, 63n, 66–9, 95–6, 127, 151–2; agitation, 33, 60, 76, 155–7; clergy, 156, compared to Co. Galway, 60, 154; emigration, 157; evictions, 53, 102; Fenians, 68, 152, 155, 157; IRB, 68, 152; Land League, 18, 33, 152–3, 155–7; meetings, 18, 33, 156; outrages, 156; proclaimed, 81; suspects, 114, 156
Mayo Tenants' Defence Association, 16
Meany, Stephen J., 78
Meath, Co., 32, 58, 134, 147

Meelick, 48
meitheal, 114
Melia, John, 114, 165
Millstreet, 143, 155
Milltown, 18
Minihan, Martin, 165
Mitchell Henry, MP, 27, 30, 35, 37, 48
Mitchelstown, 154
Mollan, Lieutenant Colonel, 46
Moloney, Miss, 108
Monaghan, Co., 62; Defenders, 62; Jail, 110, 112
Monaghan, Patrick, 146
Monaghan, Thomas, 146
Moneen, Ardrahan, 36, 56–7, 87, 108, 139
Moody, T.W., 151
moonlighters, 125; society, 64, 70
Moran, ballad singer, 78–9
Moran, Bishop, 155
Moran, Jack, 112
Moran, John, 71, 165
Moroney, Michael, 125
Morris, Constable, 108
Morris Reade, William, 44
Morrissey, Anna Maria, 108
Morrissey, John (Soldier), 92
Morrissey, Mary, 108
Morrissey, Patrick, Carrigan, 84, 86, 164
Morrissey, Patrick, Loughrea, 127, 165
Morrissey, Thomas, 84, 86, 92, 164
mortality (death rate), 11, 27–8, 148; national figures, 27
Mountbellew, Land League branch, 31; meeting, 40
Mount Carmel Convent, 94
Mount Pleasant, 93, 97
Moyode Castle, 42–3, 90, 103
Mulkern, Thomas, 161
Mullagh, 50
Mullavel, Martin, 110, 164
Mullingar Jail, 140
Munster, 70; Invincibles, 71; Right Boys, 62; winter assizes, 134
murder (killing), accessory to, 99–100, 117, 159, 164–6; agrarian and political, 60, 135; Athenry and Loughrea police districts, 60, 99; conspiracy to, 98, 163; Co. Cork, 154; Co. Galway, 155; Co. Kerry, 98, 157; incitement to, 37, 117; Letterfrack, 133; Maamtrasna, 134; non-agrarian, 88; of John H. Blake, 9, 97–8, 114, 120, 128, 138; of Walter Bourke,

95–8, 138; of James Connors, 88–9, 91, 98, 129, 159n, 163n; of landlords, 11, 37, 60, 95; of Peter Dempsey, 90–1, 95, 98, 163; of Peter Doherty, 70, 84, 95, 100, 112, 122, 127, 129; of James Linton, 73, 92–8; of Thady Ruane, 9, 97–8, 114, 120, 127, 138; of Corporal Wallace, 95–8, 138; Phoenix Park, 69–70, 123, 132; non-agrarian, 88; triangle, 88–9
Murphy, Alexander, 134
Murphy, James, 80, 90, 134
Murtagh, Constable, 11, 149, 161

Naas prison, 110
Na Buachailli Bána, 63
Naish, John, 98, 111, 133–5, 139
Nally, John, 152, 155
Nally, P.W., 17, 33, 68, 152, 155
national, arrest statistics, 117–18; campaign of agitation, 158; categories of offences, 117; consciousness, 140; emigration statistics, 28; eviction statistics, 53, 61; independence (self-government), 16–17, 30, 40, 146, 149, 154; labour force, 115–16; leaders of the Land League, 107, 113, 135; mortality figures, 27; outrage statistics, 59, 61; (political) developments, 32–3, 87; relief fund, 147; rights, 14; 'the national issue', 146; weather statistics, 21–2
nationalist, 12, 33, 36n, 39–40, 51, 71, 124; community, 49; constitutional, 16; press (papers), 107, 137, 140
National Land League of Mayo, 18, 153
nationalism, constitutional, 153
Naughton, Coleman, 143
Neely, James, 104
Nevin's Hotel, 50
New Inn, 40, 139
Newell, John, 39, 96, 167
Newell, Martin, 96
New Pallas, 83, 120
New York, 17, 35, 78
New York Herald Tribune, 16
New York Herald Tribune Fund, 24, 28
Nicholson, M.J., 24
Noakley, James, 113, 164
Nolan, John, 26–7, 30, 48, 112–13
Nolan, Patrick, 104
Noud, Michael, 85
no rent, 17, 35, 126; agitation, 35, 26; banner, 104; manifesto, 107; policy, 37n, 107–8

Nugie, Andrew, 46–7
Nulty, Dr, 147

Oatfield, 48
O'Brien, P.J., 25, 30, 84–5
O'Brien, Thomas, 99, 166
O'Brien, William, MP, 9, 107, 134, 151
O'Brien, William, judge, 57
O'Callaghan, Margaret, 99, 117
occupational analysis of suspects, 114–16
O'Connell, Daniel, 14
O'Connor, Head Constable, 66
O'Connor, John, 66
O'Connor Power, John, 16–17, 33, 65, 68, 152, 156
O'Connor, T.P., 32, 36, 71
O'Donohue, Dr, 97
O'Donovan, Michael, 64
O'Farrell, J.C., 94
O'Farrell, Thomas, D., 94
Offaly, see King's County
O'Flaherty, Joseph, 65, 72
O'Flynn, William, 99, 166
O'Gallagher, Francis B., 162
O'Hagan, Lord, 76
O'Halloran, Martin (Maurtheen), 37–40, 50, 70, 81–2, 146, 164
O'Keane, John, 17, 33, 68, 152, 155
O'Kelly, James J., 32, 47n, 67, 107
O'Leary, John, 68
O'Leary, Revd, 157
O'Loughlin, John, 72
O'Loughlin, William, 146
Omagh Jail, 110, 113, 143
O'Neill, Fardy, 127, 166
O'Neill, Bridget, 9
O'Neill, Tim P., 53
Orange Emergency Committee, 79
Oranmore, 38, 95; typhus fever, 28; Whiteboyism, 62
Orridge, Andrew, 61
O'Sullivan, Michael Malachy, 15–19, 36, 38, 68, 80, 152–3
O'Sullivan, W.H., 19
O'Toole, John, 24, 93
outdoor relief, see relief

Paine, SI, 111
Palmer, N.D., 23
Paris, 17, 69, 107
parliament, member of (MP), 19, 26, 30, 35–7, 47n, 48, 66n, 73, 80, 82, 104n, 107,

112–13, 131, 143, 147, 155; parliamentarians, 17; in Ireland (College Green), 40
parliamentary, 15, 27, 33, 84, 126; debate, 52, 65, 158; elections, 12; Parliamentary Party, Irish, 33, 104, 156; obstruction, 80
Parnell, Anna, 108
Parnell, Charles Stewart, 16–20, 24, 27, 29, 31–2, 36–7, 43, 47, 61, 68, 78, 82, 85, 104, 106–7, 113, 126–7, 146, 149, 153–4; arrest, 105–6, 113; release, 126; state trial, 80, 92
Parnell Special Commission, 37, 39–40, 65, 72
Pastorini, 62
Paul, W.J., 38, 48, 67, 87, 111, 149
Payne, HC, 140
peace, 45, 109, 111, 113, 122, 131, 137, 142, 144–5; justice of the, 24, 44, 90, 121, 135, 143; public, 131, 142
Peace Preservation (Ireland) Act 1875, 76
Peace Preservation (Ireland) Act 1881, 81
Pearse, Colonel, 46
peasant, 14, 62–4, 93, 138; peasantry, 14, 62, 82, 152, 154; proprietary, 16, 19, 32, 37, 103–4, 146; proprietor(ship), 14, 16–17, 30–1, 103
Pelly, J., 90
penal servitude, 133
penalties, 49, 100
Pendergast, Thomas, 122, 166
Pendleton, chief magistrate, 62
Persse, Algernon, 56–7, 139
Persse, Burton, 42–4, 46, 86, 90, 103, 129
Persse, Dudley, 42, 48
Persse family (the Persses), 42, 56, 138
Persse, Henry, 44, 90
Persse, William B., 46
Peterswell, 25, 49
petty sessions, 56; Ardrahan, 45, 57; Athenry, 112; Gort, 95; Loughrea, 34, 141–2, 149; special, Tuam, 138
Phillips, John D., 94
Phoenix Park, depot, 69, 120; murders, 69–70, 123, 131
Piggott's Lane, Loughrea, 97
Pilkington, Henry L., 38, 104–5, 109, 146, 164
Plan of Campaign, 37, 73, 157
Plower, Peter, 113, 164
Plunkett, Thomas Oliver, 109, 119

police(man), 11, 30–1, 33–5, 39–41, 49, 53, 59, 60–3, 65–6, 68–9, 72–3, 75, 77–8, 81–2, 88–96, 98, 100–1, 105, 108–9, 112–13, 120, 122, 127–9, 131–2, 136–7, 139–44, 148–50, 153, 159–61; and military, 11, 31, 44, 48–9, 55, 58, 77, 88, 95, 99–100, 105, 109, 111, 118, 120, 122–3, 128–9, 144, 155; and protection tax, 122; barracks, Loughrea, 141, 143, 161; depot, 69, 120; districts, 11, 60, 119, 120; Connacht, 63; Loughrea and Athenry, 11, 60, 96, 99, 112, 114, 116, 127, 135, 164; Dublin Metropolitan, 69; escorts, 56, 76; hut, 11, 109, 120; informer, 60, 69, 71–2, 100, 153; protection, 35, 41, 92, 101, 144; report, 65–6, 72, 75, 91, 96, 98, 153; station, Ballinasloe, 161
political assassination (murder), 60, 71, 93, 98–9, 129, 131
Pollok, John, 44, 48–9, 52, 82
poorhouse, 27
poor law guardian, 15, 24, 38, 57, 109, 129, 147
poor law union, Gort, 11–12, 21–3; Loughrea, 11–12, 21–3, 29, 38, 83; board of poor law union, 38, 83
population, 27, 62, 132; changes, 12; rural and urban, 116
Portarlington, earl of, 155
Portland Prison, 81, 107
Portumna, arms, 65; distress, 27; land meeting, 40
Poulnabonny, 128
press (papers),; control of, 137; editors and proprietors, 131, 135, 137, 140; local, 61, 137; national, 12, 142, 148; London, 148; nationalist, 107, 137, 140; reporters, 140, 148–9
Prevention of Crime (Ireland) Act of 1882, (Crimes Act), 11, 49, 131–45, 148, 150; administration, 132, 144; introduction, 11, 136; provisions, 131, 140, 142
prison, see jail
prison conditions, 83–7; solitary confinement, 86
Prisoners' Sustentation Fund, 108, 113
process, server(s) (serving), 31–2, 60, 79
Property Defence Association (PDA), 79
Protection of Person and Property (PPP) (Ireland) Act 1881, 9, 11, 43, 81–3, 91, 106, 118–20, 164, 168; aims, 81, 106, 135;

arrests, 38, 44, 81, 83–4, 87, 91–2, 94, 97–8, 100, 109–20, 122–3, 127, 135–6, 155–6; Bill 1881, 80; cessation, 125; main offences, 81, 117, 119, 126
public order, offences, 131, 140, 144

Queen's, College, Galway, 22, 84; County (Laois), 154–5
Queenstown, 28
Quinn, Lewis, 165
Quinn, Patrick J. (also J.P.), 17, 107, 162
Quirke, Mrs, 161

rack-rent(ing), 19, 43, 51, 58
Rafferty, Patrick, 97
Raford House, 63, 103
Raftery, Patrick, 165, 167
Rahasane, case, 49; House, 11, 33, 95–6, 102; tenants, 102
Raifterí, Antoine, 63
railway, 78, 147; officials, 70; station, Amiens Street, 55, 161; Athenry, 87; Ballinasloe, 161; Broadstone, 161; Craughwell, 41; Gort, 125; Navan, 147; Tullamore, 125; Woodlawn, 110
Rathcosgrove, 128
Rathruddy, 99, 167
Rathville House, 97
Red Branch Knights, 162
Redington, Christopher, 106; family, 43
Redington, sub sheriff, 56, 79
Redmond, John, 71
Redpath, James, 83, 138
Reed, Andrew, 57, 69–70, 72, 136, 145
relief, 23–5, 27, 30, 33; local committees, 26–8; Relief of Distress (Ireland) Act 1880, 26; Relief of Distress (Ireland) Bill, 27; funds, 23, 31; Mansion House Relief Committee (MHRC), 24–7, 168; Fund, 24, 28; measures, 23, 26; outdoor, 25–8, 57, 83; works, 23, 25; workhouses, 28; relieving officer, 27
rent, 19, 22, 26, 30–8, 403, 50–3, 55–7, 60–1, 66, 78–80, 91, 94, 101, 105–8, 111–14, 117, 128–30, 137, 139, 147, 151–2, 155, 162, 164–5; 'at the point of the bayonet', 35, 157; fair, 14, 17, 19, 37, 42, 50, 82, 103–4; no rent, 17, 35, 126; no rent agitation, 35, 26; no rent banner, 104; No Rent manifesto, 107; no rent policy, 37n, 107–8; rack-rent(ing), 19, 43, 51, 58

repeal association, repeal of the Union, 14
resident magistrate (RM), 44, 48, 67, 69, 71, 76, 81–2, 98, 109–10, 124, 136, 140
Ribbon societies, 67
Ribbon-Fenianism, 67, 69–71, 153
Rice Henn, T., 167
Richards, Edward M., 65
Richmond Commission, 19, 51; assistant commissioners, 51, 151
Rickham, James, 27
rights, constitutional, 107; of property, 76, 79, 141–2, 154; of tenants, 19, 34–5, 42, 53, 108
Right Boys, 62
Riverville, 35, 37, 42, 52, 56, 80, 90, 92, 101, 103, 149
Robertson, Major, 151
Robinson, Sergeant, 47, 94
Roe, Constable, 161
Roe, Mr, 163
Roland, Martin, 167
Rory of the Hill(s), 14, 41
Roscommon, 85; Co., 134; MP, north, 47n; police district, 120; south, 15
Rotunda, Dublin, 32, 82
Roughan, Dr, 26–7
Roveagh, 79, 108, 128
Roxborough, 42, 48, 56, 63
royal commissions, 51
Royal Dragoon Guards, 95
Royal Irish Constabulary (RIC), 101, 112–13, 118, 137, 143, 155, 161; deputy inspector general, 66; detective department, 69n, 89; inspector general, 69
Ruane, John, 45
Ruane, Patrick, 165
Ruane, Thady, 9, 97–8, 102, 114, 120, 127, 138
Rush, Edward, 24
Ryan, John, 90, 163–5, 167
Ryan, Mark, 52, 65
Ryan, William, 141

St Brendan's College, 24, 161
St Clerans estate, 11, 63
Sams, John Berwick, 47, 102
Scanlon, John, 65
Scanlon's Hotel, 92, 98
Seed Supply Act 1880, 26
Seefin, 63
Select Committee on Outrages 1852, 64
Sellars, J., 163

Sellars, P., 163
Sexton, Thomas, 32, 71, 80, 107
Shanaglish, 72; Ladies' Land League branch, 108
Shanbally, 121, 167
Shaughnessy, Michael, 72
Shaw Lefevre, G., 110
Shawe-Taylor, Mr, 95–6
Sheehy, Eugene, 83, 106, 112, 119
Sheill, John, 166
Shepherds' Association, 140
Sheppard, Frank, 89
Sheridan, P.J., 68, 71, 83; family, 128
shopkeeper(s), 12, 42, 56, 110, 135–6, 151, 154
Sigerson, George, 28
Skehill, Peter, 167
Slacke, Owen R., 44
Sligo, 90; Co., 39n, 71; summer assizes, 90, 94; winter assizes, 57, 134; trial venue, 134–5
Smith, Philip, 140
Smyth, Captain, 30, 41
Smyth, John, 24
Smyth, T., 68
Snider rifle, 67, 90, 95
Snow, Captain, 129
solitary confinement, 86
Solow, Barbara, 51, 53, 151
Special Commission of Judges, 131–2
special, court, 140; juries, 131–5; petty sessions, 138
special resident magistrate (SRM), 11, 57, 72, 81, 98, 110–12, 119, 123
Spellman, Martin, 85, 164
Spencer, Earl, 9, 69, 81, 95, 98–9, 111, 118, 123, 126–7, 135–7, 140, 144, 147
Spiddal, 31
stopping the hunt, 42–9, 147
Stratford, Bernard, 165
Stratford, Michael, 165
Stratford, Thomas, 150, 167
Strattan, William, 24
Stritch, Clara, 108
Stritch, John R., 47
Strokestown, 82
Sullivan, Alexander Martin, 36
Sullivan, Timothy Daniel, 36, 147
summary, judgments, 140; jurisdiction, 131, 140, 149; prosecution, 131, 135
suspect(s), prisoner(s), 9, 43–9, 56–7, 59, 71–3, 81, 83–4, 86–7, 89–94, 98–9, 108–20, 122, 126–8, 134–5, 138, 141, 143–4, 146, 149–50, 152–7, 159–63
suspension (repeal) of habeas corpus, 58, 76–7
Sweeney, Michael, 97
Sweeny, Alice Bridget (Siss), 9, 159
Sweeny, John, 9, 65, 72–4, 78, 83–6, 91, 110, 141, 146–8, 153, 157, 159–60, 164
Sweeny, Lizzy, 161
Sweeny, Martin, 161
Sweeny, Mary Agnes, 159
Sweeny, Mrs John (Bridget O'Neill), 9, 49
Sweeny, Patrick, 127, 143, 166
Sweeny, Peter, 39, 110, 127, 159, 161, 165
Sylver, Michael, 45, 47–8

Taylor, John F., 67
tenant(s), 51–2, 138–9, 146, 154–6; associations (leagues, movement), 14–15, 18; defence associations, 18, Ballinasloe, 15, 17, 152; Mayo, 16; farmers, 15, 17, 19, 26, 30, 34–5, 37, 40, 42, 45, 50, 65, 105, 107, 112, 126, 146–7, 151, 155, 157; in arrears, 55, 104, 113, 126; right(s), 19, 34–5, 42, 53, 108; Landlord and Tenant (Ireland) Act 1870, 15–16
Terry Alt, 63
the '3 Fs', 14–15, 17, 37, 52, 78, 103, 113; Meany's version, 78
Thurles, 73
Tiaquin, 112
Tierney, Martin, 37
Tipperary, Co., 44, 73, 134
Tithe War 1830s, 58
Toledo Blade, 138
Towerhill, 55
Townsend, Mr, 89
Townshend, Charles, 154
town commissioners, 24, 114; elections, 78; Loughrea, 78, 99
Traill, RM, 67
Tralee, 17, 85, 157
Treacy, James, 130
treason, 117, 132, 149; treasonable, 34, 81, 106, 125, 137, 164; treason felony, 155
Trevelyan, George Otto, 98, 133, 143
trial(s), 47n, 91, 101, 119, 133–4, 138; internment without, 11, 58–9, 81; of, Edward Barrett, Nicholas Barrett, Thomas Cunningham and James McDermmot, 142 (150); Michael and

Mary Anne Clarke, 94; Craughwell prisoners, 135; Anthony Daly, 63; Michael Dilleen, 94; Francis Hynes, 134; Patrick Keogh, 90; John McCarthy, 93; John McPhilpin, 138–40; Parnell and others, 80, 92; John Ryan, 90; Michael Walsh, 133; Patrick Walsh, 133; venues, 131–5
Tuam, 47n, 104; archbishop, 17–18; arms, 67; Fenians, 65; land meeting, 18; Right Boys, 62; special petty sessions (court), 138, 140
Tuam Herald, 19, 138
Tuam News, 57, 73, 87, 128, 137–8, 143
Tubbercurry, 71
Tuke, J.H., 55
Tulla, 120, 125, 145; Workhouse, 125
Tullamore, 125
Tullira, 96; Castle, 106
Tully, Jasper, 83; Tully family, 128
Tuohill, Patrick, 113, 164
Tynagh, 104, 146; land meeting, 40
Tynan, P.J.P., 67–8, 71, 96
typhus fever, 28
Tyrone House, 96

Ulster, 15, 71
United Ireland, 47n, 85, 138
Ussher, family, 45; Christopher, 44

Vaughan, W.E., 51–3, 55, 58
venue of trials, change of, 131, 133–5

'Walks' fields, Loughrea, 33
Wall, Mrs, 55
Wallace, Fanny, 102
Wallace, Robert, 95–8, 102, 138
Walsh, Michael, 133
Walsh, Patrick (Pat), 133
Walshe, John, 17, 152, 155
war office, 65, 109, 123, 132
Ward, Michael, 165
Waterford, Co., 44, 69
weather conditions, 22, 29
West, Augustus, 79
west of Ireland, 15, 21, 23, 28, 76, 151–2; West Riding (Galway), 12, 52–3, 55, 59–60
western division, 136
Western News, 28, 122, 137, 140, 149–50
Westmeath, Co., 58, 134, 162
Westport, 16–18, 152
Whelan, Martin, 167
Whiteboy, 62–3, 155; Act 1831, 38
Wicklow assizes, 73
Woodford, 49, 62, 65, 82
workhouse, Donoughmore, 155; Loughrea, 25, 56, 130; Tulla, 125

Young Irelanders, 14